Personnel Planning and
Occupational Choice

Personnel Planning and Occupational Choice

STUART R. TIMPERLEY

Lecturer in Organisational Behaviour/Manpower Studies
London Graduate School of Business Studies

London · George Allen & Unwin Ltd
Ruskin House · Museum Street

First published in 1974

© George Allen & Unwin Ltd, 1974

ISBN 0 04 658208 8

Printed in Great Britain
in 10pt Times roman type
by Cox & Wyman Ltd,
London, Fakenham and Reading

To Veronica

PREFACE

The basis of this book is that the processes by which organisations (and larger entities) attempt to influence their populations (and prospective future populations) are capable of systematic analysis, and that this process of understanding becomes more meaningful when considered in conjunction with a similar analysis of the process operating on one key area of behaviour, namely individual mobility within and between the occupational and educational sectors.

The first part of the book is therefore concerned with a detailed discussion of the areas of personnel planning and occupational choice. Through this discussion an attempt is made to distinguish the major theoretical and practical contributions and to co-ordinate them into coherent individual and linking frameworks. Thus, the relationship between prediction and control in a planning context, and the relationship between aspirational bases of educational, occupational career and job decisions and the structural limitations on such decisions, and hence on mobility, are both considered as parts of a closely related process. Later chapters are based on empirical studies which focus on different stages in the career and mobility process to illustrate the effects of the major constraining and influencing factors on the attitudes and behaviour of individuals treated at these stages. An examination of the process of mobility, from the higher educational system into the occupational system in Chapter 3, highlights the role of structural factors in this process, and indicates the existence of a process of mutual influence and adaptation. In Chapter 4, a discussion of the job and career attitudes and behaviour of graduates in industry and commerce is based on a series of studies in eight organisations, and highlights the variations in reaction to the range of organisational personnel policies (taken as the basis of organisational control). A final chapter attempts to further discuss the working of the process by which organisations attempt to influence and control their manpower, and the reactions of employees to this process. Through the use of functional analysis some of the problems of 'fit' between organisational control mechanisms and individual responses are discussed.

The author would like to express his thanks to the organisations and individuals who so readily gave their time in co-operating with the various studies involved. Thanks are also due to Alison Gregory and Charles Foley who assisted with interviewing at various stages, to Andrew Young whose work and help provided a focus for my interest in manpower planning, and to Dennis Chapman whose advice and insights over a number of years were of immense value. Final thanks are due to Kerry Jones, and Anna Raeburn for their excellent typing of the manuscript at its two stages.

SRT

CONTENTS

CHAPTER 1

An Integrated Approach to Manpower Planning

The considerable attention now being given to manpower planning is one manifestation of the increasing awareness at all levels of the importance of the effective utilisation of human resources. It is this awareness which Ginzberg has suggested has led to a 'new discipline of human resources',[1] and whilst this may be premature, it does highlight the present concern with all aspects of manpower. Certainly, it is becoming apparent that one of the key elements of organisational success is the effective development of human resources. The case for the development and planning of manpower is well put by Vetter who suggests that

'. . . manpower is an asset which enables an enterprise to distinguish itself in performance from other enterprises. Manpower is more than a mere current resource used in the production process. It has a long economic life which deserves the same planning attention given to other assets with long lives. Actions taken today in the manpower area influence the quantity and quality of the company's future manpower.'[2]

It could be argued, however, that it is the complexity of the human resource area which distinguishes it from the other organisational functional areas. A simple model of organisational manpower planning, for example, would only take account of wastage in the form of retirement, death and voluntary resignation, and seek to redress this by recruitment and promotion; yet useful as this is, it only highlights an existing or predicted situation when from a standpoint of organisational policy what is essential is understanding of the dynamics of the behavioural process.

It is the concern of this opening chapter to discuss the concept and implications of 'manpower planning', to develop a working definition of the concept, and then to examine the case for manpower planning particularly in the light of present approaches to human resource management. This will involve description and discussion of both quantitative and qualitative considerations in planning, and an examination of such issues as the process of personnel flow and the ways in which such movement can be influenced. It will be argued that manpower planning is not simply a question of predicting future requirements, but rather a question of utilising quantitative and qualitative information as a basis for the formulation of personnel policies which are aware of, and adequately account for, the complexities of organisational life and personnel movement.

The primary consideration of this book is with organisational manpower planning and with the ways in which organisational policies will affect the behaviour and attitudes of staff at all levels, but it is obviously essential to highlight the important relationship between planning at this level and manpower planning at both industry and national levels. In this context, in fact, Smith[3] has emphasised that manpower planning at national level (i.e. the planning of a large socio-economic system) and the planning of the manpower sub-systems of the economy (i.e. an industry or an organisation) should be looked on as interdependent aspects of the same process. Similarly, Galbraith in discussing what he terms the 'principle of consistency' has suggested that 'the relationship between society at large and an organisation must be consistent with the relation of the organisation to the individual, and there must be consistency in the motives which induce organisations and individuals to pursue these goals'.[4] This, of course, is a normative view, and in practice there is often considerable disparity between the views of society, organisations and individuals. Unemployment, for example, could possibly be looked upon, albeit indirectly, as a form of economic control at national level, but for individuals affected by it the reaction may be quite different; alternatively some organisations, possibly misguidedly, could look to unemployment to provide a more stable and conformist work force. Conflicts of interest and conflicts of goals exist as, of course, do pressures for consistency.

However, before examining in further detail the interrelationship between the various societal elements and their respective goals in planning terms, it is vital to examine manpower planning in terms of the different interpretations given to it, the purpose being to formulate a working definition of the concept. On the basis of this interpretation it is intended to develop a framework within which the manpower planning process can be examined, and elements of the process monitored.

MANPOWER PLANNING – SOME PARAMETERS

Manpower represents one of a number of national or organisational resources, and it is important that this fact is adequately accounted for in any attempt to plan manpower requirements. Generally the overall objective of the nation or of individual organisations is to make the most effective use of all its resources, with this often being seen in terms of return on investment and the maintenance of financial viability.[5] To achieve this aim, given the increasing rate and complexity of change, it is increasingly being advocated that thought and action take place within an overall planning framework. The growth of corporate planning as an activity does not, of course, mean that planning has been ignored in the past, rather that given the above-stated complexity and speed of change and the implications of this, there is an acceptance that it is becoming increasingly necessary to co-ordinate different planning activities and to formalise the overall planning process.

It is generally accepted that growth and progress are dependent on the effective deployment of, and economic co-ordination of, all available resources, with the end result of achieving established objectives and securing optimum performance.[6] There is in, addition, the problem of defining economic efficiency or social welfare, and also there is exactly what is meant by growth and progress: is this seen as the problem of the acceptability of established objectives?[7] At this stage, however, it is intended that the framework for the later empirical work which will illustrate the dynamics of the manpower planning process. Thus, returning to the concept of planning, the question to be answered is 'what is planning?', rather than 'what are we planning for?'

Russell Ackoff in discussing the concept of corporate planning, highlights the two key elements in planning when he says that 'planning is the design of a desired future and of effective ways of bringing it about'.[8] Thus, planning is regarded as an anticipatory decision-making process, a process which involves a set of interdependent decisions if the desired future is to be met. The two elements of design and procedure referred to above are illustrated clearly by the parts of the planning process: the specifications of ends; the means by which the ends are to be pursued; the determination, acquisition and allocation of resources; the implementation of the plan; and finally the design of a system of control to monitor, and where necessary correct, the progress of the plan.

Ackoff's view of corporate planning is based on the establishment of desired objectives as well as on the planning process itself, and this two-stage approach is also a characteristic of the approach of Ansoff,[9] who stresses the importance of recognising that plans are based on certain assumptions which equate with the basic strategies and policies of the organisation, and that such assumptions will have a determining influence on the plan itself. For Ansoff, therefore, the plan-making process requires firstly, the solving of the planning problem, and secondly, the preparation of a plan based on the solution – different yet closely related steps in the process.

One of the most important functions of any planning activity is to enable the organisation to interact with, and react to, the changes taking place in the environment. The definition of corporate planning put forward by Chambers as 'a systematic way of running a company so that it anticipates and can profit from change'.[10] reflects this view of the organisation interacting with its environment and responding to social, economic and technological changes. This dynamic view of organisation is also a characteristic of many of the models put forward by social scientists to assist explanation of the function and operation of organisations in a constantly changing environment.[11]

One major approach which has considerable implications for planning purposes, is the analysis of the characteristics of enterprises as systems, and it is useful to examine some manifestations of 'systems' approaches in this context. The view that methods of work to be employed are determined by both work to be done and the technical and human resources available, could be taken as representative of a current managerial philosophy.[12] Here the significant feature is the interrelationship of the social *and* technical systems. This systems approach, successfully adopted in early empirical studies of organisational structures and behaviour by Blau,[13] Gouldner,[14] and Jacques tended to reflect an approach, which though it allowed for the analysis of organisations as complex social and technical systems, often failed to relate differentiation between 'closed' and 'open' systems. It is rigidly applied in the physical sciences,[15] and in the study of social organisations, Emery and Trist[16] have distinguished between the two, indicating that the organisation is sufficiently independent to allow its major problems to be analysed with reference to its internal structure. In contrast to this the open system approach to organisations, as described by Katz and Kahn,[17] and successfully utilised by the Tavistock Institute,[18] suggests that organisations are not simply self-contained entities but affect, and are affected by, the external environment. Katz and Kahn constructively highlight the arguments for an open-systems approach, by emphasising the limitations of the closed-system approach in commenting that

'traditional organisational theories have tended to view the human organisation as a closed system. This tendency has led to a disregard of differing organisational environments and the nature of organisational dependency on environment. It has led, also, to an over-concentration on principles of internal organisational functioning, with consequent failure to develop and understand the processes of feedback which are essential to survival.'[19]

In a sense the concept of an open system can be likened to the earlier mentioned dynamic models; in fact, the concept of 'dynamics' used by Fiebleman and Friend[20] can be equated to the concept of an open system. In their approach, they refer to the concepts of 'statics' and 'dynamics', with a static (closed) approach referring to organisations as being independent of their environment and, thus, in some way isolated from difficulties of interacting with other organisations, and a dynamic (open) approach referring to organisations as being to some extent dependent on their environment and thus involved in interacting with other organisations. The important aspect of the work of Fiebleman and Friend, however, lies in the way that they relate the two approaches to the functioning of organisations, illustrating that although the division is not absolute (since all organisations have structure and suffer functional change) there are logical grounds for abstracting the two and advocating that the dynamics of organisation cannot be properly understood without some understanding of statics.

It is accepted here that a useful basis for planning is the adoption of an open-systems approach to the structure and functioning of organisations. Here we are concerned with the nature and constraints on planning from an organisational standpoint, and the approach to be adopted recognises that organisations, which are seen as complex socio-technical systems, operate in a dynamic external environment. Thus for planning and policies to be effective they must be realistic, which means taking account of the interaction between the organisation and the external environment.

MANPOWER PLANNING – AN INTERPRETATION

The above description of the overall planning process, and the argument for the adoption of a systems approach to any planning activity provides a useful frame of reference for a detailed analysis of the concept of manpower planning, as well as highlighting the need for any attempt to plan manpower requirements and structure, to be closely related to other organisational (or national) objectives and plans. Manpower planning, in other words, is part of overall corporate planning, and accordingly manpower objectives and manpower policies must relate to national or organisational goals and policies. Acknowledging the need for the planning activities of the major resource areas to be closely integrated, it is now intended to look in some detail at the human resource area, initially in terms of the elements involved in the planning of such a resource, and then in developing the implications of such an activity for the formulation of 'personnel' policies and the practice of 'personnel' management.

Any attempt to discuss the nature, scope and content of manpower planning is severely hampered by the many different definitions attributed to the concept. In order to put forward a meaningful interpretation, it is important to examine those aspects of manpower planning given particular emphasis in the different definitions. A useful point to start such an activity is with what might be termed a 'general' approach – that taken by the Department of Employment and Productivity in its booklet *Company Manpower Planning*. Here, manpower planning is looked on as a wide ranging activity, 'a strategy for the acquisition, utilisation, improvement and preservation of an enterprise's human resources'.[21] Implicit in this activity is the need to evaluate present resources, the need to forecast future manpower requirements, and the need to take certain measures to enable such resources to be available as, and when necessary. The significance of the above definition lies in the fact that it accounts for both quantitative and qualitative elements in the manpower planning process. In the DEP interpretation both elements are seen as aspects of the manpower planning process, yet other interpretations would appear to draw distinctions between the forecasting or predictive element and the control or policy element. It is argued here that the distinction between what could be called manpower forecasting, and manpower management, can be accounted for under the general term of manpower planning, and that with such an integrated approach manpower planning has the opportunity to become a realistic and effective activity.

However, as yet there does not really exist, as Walker[22] has pointed out, a general or integrated approach to manpower planning, despite such exceptions as the DEP approach. Geisler,[23] in a study of manpower-planning activities in American companies demonstrates quite clearly the unsettled nature of manpower planning, and suggests that a variety of activities – from gross number forecasts of manpower requirements to the whole personnel function are deemed to constitute manpower planning. Certainly it is not unusual to find manpower planning interpreted as being synonomous with personnel management (see, for example, Barber,[24] Hood[25]), nor is it unusual to find manpower planning interpreted in terms of mathematical techniques for forecasting purposes with only marginal attention paid to the problem of developing measures to ensure that forecasts can be met (see, for example, Gascoigne,[26] Lane and Andrew[27]). What would seem to be missing is a framework for, and definition of, manpower planning which would allow for the integration of both quantitative and qualitative approaches.

One serious attempt at such integration has been by Vetter at the managerial or high talent level; here manpower planning is defined as 'the process by which management determines how the organisation should move from its current position to its desired manpower position'.[28] This definition incorporates the two approaches or orientations discussed above; illustrating that undertaking personnel development programmes in isolation from quantitative information about future manpower needs is as ineffective as simply estimating future manpower requirements and hoping that the quantitative aspect of development will be met by a natural development process. In many cases it would appear that the two elements are considered separately (if they are both considered at all), but for Vetter the two are inseparable, as can be seen from a brief analysis of the phases involved in his interpretation of the manpower planning process. Four major phases are identified – the developing of manpower inventories and forecasts which refers to the obtaining and analysis of data; the establishment of manpower objectives and policies; the design and implementation of plans and action programmes; and the control and evaluation of such plans and programmes – and though each particular phase will require specialist activity the significant thing is that for any phase to be meaningful it must be incorporated into the process as a whole. This view of manpower planning, therefore, which is in many ways similar in its comprehensiveness to the DEP view, looks upon it as a process which contains a number of different but related elements.

The need for a comprehensive and integrated view of the manpower-planning process cannot be overemphasised, but unfortunately, it would appear that many manpower planning attempts suffer from either a superficial or specialised view of what such an activity entails. Thus, it is not, perhaps, surprising to see manpower planning often interpreted literally as a means of enabling the supply and demand aspects of the manpower situation to be matched. This view of manpower planning which sees it in terms of trying to forecast the future requirements of all types and levels of employee and matching these with the probable availability of such people, is not incorrect, on the contrary it is possibly what it eventually comes to, but it is the implications of this matching process, and the means of being able to carry out this matching process which are surely more significant. This is certainly recognised by Pym,[29] who suggests that if manpower planning is to be economically viable then the supply/demand interpretation needs to be extended to include measurement and control of the variables affecting the supply of and demand for skill: these he identifies as education, vocational training, utilisation and innovation. Similarly, Bell *et al.*,[30] though defining manpower planning in terms of two stages – the demand forecast, and the internal and external supply forecast – use this as a basis for a discussion of the factors which have a considerable bearing on the realities of the supply and demand situation. Thus, one finds a useful review of work done on, for example, manpower utilisation, as well on factors affecting the flow of personnel in relation to the organisation. In addition, Mcbeath,[31] has suggested that manpower planning covers a good deal more than simply planning future requirements, and divides the manpower planning process into two stages: firstly, the detailed planning of manpower requirements for all types and all levels of employee throughout the period of the plan; and secondly, the planning of manpower supply to provide the organisation with the right types of people from all sources to meet planned requirements.

Implicit in the concept of manpower planning is the idea of moving from a present position to a future position. This emphasis on the element of forward movement is characteristic of Vetters's interpretation of manpower planning and Denerley and Plumbley[32] have also stressed this, in pointing out that a manpower plan should take account of the main staffing changes which an organisation will expect to take place over a period of years. The need to be more specific in terms of the actual time period involved in the forward movement has been illustrated by Walker,[33] who, in discussing manpower forecasting, suggests that it is helpful to highlight the demand and supply functions appropriate for each of three planning periods: these he defines as short range (0–2 years), intermediate range (2–5 years), and long range (over 5 years). Walker is essentially referring to manpower forecasting in organisations, and his differentiation between periods of forward movement obviously relates to this fact, but this pattern of differentiation can have relevance to national manpower planning as Cassell[34] has shown. He has postulated that the role of government can best be understood by breaking manpower planning down into long range (10 years), intermediate (3–5 years), and short range (1 or 2 years), and suggests an important link between these different periods in that the framework of long run policies will determine the need for, and the character of, the sub-policies of the intermediate and the short run. It should be pointed out, however, that the length of planning period will vary considerably, depending on the particular technological, economic, or social circumstances. One of the key factors which determines the planning period in this country, for example (and which also reflects the link between national policy and organisational practice), is the statutory period of notice for termination of employment; this might vary from daily or weekly for manual workers, to monthly for managerial staff, and three monthly in the case of the education sector. For practical purposes, therefore, the length of the planning period in practice will often be considerably shorter and in some cases more fixed, than the ideal planning periods described above. Certainly in the public sector, planning periods are generally rigidly adhered to – the universities' quinquennium period is a case in point.[35]

Manpower planning, therefore, is an activity or process which relates to the future, and is generally regarded in terms of the planning of a desired future both in terms of the effective utilisation of resources, and 'human satisfaction'. The important difference, though, between human resources and other resources is that manpower can be both a means and an end, and as Ginzberg has pointed out the key is the quality of human life.[36] In this respect, therefore, it could be argued that manpower policies should attempt to reflect both organisational or national objectives, and personal objectives. This of course, does not always happen, and it is becoming increasingly obvious that simply providing gainful employment without recourse to the objectives and demands of individuals is an unrealistic objective. In this context, Miller has aptly commented that 'rising aspirations ... may soon place greater demands upon employers than current personnel practices are prepared to handle'.[37] This need to relate organisational policies and programmes to individual expectations is certainly a major justification for manpower planning, particularly in the light of the argument that the effective utilisation of human resources will contribute enormously to economic growth.

The justification for manpower planning often rests on economic arguments. This economic approach to manpower planning rests largely on the concepts of investment and cost. An organisation makes an investment in manpower resources, and this in itself represents a major reason for undertaking the planning of that resource; the organisation, as it does with all other resources, wants a return on its investment. The economic difference between having manpower planning and not having manpower planning represents the economic argument for manpower planning. The economists viewpoint is illustrated by Vetter,[38] who stresses two considerations, firstly the relationship between an organisation's use of its manpower and the value of such manpower, so that the more intensively manpower resources are utilised (in terms of capability and capacity), the more valuable it tends to become; and secondly, the relationship between the ability of the organisation to adapt to change and economic success, which implies that economic success requires a work force capable of successful adaption to changing conditions.

When an organisation recruits an individual it is undertaking a considerable commitment. Certainly the individual is making an investment, and this aspect will be discussed in the following chapter, but so also is the organisation. Gradually, organisations are beginning to cost different personnel activities, for example, the cost of recruiting graduates, the cost of training different levels of employee, the costs of replacing different types of employee in terms of the investment made; and there is considerable interest being shown in the concept of social accounting. However, as Haire[39] has pointed out, all too often organisations do not assess the value of human resources in balance sheet terms. The question of cost effectiveness of manpower also demands an analysis of the productivity of an organisation's human resources, and in this respect Buckingham and North[40] have produced an interesting analysis of manpower planning in relation to productivity bargaining, in which they suggest that the purpose of manpower planning is to safeguard, economically, the future manpower needs of the organisation by the development of manpower plans and programmes which would satisfiy those requirements. Thus, in making a productivity bargain, an economic analysis of manpower needs is necessary. It is significant, too, that this economic honesty is regarded as essential in another way, from the employees side, where the concern is with the fact that management should treat any possibility of having to terminate employment with the care and attention its importance warrants. Manpower planning, therefore, implies a social obligation on the part of the organisation to take reasonable steps to ensure continuity of employment, as well as an economic obligation.

This is, perhaps, an opportune time to comment on the dilemma which organisations face in terms of their economic and social obligations. The problem is neatly posed by Sofer who suggests that two principles are in operation within an organisation, 'one is a principle of intellectual objective rationality . . . the other is reasoning based on the consideration of history, past commitments, power structure, relations between individuals and groups, feeling and estimates of probable reactions'.[41] Organisations, therefore, whilst having a responsibility to shareholders to provide a reasonable return on investment, also have an obligation to their employees and to the community. These different, yet not mutually exclusive, obligations are sometimes formalised by organisations in the form of written objectives. One of the largest organisations in this country,[42] recently set out a written statement of its objectives and policies which illustrates clearly the need to reconcile economic and social obligations (to its employees and to the community). Thus, the primary concern is with maximising the company's contribution to the long term profitability of the larger group, yet recognising that the resources it utilises are part of the total resources of society and must be protected, developed and managed as such. Implicit in both these objectives is a further objective which refers to creating conditions, in which employees at all levels will be encouraged and enabled to develop and to realise their potentialities while contributing to the company's objectives. The way to achieve such objectives is seen in terms of a principle of joint optimisation which suggests the management of both a social system and a technical system. Of course, simply setting down objectives, and an organisational philosophy, or even policies to be followed, does not necessarily mean that the objectives will be achieved. There is often a considerable difference between stated policy and actual practice, which will be discussed later, but it does perhaps illustrate that, for whatever the reasons might be, organisations are aware of the social obligations upon them; the next step is to ensure that policies are successfully implemented. At national level, too, the problem of reconciling economic and social obligations is continually occurring, though whether particular government's accept that there is a problem is another question. Unemployment, for example, as Faunce[43] has pointed out can be regarded as a valuable economic measure or as a social problem. However, the difficulty of reconciliation does exist, and manpower planning is often seen as one way of solving this difficulty in that it is sometimes interpreted as a means of interrelating the two. Thus, Lester[44] sees manpower planning at national level as seeking to improve the human resources of the country and to enlarge, in the long term, their economic effectiveness, and as a result of this it aims to raise the productivity of the economy.

The suggestion is often made that the reasons for undertaking manpower planning are considerable, and that the more immediate reasons for such planning involves the need to ensure that future labour requirements will be available, the need for greater productivity within the organisation and the need for organisational change.[45] More detailed practical reasons for the activity are suggested by the Department of Employment and Productivity in their discussion of company manpower planning, and include the determination of recruitment levels as a basis for effective recruitment policies; the anticipation of redundancies and the avoidance of unnecessary dismissals; the determination of optimum training levels; the provision of a basis for management development programmes; the costing of the labour element in new projects; and the provision of assistance with productivity bargains.[46]

There are, of course, a great many constraints on manpower planning and the existence of such constraints, it could be argued effectively inhibits the manpower-planning activity. Thus, there are immense difficulties in anticipating the rate and direction of technological change, and associated with this the numbers of scientific and technical staff who will be needed and available in the future. Similarly, the educational trends in society and the different approaches to conventional education and training will also create difficulties. It might also be said that the quality of applicant for future employment is likely to increase markedly, given the higher school-leaving age, the growth of higher and further education, and the importance of qualifications; it could be suggested that this situation has the effect of both reducing the initial labour supply available and also changing the quality of the applicant. The situation, of course, presents a problem, but a problem that necessitates acceptance, and action taken to ease or solve it. It is sometimes argued that the trade union movement provides an example of this position, the suggestion being that the major source of recruitment for trade union officials was for many years the early school leavers. This meant people left school at the minimum age, and the unions could be highly selective; also from the point of view of the abler leavers, the trade union represented an outlet for the utilisation of their abilities. Given that the staffing structure of trade unions has not basically changed[47] and that there has been considerable growth in further and higher education (allied to the fact that the school-leaving age has risen) the result has been that the traditional source of trade union recruitment has diminished. This argument is, of course, based on a rather simplistic view of the workings of the educational system, i.e. that it is possible to identify 'ability' and that the educational system functions in this way. Perhaps a more realistic assessment of this would be that the extent to which the education system is successful in this respect depends on the extent to which people are capable of utilising the opportunities available.

On a more general, or theoretical level, Walker[48] has highlighted two major reasons for pursuing manpower planning which also reflect his interpretation of the activity. He suggests, firstly, that as a result of the increasing costs of obtaining, training and keeping the skilled manpower which is now required by organisations, new concepts are needed for manpower planning because managerial responsibility in this area has increased markedly in recent years. The second reason that manpower planning is increasing is because the size of organisations is continually increasing, and this means associated increases in manpower requirements and in the complexity of managing human resources efficiently. This complexity, however, and the constraints which exist to prevent or inhibit effective planning are surely major reasons for undertaking the planning activity in the first place. The fact that conditions are likely to change and increase in complexity presents a clear-cut situation for most organisations: either to react to changing circumstances which they have deliberately avoided trying to predict or understand, or alternatively to attempt to plan ahead and forecast what is likely to happen by monitoring outside trends and circumstances; by ascertaining what they would like to achieve, and given the information they will require for the monitoring and forecasting processes, a serious attempt could be made to control their situation in order to achieve their desired future. As Gray has said, 'this complexity is . . . a challenge to ingenuity and persistent efforts at mitigation . . . not an excuse for withdrawal'.[49] It is perhaps useful to draw an analogy with the problems of planning and population control in organisations by reference to Professor Myone Stycos,[50] who in discussing the problems of fertility control in underdeveloped areas, refers to what he terms the real problems in population planning and birth control, namely, ignorance (about what can be done); indifference (because of a lack of information); ambivalence (of attitude); and late motivation. All of these problems could be said to apply in varying degrees to many organisations, and perhaps none more so than the problem of late motivation, which could be defined as the problem of organisations only becoming seriously interested in planning and control when the manpower problems are upon them (problems which might well have been avoided by taking measures in line with desired objectives). The argument is taken to be that organisations exist in a society which experiences considerable change, and as a result few organisations are static; in this context planning is regarded as necessary, and in every way preferable to a reactive approach with expediency as its justification.

To return more specifically to the difficulties involved in manpower planning due to the different interpretations of the concept, it would appear that many activities are referred to as 'manpower planning', and that progress in this field is hindered because of this fact and also because the difference in emphasis on different aspects of the process has led to a fragmentary approach, with the existence of a number of separate activities, with responsibility for recruitment planning, succession planning, manpower forecasting and so on. What would appear to be lacking is a comprehensive approach which is capable of providing a link between the various aspects of what is commonly regarded as manpower planning.

Such an approach to manpower planning should particularly allow an integration of approaches that have stressed either quantitative or qualitative considerations, given that there would appear to be a consensus in most discussions of manpower planning that the aims of such an activity is to assure the organisation both quantitatively and qualitatively of sufficient manpower to satisfy its future development. In this context, manpower planning is taken to have two distinct yet interrelated elements: prediction or forecasting, and control. This is in line with Gray's view that 'the

objects of planning are prediction and control',[51] and the interpretation of Walker[52] who regards an integrated approach to
manpower planning as combining the elements of forecasting,
and the design of activities. However, what our interpretation
does not do is to differentiate completely between the elements of
forecasting and control. It does happen that these two elements are
taken as separate concepts, which might be termed manpower
forecasting and manpower management. An example of this
would be the approach taken by Moss, who distinguishes clearly
between manpower forecasting and manpower planning in the
following way, 'manpower planning is considered as a three-stage
operation which attempts to explain, predict, and influence
manpower changes in relation to the changing economic, technical
and social situation of establishments. Manpower forecasting is
concerned with explaining and predicting'.[53] The difference, in
other words, lies in the question of influencing or controlling the
situation. This, on the surface would appear to account adequately
for the situation, but the difficulties occur when Moss goes on to
discuss training in terms of a manpower-forecasting approach, and
inevitably has to attribute to manpower forecasting the very
characteristics he suggests are the basis of manpower planning, in
saying that manpower forecasting would appear to have to ensure
an adequate supply of trained men and women at all levels of
industry.[54] The ensuring of an adequate supply of manpower is
surely a control or influencing function? The point to be made is
that forecasting and control are best looked upon as important
parts of a process, and it is argued here that it is more constructive
and effective to highlight the integrative aspects of the process
rather than the distinctions. Thus rather like a pluralistic view of
industrial relations,[55] or a realistic view of conflict,[56] it is necessary
to accept the fact that differences exist and require accommodation.
In manpower planning terms, therefore, it is accepted that there
are distinct elements in the process but it is regarded as more
important that these are pursued within a comprehensive and
integrated framework.

The interpretation of manpower planning adopted here is,
therefore, that manpower planning is concerned with two elements: firstly manpower forecasting, which entails forecasting
overall organisational manpower requirements (age, type, etc.),
this will also involve the setting of manpower targets and must be
integrated with general business planning; and secondly, manpower management or control which refers to the control of the
population in terms of formulating personnel policies and

personnel programmes. One further, yet vital point needs to be made at this stage in the context of the above approach, and this is the relationship between organisation structure and planning. One of the important tasks for any organisation is to relate, as closely as possible, the number and structure of jobs to be done, and the size and structure of the population; these factors will change over periods of time and as a result the manpower planning process will need to be a continuous process. The changes will be due to changes in both the internal and external environment, and there is an important difference here, in that an organisation can monitor or have early warning of internal changes, but organisations are subject to outside forces – not the least of which is national level intervention – and these changes will necessitate a constant changing of manpower plans.

Before analysing in more detail the two key areas of forecasting and control – the quantitative and qualitative considerations of manpower planning – it is essential to pay some attention to the point raised above, that is the constraints presented by outside environmental factors, and particularly the question of national level intervention and national manpower policies (the more immediate environmental features which relate to the careers of individuals are regarded here mainly as aspects of the 'control' features of manpower planning, as are the questions of organisation planning and organisation structure, and will be integrated into the discussion of qualitative factors later in this chapter.)

NATIONAL MANPOWER PLANNING – SOME ISSUES

The same characteristics involved in manpower planning at organisational level are taken as being relevant to national manpower planning, which means that consideration of planning at national level will be concerned with both forecasting, and with policies or control.

The need for manpower data to be more readily available and more accurate has been stressed by Hall, who in arguing for an improvement in manpower information systems suggests that the data being compiled in industry represents an untapped statistical source of immense national value.[57] It has been pointed out that the statistics which relate to manpower in this country are extremely good,[58] and certainly there would appear to be almost a surfeit of manpower information on certain topics; however, there are problems particularly with regard to the irregularity of the publishing of some statistics, the division of responsibility amongst government departments, and the time lag between collection and publication. Some improvement in manpower statistics in specific areas might also be useful.

The statistical information is of course, particularly relevant to the forecasting element of national manpower planning; but it should be stressed that there are two distinct elements in the forecasting function – the forecasting of the availability of manpower, and the forecasts of manpower needs. The question of forecasting manpower supply is, perhaps, the less difficult part of the process and there are, of course, already in existence the projections of future population. Attempts have been made, too, to predict the size of the future labour force,[59] and also the size of special occupational groupings.[60] There, is however, considerable potential in the area concerned with forecasting manpower supply, particularly with regard to the question of personnel flow, since not enough is known about the mobility of the population. The collection of such flow information would represent a significant advance.

The forecasting of manpower demand as characterised, for example, by the National Plan[61], and the Ministry of Labour's Pattern for the Future,[62] is a highly complex activity fraught with a great number of problems. As Evans has pointed out, 'surveys of this nature are inevitably crude. Apart from the weakness (or absence) of statistics, they are based on many assumptions that may prove false, notably concerning migration and activity rates'.[63] It is not the intention here to become involved in a discussion of the problems, but it is worth noting that an excellent discussion of the major techniques of projection (time series extrapolations, cross-section comparisons, survey questionnaires, and models) is given by Leicester.[64] The problems involved are also noted and can be classified as problems of forecasting technological progress, the role of factors that may determine employment patterns, and the problem of drawing up a taxonomy of occupations. One could also suggest that there remains another key problem inherent in any attempt to forecast future manpower demand, which applies at both industry and national level; and this is the problem of manpower utilisation. To project past information, which could well reflect manpower misuse of one kind or another, into the future is obviously likely to lead to an artificial situation; what is obviously needed is much more detailed analysis of manpower utilisation before forecasts can be made with any degree of certainty.

That the forecasting situation at national level could be

improved by the provision of more information – perhaps by means of a national manpower grid as suggested by Hall[65] – is difficult to contest. It is difficult, however, to accept the view of the Edinburgh Group who in their discussion of manpower planning at national level suggest that 'there is such a complete lack of information on manpower forecasts of demand and supply in this country that to talk of manpower planning, at a national level, in what ever form it might be practised, is simply not feasible today'.[66] If one accepts that manpower planning involves both forecasting and control (in the form of manpower policies) then it certainly is feasible to talk of national manpower planning, and for two reasons: firstly, because despite the Edinburgh Group's reference to a complete lack of information, there is in existence in this country a considerable amount of information on manpower matters (even allowing for the admitted weaknesses); and, secondly, that national manpower policies (including social and economic policies) are formulated and put into practice, in order to influence the quantity, quality, distribution and mobility of labour. National manpower policies are a reality; they may vary in effectiveness but they do represent an influence on the manpower situation at national and organisational levels. Manpower policies at national level represent both an attempt to control the overall manpower situation, and a framework within which organisations have to plan their own manpower policies.

National manpower policy itself must operate within an important international framework and must obviously concern itself with a consideration of such forces as immigration and emigration. In this context, the staffing of the National Health Service is an excellent example of the importance of international manpower considerations. The primary consideration, however, of national manpower policies would appear to be with the achievement of economic growth. Johnston,[67] for example, has pointed out that British governments see manpower policy as a major instrument for the achievement of national manpower objectives, whilst Hunter and Reid have suggested that the encouragement of manpower mobility is a key objective in an active manpower policy for achieving economic growth, the full productive utilisation of manpower, and reasonable price stability.[68]

The area covered by national manpower planning could be said to include those elements in the manpower situation which are the product of society – its beliefs, values, its rate and direction of growth – in other words matters over which no one element in society has control. Such features as the total supply of, and demand for, labour, manpower mobility or immobility, the quality and availability of education and training, and general economic and social policies which would affect the manpower supply and demand position, would be relevant in the national manpower context. The justification, too, for national manpower planning rests largely on this concept of the goals and values of society, although there is also a more practical argument which refers to the fact that it is being increasingly realised that the labour market does not respond to free market processes, and that economic, personal, sociological and institutional factors hinder the operation of such a market; accordingly, intervention at national level in the manpower system has become accepted as necessary.[69]

National manpower policies operate within a time scale, reflecting long and short-term objectives. There is surely a need to understand the interrelationship of policies designed to affect the situation in the long or short term, and this understanding will only occur if the differentiation between manpower policies in terms of time is also fully understood. A most useful discussion of this theme is presented by Cassel[70] who relates the role of government in manpower planning to long range, intermediate range, and short-range policies, and suggests that it is the framework of long-range policies which determine the need for, and character of, the sub-policies of the intermediate and short run. Thus, the failure of long-term policies to produce, for example, enough scientists and engineers might have to be overcome by more immediate policies which might include the liberalising of immigration, or a particular emphasis on the encouragement of mobility. It is obviously important to make more effective the longer-range policies and reduce the need for improvisation and this highlights the need to improve the forecasting of, and dissemination of, manpower trends and information. This in itself suggests an important link between national and organisational manpower policies, for, as Johnston has argued, it is of the highest importance that we should ensure that national manpower programmes are properly understood and implemented at the company or 'grass roots' level.[71] In other words there is a distinct need for integration between national and organisational levels in terms of co-ordinating manpower policy.

The particular policy areas at national level which obviously affect the organisational situation would cover the areas of health and population, immigration and emigration, education and training, foreign affairs, the organisation of labour, and general policy regarding the development of particular areas. This latter point would cover the need felt to develop certain underdeveloped regions or 'grey areas', [72] location of industry policy, characterised, for example, by the allocating of grants for the building of factories in particular areas, and, given the importance of the government as an employer, the siting of government institutions in particular regions.[73] The issues of health and population can, to some extent, be thought of as interrelated since certain policies with regard to health will obviously affect the size (and quality) of the population; thus, the provision of a minimum standard of living through the provision of social security benefits, the payment of family allowances, and the provision of birth control information and advice, represent possible influences on the general population, and hence on the working population. Similarly, immigration policy represents an important influence on the size and nature of the work force, and also policy in foreign affairs – the question of entering the Common Market – will affect the nature of the labour market.

One of the key areas of national manpower policy lies in the field of education and training. Educational policies at national level will affect the quality and quantity of the supply of educated manpower available to employing organisations. This important relationship between the education system and the employment system means that any change in educational policy – the growth of polytechnics and technological universities, the development of comprehensive education, the possible replacement of student grants by loans – will have repercussions at organisational level. Similarly, government intervention in the field of industrial training through the introduction of the 1964 Industrial Training Act with its associated levy grant system, represents a financial pressure on companies to implement the national policy for industrial training.

Johnston,[74] in fact, has argued very forcibly for organisational manpower activities to be conducted in a way that enables them to be encompassed within a national framework, and has illustrated four important links between state policy and company practice: the Manpower Research Unit of the Department of Employment and Productivity, the Public Employment Service, various 'early warning' systems (e.g. periods of notice, the Redundancy Payments Act, and the Contract of Employment Act), and the Industrial Training Act. Though there are deficiencies in the operation of these links at the present time, it can certainly be argued that they are important sources of contact between national and organisational levels, and that further attention should be paid by both sectors to ways of improving the two-way flow of ideas and information. Thus, we can think of manpower planning at company and at national levels as parallel and not dissimilar activities.

National manpower planning can be considered as the major framework within which company planning has to operate, but there are other constraints in existence which need to be considered, particularly the manpower planning which takes place at industry level, and the attitudes to manpower planning by trade unions. At industry level, the need for manpower forecasting on an industry wide basis has been continually stressed,[75] and the Manpower Research Unit of the Department of Employment and Productivity has played a major part in carrying out this function. In terms of manpower planning or control, the Industrial Training Boards were set up with the intention of improving the manpower situation in their respective industries, and though there has been much controversy about the working and effects of the various boards, there is evidence to show that they represent a major influence on company manpower policies.[76] There are, of course, considerable difficulties in manpower planning at industry level, not the least of which is the fact that manpower planning for an industry may not be in the best interests of particular firms, or possibly occupational groups. In addition, as Yewdall[77] has pointed out, there are difficulties in forecasting at industry level, such as the importance of a thorough understanding of the nature of an industry's utilisation of its manpower, and the problem of reconciling approaches which on the one hand assume an equalisation of pressures when calculating the whole, and on the other, attempt to assume the forecasts of individual companies to arrive at the whole. However, it could be suggested that providing the information collected at industry level (e.g. the level of employment, occupational breakdowns, and mobility estimates) is sound, then an effective integration can take place between national, industry and organisational levels.

The trade union role in manpower planning cannot be overestimated. If manpower planning is interpreted in terms of forecasting and control, then the attitude of the trade union sector to both forecasts of manpower requirements (which rely on analyses of utilisation) and to methods of controlling manpower, can greatly affect the outcome of any attempts to improve or change the manpower situation. The trade union movement would appear to accept the need for manpower planning; the Amalgamated

Engineering Union[78](Amalgamated Union of Engineering Workers) in their evidence to the Royal Commission on Trade Unions' and Employers' Associations, appeared to accept the need for such an activity, and the General Secretary of the Transport and General Workers' Union, Mr Jack Jones, has argued that trade unions do accept the need for greater flexibility in the use of labour, and that this has been shown by the extension of productivity bargaining.[79]

In practice, there is often a good deal of difficulty in obtaining speedy joint agreements to improve the manpower situation, such as the extension of shift working, the improvement of the traditional apprenticeship system, the reduction of overmanning and the cutting down of overtime. Success will depend quite naturally on whether the trade unions (employees) perceive the outcome of such attempts to be favourable, i.e. an improvement. Such factors as the speed, nature and extent of such changes are, therefore major considerations. The point at issue here is that trade unions are often in a position to be able to radically affect – one way or another – manpower planning proposals, and as such represent an important influence on any attempt to plan and improve the human resources situation in an organisation. The role of trade unions in manpower planning is an obvious basic consideration.

The above discussion of the factors involved in manpower planning at national level, has hopefully indicated, firstly, that at this level, manpower planning has many of the basic features of planning at organisational level, and secondly, that national planning activities must be looked at as a framework for all organisational planning activities. There are certainly deficiencies in the integration between the different planning levels, but regardless of such weaknesses the significant point is that any attempt to plan manpower in organisations must take account of the constraints imposed by government planning, and by the attitudes and activities of other key sectors of the labour market. Manpower planning at organisational level, if it is to be viable, must be realistic; constraints do exist, and must be catered for if both the forecasting and control elements of manpower planning are to be effective.

MANPOWER PLANNING AT ORGANISATIONAL LEVEL

This book is primarily concerned with organisational attempts to control human resources, and the emphasis in this latter part of the chapter will be on a detailed analysis of the two key elements in the manpower planning process, which have been identified as prediction and control. It will be argued that for the planning activity to be successful the two approaches must be looked upon as closely interconnected and that information received from predictions and analysis is essential for the formulation of realistic and effective personnel policies. The relationship between forecasting and control, therefore, is taken to illustrate that effective control is dependent upon an analysis of the present manpower position and subsequent predictions made on that basis. The fact that such a manpower analysis is a necessary first step for predictions and subsequent policy formation requires a greater understanding of the process of analysis, and in this respect, two important aspects of manpower analysis will be discussed; firstly, the provision of relevant information on manpower matters, and secondly, the need for a detailed study of the utilisation of present manpower.

A manpower information system with at least the basic data on employees is a necessity for any attempt to plan or manage manpower. As the Edinburgh Group have said, 'in order to be able to assess the forward needs of the company for manpower, to anticipate the consequences of reorganisation, to prepare a new wage structure, or to carry out other studies in a manpower programme, there is the prime need for a manpower information system of the organisation's human resources'.[80] Exactly what information will be required, and the associated detail, will depend on the problems to be examined and the needs of the institution, but obviously more than an awareness of numbers is needed. A useful first step might be to divide the organisation into cohort groups, and then to obtain information about numbers, age distribution, performance and potential for promotion, retirement data, particular skills, salary and salary progression, present job and job progression, general experience and qualifications. With such records and information it should certainly be possible to initiate a manpower planning operation.

It has been suggested that one area in which progress could be made is in the development of a system of occupational classification,[81] and this inevitably relates to the computerisation of personnel records. Hall,[82] in arguing for the development and standardisation of personnel data by means of a personnel tape, has suggested that the computerisation or the mechanisation of payrolls, offers revolutionary possibilities in handling the main ranges of personnel data. Certainly, as Newton[83] indicates, given a computerised system it is possible to develop occupational classification systems which might range from those using a single axis of classification, (i.e. long list of jobs under various headings) to multi-axis classification systems which would look at the job in several different dimensions. Cox,[84] has shown that a multi-dimensional system of classification of jobs can be successfully developed, and her work in developing such a system in the Ministry of Technology would appear to lend support to both her arguments: firstly, that to undertake manpower planning we must be able to define and identify the jobs we must plan for; and secondly, that the development of such job classification systems provides an important link between organisational and national manpower planning. Hall, too, has emphasised the importance of standardising information possibly by standardising codings for educational and occupational information, and possibly by the development of what he refers to as a 'national manpower grid'.[85] Such developments are to be welcomed, but to return to the more specific problem of adequate personnel information for man-power purposes at organisational level, the key point remains that such personnel records should provide information about human resources that is both quantitatively and qualitatively relevant to the purposes of forecasting, and to the formulation of personnel policies. There are, of course, problems involved in the develop-ment of a manpower information system: the lack of uniformity in record keeping throughout the organisation, the difficulties in retrieving information even where it exists, and the problem of continually updating information – and the aim must be to ensure that there is a standardisation of personnel records which will enable manpower planning to be undertaken. One approach is through the computerisation of such information, and certainly if the system is computerised then the possibilities for a more sophisticated manpower planning exercise increase. It is perhaps useful to quote Vetter in this context, who, in emphasising both the need for manpower inventories and the capability of the computer in this area, refers to the fact that

'the inventory should enable the analyst to determine the existing manpower significant categories (function, experience, training, age, performance, quality, and the like), where it is being utilised and how it is being utilised. These data can be integrated into matrices for analytical purposes. To be effective and economic, the inventory effort should be co-ordinated with the data retrieved systems and performance and potential appraisal programmes'.[86]

The other vitally important area of manpower analysis refers to the fact that before any manpower planning is attempted there is a need for a detailed study of the utilisation of present manpower. That the underemployment and misemployment of human resources represent a problem in this country is continually being stressed. The late National Board for Prices and Incomes drew attention to this in a number of their references; for example their report on railwaymen's pay suggested that the railways were over-manned,[87] and their report on overtime working in Britain illustrated the high degree of overtime being worked in this country.[88] Similarly, the development of productivity bargaining has drawn attention to the extent of restrictive practices, and has illustrated, in some cases, the more efficient utilisation of manpower that can be achieved; and at a more specialist level, Pym had demonstrated the underutilisation of engineers and scientists.[89] Certainly the 'problem' of white-collar redundancies might be looked upon as a consequence of a wholesale analysis of utilisation by employing organisations. One of the difficulties, however, would appear to be in distinguishing – in productivity or performance terms – between analyses primarily concerned with numbers employed (for example, manning comparisons), and analyses which are more concerned with actual utilisation, or the quality of performance. For the purposes of forecasting and planning manpower requirements, whilst manning indices and comparisons are useful in highlighting deficient areas, it is suggested that a rather more detailed analysis is required of all aspects of manpower utilisation.

The analysis of manpower utilisation can be looked at from a number of standpoints, such as the measure of utilisation, whether utilisation deficiencies are caused by misemployment or underemployment, the barriers (in all forms) to improving utilisation (and whether these are likely to be overcome), and ways in which improvements might come about. Perhaps, too, some consideration should be given to the wider implications of an increase in the utilisation of manpower. All of these factors require acknowledgement and consideration.

Measurement of productivity can be extremely complex, and measurement is often linked with particular techniques for improving utilisation. Significantly, much of this activity is concentrated at the lower levels of organisations where many of these techniques are easier to apply. Thus, activity sampling, and the drawing up of manning indices, can be used to analyse what is actually occurring in the way of performance, whilst techniques such as work study, cost benefit analysis and critical path analysis can highlight the difference between the present situation and what could, or should, be the position. In addition, there are available such techniques as performance appraisal and management by objectives, which could be regarded as having implications for both actual performance, and desirable performance.

Analysing manpower utilisation in an organisation is, of course, simply a first step which reflects the relative success of the methods of analysis. What is far more important is an analysis of the reasons for performance levels, which should highlight the structural, attitudinal and behavioural reasons for performance. In structural terms this could cover the effectiveness of the present design of the work process, various aspects of the structure of the organisation, and particularly the design of jobs. In addition, the effects of organisational policies on behaviour (which might represent utilisation) will need assessing. Similarly, some investigation is needed of other factors in the work situation which affect the behaviour of individuals in their jobs; outside influences, the importance of custom, career aspirations, the importance of trade unions. Many of these factors might be outside the organisation's control, but it is important to be aware of the relative influence of factors affecting manpower utilisation. At least the organisation might then be in a position to know the areas in which it might effectively discuss change.

The Edinburgh Group[90] make an important point when they suggest that studies of manpower utilisation only become meaningful when studied against a background of the ideal or expected pattern of manpower development. This is a question of both organisational and job objectives, and involves examining the present situation – as revealed by manpower analysis studies – against standards which the organisation has specified as being desirable. The movement from the present position to the desired one, might, of course, be hindered by any of the factors mentioned earlier, but if the objectives set are realistic then some account would presumably have been taken of their influence. One other point which is relevant at this stage, however, refers to the fact that manpower is not an independent variable, but is interchangeable with capital. Thus, any change in the capital situation will affect the manpower position to an extent which will need careful analysing. Similarly, any capital decision will need studying in terms of the likely manpower effects.

The position adopted here is that the utilisation of manpower is a key concept in manpower planning, and this is in line with Pym's emphasis on the futility of any manpower planning exercise which does not take the utilisation of its labour force as a starting point. Manpower utilisation is taken to represent behaviour in the work organisation, and on this basis the influence on this behaviour became crucial. It is not intended to enter into detail about the various considerations that are known to affect organisational behaviour at this stage, but it is relevant to comment that, though there are approaches which emphasise the motivational aspects of behaviour,[91] approaches which emphasise the prior orientations of individuals,[92] and approaches which emphasise the importance of structural features in the work situation,[93] the fact remains that to an extent, which needs determining, the organisation can influence the behaviour of its members. It is for this reason that an analysis of manpower utilisation must take into account the causes for the present level of utilisation.

Detailed analysis of manpower utilisation is a vital prerequisite for any attempt to forecast or plan ahead, and this relationship has been emphasised by a number of writers. Newton,[94] for example, makes the point that simply to equate the supply and demand aspects of manpower is inadequate, since this will only perpetuate the misuse or underuse of manpower where this exists, and the Edinburgh Group[95] have argued that before entering into a forecast of manpower demand, it is necessary to ensure that the present resources are those most appropriate to the tasks being performed. Walker[96] too, has made the point that attempts to forecast from historical data alone are marked by a built-in capacity to optimise the utilisation of human resources, whilst on similar lines Vetter[97] has commented that when historical data is used exclusively the emphasis is on what *has* been rather than on what *ought* to be. There is a need for organisations, when attempting to forecast their future demand for manpower, to assess the present situation in some objective way (i.e. meaningful to them), and to analyse the reasons for present utilisation. For it is obviously desirable that any present misuse of manpower is not carried into the future. Manpower forecasting and manpower planning need a sound base, which implies detailed studies of manpower utilisation.

MANPOWER FORECASTING

The role of forecasting in the manpower planning process encompasses two distinct yet interrelated areas: the forecasting of organisational manpower requirements, and the forecasting of available manpower supply (both internally and externally). The intention is to analyse the two areas separately, and then attempt to discuss them in terms of the overall role of forecasting. This will then be linked with the control aspect of the planning process, with the intention of suggesting an integrated approach to the management of the forward movement of organisations and manpower.

The establishment of organisational manpower requirements, the demand function, is linked with the overall plan for corporate growth. The closeness and nature of this link will obviously vary with differing circumstances, but as a general principle it could be suggested that planning manpower requirements without reference to the corporate plan could at best be irrelevant, and at worst potentially disastrous. Despite the fact that there will be some variance in the information provided by the corporate plan in different situations, a minimum base of information in certain cases is obviously necessary, if the manpower plan is to be viable. Heneman and Seltzer,[98] for example, suggested that this minimum base should include facts on product demand (sales and work load); efficiency (technological and administrative change); expansion (facilities expansion, new products); budgets; internal labour supply (quality of manpower, labour turnover); and external labour supply. Further after identifying these factors they have attempted to crystallise the various relationships between the factors, implying that accurate manpower forecasting necessitates identifying, eliminating and weighing the relevant factors.

The importance of the corporate plan for the determination of manpower requirements has been well illustrated by Chadwick[99] with particular reference to the British Petroleum Company. Three major factors are seen as most likely to affect manpower requirements, the general pattern of trading and production, technological change, and social and economic change, but the important point is made that it is perhaps more meaningful to study the manpower implications of such factors on individual sections and individual categories rather than to look at the overall effects of such estimated changes. A similar interpretation of the key factors to be considered is presented by Newton[100] for the Royal Dutch Shell organisation, in that he isolates two main factors which affect manpower demand – trading and production patterns, and technological change. The impact of production plans and of technological change are also referred to by Hodgson[101] in his discussion of manpower forecasting at Ford's; he suggests that for forecasting purposes, data is required about assumptions made about product and profit plans, current manning standards and projected changes (due to method changes, technological changes, or blind faith), and a variety of historical data from which behavioural projections can be made. There are particular problems associated with manpower forecasting in relation to technological change as Wedderburn[102] and Kuhn[103] have pointed out, and the answer could well be that manpower can only be planned ahead in relation to the degree of technological knowledge.

Attempts to forecast demand for manpower in relation to the corporate plan, are likely to be unrewarding unless the overall requirements are formulated after consideration of requirements at each functional or divisional level. This is an important point, emphasising the need for detailed analysis of the present manpower position at functional level (and below), and then the forecasting of requirements on the basis of both this analysis and of perceived changes. It may be useful in this respect to look at functions as sub-systems, or small organisations in their own right, and it may be observed that given an overall rate of expansion for an organisation then the rate of expansion of the functions or sub-systems may be greater or less than the overall rate. Given the need for such a forecast base, it is important that each function is examined in terms of category of employee. The relationship between the corporate plan which will depend on economic, technological and financial forecasts, and manpower forecasting, is a two-way relationship; the corporate plan will be affected by manpower forecasts, and similarly the corporate plant will affect the forecasts of manpower emerging at functional level.

The forecasting of the demand for manpower represents one important area of the manpower forecasting process; the other is the forecasting of the supply of manpower, and manpower supply itself is represented by two distinct elements: manpower which might be available from outside the organisation, and the internal manpower supply. Forecasts of the external supply of manpower will be based on information obtained from a number of sources concerning various aspects of the likely manpower position. Population predictions will relate closely to the likely size and nature of the labour force (such as sex, age and occupational structure). Estimates of the total labour force and of occupational groupings will obviously need to consider the number of people emerging from the educational system at all levels, and also the rates of emigration and immigration. Of course, this information is purely quantitative and refers to the potentially available manpower; whether an organisation will be able to recruit the manpower it requires will depend on a variety of factors, some outside its control (for example the general desire of married women to work, the occupational choices of individuals, and the influence of the social security system and so on), and other factors over which it does indeed have control, and which relate to the area which we shall call 'personnel policy' and to which we shall refer shortly.

The supply of manpower available internally is usually ascertained by analysis in certain areas. Initially, of course, it is necessary to prepare a detailed assessment of the manpower position at the present time, and for this information to be readily available. The other important area relates to the numbers of people actually leaving the organisation at present, and the estimated future wastage rate, and it is this area which will be dealt with in some detail, since in many ways it provides a linking point between the more quantitatively based forecasting area, and the qualitative or control side of manpower planning.

In a useful discussion of the development of manpower planning policies, Bryant [104] has pointed out that much of the early work in this field dealt with labour turnover problems, and certainly there would appear to be some justification for treating labour turnover as a subject in its own right, given the amount of work conducted into the problems of wastage. However, simply to take the crude wastage rate – the number of employees leaving during a period divided by the average number employed during the period, as a percentage – is often unrevealing, and it is often useful to develop some form of 'stability index' to highlight wastage amongst longer service employees. Certainly it is more useful to analyse turnover for specific areas – functions, departments, job categories, age, sex, reasons for leaving – rather than simply to rely on the crude wastage rate.

Most of the early work on labour turnover was initiated by the Tavistock Institute of Human Relations and particularly by Rice, Hill and Trist.[105] This work identified labour turnover as a quasi-stationary process and involved an examination of survival patterns and the formulation of survival distributions. Perhaps the most significant thing about this work is the way in which it attempts to put forward behavioural reasons for the various survival distributions, identifying three major phases in the turnover process: the period of induction crisis, the period of differential transit, and the period of settled connection. The work of the Tavistock researchers highlighted a number of important characteristics of the labour turnover process, and these have been well documented by Silcock[106] in an important paper. As these characteristics have considerable implications for the development of measures or policies to control wastage, it is useful to mention the major characteristics: these would include the fact that the rate of turnover varies widely between different firms; most terminations are at the request of the employee; wastage decreases as length of service increases; wastage decreases as the amount of skill exercised increases; and that wastage is higher among females, and is higher among married women than single women. Similar characteristics are identified by Gaudet,[107] and by Hedberg.[108] The identification of such characteristics obviously provides a most useful basis in attempting to understand and control wastage, but it could be suggested that it is on Silcock's description of *possible* characteristics (i.e. characteristics on which the evidence is fragmentary) that attention should be focused, for it is in these areas that the sociological and psychological features of labour turnover occur, and it is strongly argued here that in order to obtain a realistic understanding of labour turnover it is necessary to understand the relationship between organisational policies, conditions, and features, and the orientations to work and careers displayed by individuals. Silcock himself would appear to recognise this, when he suggests that the interaction between the characteristics of the institution and the individual may result in a constant force of separation, and that this constant force varies from one individual to another with a given probability distribution.[109]

It was stated earlier that the phenomenon of wastage represented a meeting point for the quantitative or forecasting approaches to manpower planning and the qualitative or control approaches, and this can be seen particularly in the area of prediction. In this context, prediction is taken to mean something beyond forecasting which is really concerned with assessing manpower requirements, forecasting manpower supply, and highlighting various factors which might influence the situation. Prediction is related to policy, and Chadwick [110] presents a clear picture of the role of prediction in manpower planning – as a means of assisting in policy decisions, detecting trends, indicating the future consequences of present courses of action, and the probable future consequences of alternative possibilities – with particular reference to the use his organisation makes of mathematically based prediction techniques. Thus, a projection of the structure of the labour force for a stated number of years can reveal areas of concern for the manpower planner, and mathematical or operational research techniques can be used to show the probabilities of individuals or groups remaining with the organisation after a given number of years.

Bartholomew[111] has provided a detailed discussion of many of the mathematical techniques available, and his own approach is also worthy of comment. Essentially, Bartholomew uses the concept of renewal to discuss the labour turnover process. He initially considered labour turnover as a renewal process, with wastage being made up by means of a self-renewing aggregate,[112] thus the renewal problem for organisations, a problem involving both wastage and length of service, could be solved given certain assumptions, and predictions made about recruitment needs. In terms of predicting manpower requirements for new or expanding organisations, Bartholomew suggests that an adequate supply of manpower is initially required, and also that the rate of required replacement will need to be much higher than for a more traditional organisation. The later development of renewal theory by Bartholomew has been concerned with the development of a theory of a multi-stage renewal process, where the size of the stages are fixed, and the transfer rates are treated as random variables.[113] Applications of this theory have been discussed by Bartholomew with reference to the prediction of manpower needs in a newly established organisation, the behaviour of a contracting organisation and the prediction of recruitment, wastage and promotion rates in simple hierarchical organisations[114] The significance of this sort of theorising about manpower planning problems, is that it does draw attention towards the areas in which detailed information is required. Thus the suggestion that it would be useful to know how propensity to leave depends on grade and length of service in the organisation, and seniority within grade, is particularly apt, and certainly his approach is useful in highlighting the problem in manpower planning of understanding the relationship between organisational policies, and the attitudes and behaviour of individuals. This understanding is essential if the predictive element in manpower planning is to become more sophisticated.

The development of mathematical models for application to manpower problems represents one area where considerable progress has been made, and where future progress will depend, as Young has indicated, 'on how well mathematicians and behavioural scientists can co-operate with each other to transfer sociological observations into mathematical models.[115] There are a variety of types of mathematical models proposed for the study of manpower systems, and Kendall[116] has presented an interesting discussion of three broad classes of model: models concerning supply and demand, models concerning organisation and utilisation, and models concerning industrial learning and education. Other interesting and relevant models would include the development of a model of the behaviour of hierarchical structures by Dill et al.,[117] and the utilisation of an operational research model by Eilon[118] to predict promotion and wastage situations.

Young[119] has developed and utilised, what have been termed Markovian models, in the prediction of future manpower structures. The basis of this approach can be understood by reference to two demographic models of staffing situations, the first a model of staff wastage based on the 'log normal law of distribution', and the second, a model of the hierarchical staff structure of institutions based on 'status profile analysis'. The log normal law of wastage asserts that staff leave an organisation according to a clearly definable pattern of length of service, that this pattern may be recognised early in service, and survival rates deduced, from which losses of staff can be predicted; if total staff requirements are known then recruitment needs can be predicted. The second approach, status profile analysis, is based on the assumption that recruitment, promotion and wastage patterns of staff are stable over reasonable periods of time, so that the probability that someone in a particular grade at any time will be in some other grade at a later time can be established from the detailed recent career histories of staff; using these probabilities the probable distribution of the numbers of staff in each status or category (the status profile of the organisation) at future dates can be inferred from the status profile at one particular time. The significance of modelling the flow of people through the organisation over time is, as Haire[120] has pointed out, that it makes available the power of formal analysis, which up to the present has been restricted to other issues in organisations. Thus, Young is able to observe that institutions pass through staffing cycles, and that this process involves the expansion and contraction of organisations, the effect this has on promotion and wastage, and the subsequent behavioural effects of such changes.

The above approaches can be extremely useful in highlighting future areas of difficulty such as promotion blockages and the probable future distributions of staff. It should, however, be pointed out, firstly, that these approaches are, perhaps, more relevant to larger organisations with well defined patterns of career structure, and with a sound system of personnel records, and secondly, that the manpower situation during the period in which the future probabilities were based may well have been influenced by certain significant events or changes in policy. The question of assumptions is also important in this context, and as the Edinburgh Group have said 'models are not the reality; and the answers they give are no better than the assumptions fed into them; it is for this reason that, while they should be warmly welcomed, they should be used with caution and their finding interpreted with clinical care'.[121]

Despite the cautionary note expressed above, there can be little question of the value of such models in giving warning of the situations that might develop if existing policies are continued. What is, however, also required is a more detailed and sophisticated understanding of the underlying processes of staff movement. One of the major difficulties in managing and planning human resources is the lack of understanding of the underlying processes, and the apparent complexity of the whole area of influences upon employee attitudes and behaviour. One interesting attempt to solve problems of motivation, turnover, and employee reactions to various types of organisational policy has been made by Miller[122] who attempts to integrate the predictive and behavioural elements in manpower situations, through simulating human behaviour by means of a high-speed electronic computer; basically this is an attempt to represent and manipulate causes, effects and complex interdependencies. The attempt to model and simulate behaviour in this way is certainly one area where mathematicians and behavioural scientists might continue, but the point should be made that at the present time the predictions of such simulation models of individual behaviour have yet to be validated,[123] and that it is very difficult to establish event validity for a simulation model.[124]

The manpower planner and the manpower manager are of necessity involved in the consideration and control of a great variety of behavioural processes. The quantitative approaches discussed above can be extremely useful in providing information about possible areas of overmanning and shortages, and in suggesting future probabilities of movement between grade, and future career structures. What is also required is an examination of both organisational needs and individual needs in order to understand what modifications will be required to meet these needs. This relationship between the needs of individuals and the organisation has been discussed by McLelland,[125] and though he comments that organisations and individuals are fundamentally non comparable, he does attempt to establish some parameters useful for the prediction of individual behaviour – these he terms 'career patterns'. In similar vein, Cox[126] has indicated that the aim of personnel or manpower planning must be studied from the viewpoint of both the company and the individual; he argues that it is possible to have a common plan of action which aims at an interplay between the company's requirements and supply of manpower and the personal opportunities for the employee to find his niche, and suggests that it is easier for the company to satisfy individual wishes if personnel matters are handled with the aid of long-term planning.

The basic problem is one of understanding the workings of the system of personnel flow, and also understanding the relationship between this behaviour and attempts (here termed personnel policies) to control the rate and direction of flow. It is sometimes said that one of the main functions of the social scientist is to help provide decision makers with knowledge about the consequences of alternative courses of action or inaction, and to provide them with better tools for arriving at rational decisions and executing them efficiently. It could be suggested that the provision of 'better tools' necessitates a much clearer understanding of the nature of that which is being manipulated, be it individual, group or organisation, and that, in addition, it is necessary to attempt to establish the nature of the relationship between the 'tools' and variables concerned; for example, if promotion prospects are increased or reduced, what effect will this have on say, wastage or performance? Hedberg,[127] in summarising most of the research on labour turnover, states that sociologists study labour turnover in order to clarify what motivates people to work with a firm, and what factors are of importance for their decisions to quit one job and apply for another. Though labour turnover is but one aspect of the system of personnel flow, this statement does highlight the key concept of occupational choice which can be looked at as a process influenced by sociological, psychological and economic factors. If we are to predict the behaviour of people over extended periods of time, and if we are to attempt to control their actions or choices, then it is important to know not only the characteristics of attitudes, but we must also know how and why such attitudes develop, how and why they change, and how and why such attitudes lead to action. The subsequent chapters are concerned with the analysis of attitudes and behaviour in a number of relevant situations.

What would appear to be required is for the planning and management of human resources to be organised on a systematic basis, which can relate different components of the system to each other and to the system as a whole. The quantitative analysis should provide us with information about actual numbers of people who are in cohort groups, who have joined or left the company, who have moved departments, who are in training, and so on; it should also indicate to us the number of retirements (which are a certainty), and the probabilities of employees moving in or out of the system. On this basis we can attempt to identify where shortages and overmanning will occur.

It is essential, however, to understand the nature of this system of movement, and also the influences which can be utilised to change the rate of this movement. In an organisation people can only move in certain ways: they can move in from outside the organisation, move out of the organisation, move up through the organisation, move laterally within the organisation, or they can move downwards. The major problem is that of attempting to establish the parameters of organisational influence or control, for any success in this area can lead to benefits to manpower management.

Management can certainly influence the probabilities of movement within the system, and can influence the rate and direction of movement through a range of personnel policies. These would include recruitment, selection, training, supervision, appraisal, remuneration and promotion. The way in which these policies operate and the degree to which they are related in practice will be influential in affecting the whole process of movement in the system as well as affecting what we will here term the organisational culture.

The framework, therefore, involves looking at the system in two ways. On the one hand we have certain probabilities of movement; on the other hand we have influences available to management. This enables an overall view to be taken of the problem of managing manpower, and at least we can begin to understand the probabilities of movement in jobs. What we can also do is to try and analyse what each of these influence does to the variables, e.g. does recruitment help movement up or does it help movement out.

The qualitative approach is based on the view that if you wish to predict and control the movement or non-movement of people in an organisation, you must understand the nature of the reasons for movement or non-movement. This understanding is essential for it is on the basis of this knowledge that policies will be formulated for controlling the variables. Young[128] has suggested that future progress might be made with the formulation of social models, on the basis that although patterns of group behaviour do exist, some account must be taken of the reactions of individuals. It is difficult to dispute the basis of this argument, but it could be suggested that it would be more useful to talk in terms of the behavioural aspects of the process (as distinct from purely sociological aspects). It could also be argued that in certain circumstances models of behaviour in organisations have reached a stage beyond that of infancy.

It is suggested here that it is far more meaningful when talking of behaviour in any situation to utilise the approaches of a number of disciplines which might be termed 'behavioural sciences'. Utilising an integrating behavioural science approach is far more likely to produce a more useful analysis of say mobility behaviour in organisations. In addition, there do exist a number of models of organisational behaviour which go some way towards illustrating the complexity of factors which affect behaviour in organisations. These models tend to reflect the orientation of particular disciplines, but it is fair to say that they are becoming more sophisticated as research in the behavioural science field increases. Certainly they are beyond the stage of infancy, and are now becoming increasingly complex.

Thus models of the work behaviour of individuals, indicate that such behaviour may be a function of individual characteristics (abilities), motivational factors, and situational, social or organisational factors. The difference between such models lies in the emphasis placed on the stated influences – for example, the importance of technological factors (Woodward,[129] Perrow[130]), the significance of size (Ingham[131]), the prior orientations of the employee (Goldthorpe et al.[132]), motivational characteristics (Vroom[133]), personality factors (Argyris,[134] McGregor[135]), and bureaucratic, structural influences (Fox[136]). Significantly though there does appear to be an increasing emphasis on the complexity of the interrelationships between the various influences, and it is becoming more apparent that future attempts to conceptualise organisational behaviour will need to integrate the findings of a number of disciplines. An attempt is made in the following chapter to develop such an approach to the concept of occupational choice, which is taken as an important aspect of organisational behaviour, representing not only first choice of job but also subsequent job choice and change. The analysis of occupational choice which is presented, is taken to indicate the type of approach necessary for a greater understanding of the complex behavioural process manifested in personnel flow.

SUMMARY

This chapter has emphasised the importance of human resources in relation to other organisational resources and has argued that there is a need to plan manpower on the same basis as other resources. It was suggested that the manpower planning process should be integrated into the overall corporate planning process, and that the manpower plan should reflect overall organisation objectives.

The term manpower planning has been utilised for a variety of activities from gross number of forecasts of manpower requirements to the whole range of activities in the personnel function. In this context manpower planning was taken to embrace two different but related activities – forecasting and control. Given this interpretation, an analysis was made of the nature and scope of manpower planning at national and organisational levels, and the relationship between the two emphasised. It was also suggested that the adoption of an open-systems approach at organisational level could be helpful in accounting for the considerations.

At national level the differences between forecasting for supply and demand purposes were discussed, and the point made that forecasting for demand was a far more complex activity. Some attempt at forecasting is necessary, however, given the need to control the manpower situation by the formulation of national manpower policies. The same distinction was made at organisational level between forecasting and control, but it was emphasised here, that before any planning could take place, an analysis of the current manpower situation was essential, both in terms of numbers, and, perhaps, more importantly, in terms of the level of utilisation. Given this analysis, it was then possible to attempt the forecasting element of manpower planning again making distinction between the supply and demand aspects of the functions.

The forecasting of manpower requirements at organisational level was seen to be closely associated with the formulation of the organisation's overall objectives and with the importance of forecasting requirements at all levels in the organisation; this was seen to be a complex activity involving a detailed analysis of manpower, and of perceived changes. The supply aspect has two major points of emphasis: forecasting supply from (a) external, and (b) internal sources. Information is available about the output from the total population and from various sub-sectors but, of course, organisations need to forecast what proportion of such populations they can attract. The question of internal supply led on to a discussion of the importance of predicting the wastage situation, which is in turn affected by the whole question of personnel flow, and in this context the nature and scope of mathematical models was discussed. Such models were shown to have considerable potential in assisting the formulation of policies for control of personnel movement.

The final part of the chapter was primarily concerned with emphasising the need for a greater understanding of the relationship between the attitudes and behaviour of staff in organisations, and organisational personnel policies. It was suggested that analysis of organisational behaviour is becoming more sophisticated, and that what is required is an approach which integrates the contributions of all relevant disciplines. In terms of personnel flow progress could be made by the adoption of an integrated approach to occupational choice which would attempt to account for the movement of individuals from the education system, into, and through the employment system.

CHAPTER 2

The Occupational Choice Process

This book is concerned with the planning and utilisation of human resources; and with approaches to their development. The process of 'human resource development', referred to as 'the process of increasing the knowledge, the skill, and the capacities of all the people in a society',[1] can be looked at in terms of the education system, and the aim of the process as the educational goals of the society. It could be argued that these educational goals and the operation of the education system should coincide with the economic aims of the society and the operation of an employment system, and if this is accepted, in economic terms human resource development acquires a different emphasis, and can be defined as 'the accumulation of human capital and its effective investment in the development of an economy'.[2] Much discussion at present surrounds the relationship between the sectors of society concerned with the supply and demand elements of manpower – the education system and the employment system. The concern has been on the one hand with the manpower needs of society in general and of organisations in particular, and on the other with the goals of the education system and the freedom of individual choice. It is intended in this chapter to analyse this important relationship in order to provide a framework for an examination of the concept of occupational choice.

The importance of the relationship between the education system and the employment system, and its inherent difficulties, has been commented on by Crichton in her discussion of the changing social context for the personnel policies of organisations; she states that 'education of individuals in a democratic society must necessarily be more than a vocational preparation for work. Yet work is so dominant in importance . . . that the relationship between education and employment is a vital one'.[3] In similar vein, King has referred to the fact that large-scale commitment of both money and manpower is an index of the importance placed on education in modern Britain and as such this indicates the crucial relationship between education and society.[4]

The fact that this relationship should be the subject of so much discussion, reflects the growing importance of manpower planning at both national and organisational levels, and the argument that manpower planning should be linked to both economic planning and educational planning; in this context, the view that economic planning indicates, for example, what national goals make certain employment patterns desirable in the future, 'whilst educational planning is a different activity and is concerned with the desired expansion of the education and training systems of a country',[5] is taken as being a useful distinction. At the crux of this argument is the fact that educational policies should be concerned with providing the manpower needs of the economy, and it is here that the problem arises. For the educationalists the position is clear, and is well put by Sanford[6] in his discussion of the contribution of higher education to the life of society. He refers to the three traditional functions of a higher education institution as; firstly, the development of the individual; secondly, the preservation and advancement of culture; and, thirdly, the maintenance and further development of technology. He acknowledges the fact that whilst individual development is the supreme goal of a university or college, it is interrelated with the other two goals, and that each depends, to some extent, on the other, and he further indicates that it is possible to arrange things within such institutions that all three goals are favoured, and that actions that serve one serve the others as well. The emphasis, however, Sanford argues should always be on individual development and he refers to the fact that trouble comes when individual development is sacrificed to cultural or technological advancement.

It has been pointed out that the tendency in Britain has been for education to be regarded as good in itself, and for any link with subsequent employment to be regarded to some extent as fortuitous.[7] This educational philosophy which is primarily concerned with treating education as an autonomous social system.[8] is a major reason for what Galbraith has referred to as the split between the intellectuals and the business community in contemporary Western society.[9] There are, of course, certain consequences of a divorce between the education and employment systems, and Carter[10] has highlighted two important consequences in Britain: firstly, the development of an academic tradition in many schools which is deliberately cut off from industry and the outside world; and secondly (and allied to this 'repudiation of the non-academic'), the fact that many of the brighter school leavers have been guided away from industry. Further, in suggesting that the education system is not directly geared to employment he stresses that the main aim of schools is not to prepare pupils for particular occupations.[11] That this is a valid comment can be seen by an examination of the objectives of a representative body of educationalists set up to make proposals for curriculum and examinations for sixth forms; amongst these proposals we find the view that the 'the curriculum must not take its shape from external pressures exerted in the interests of some narrow view of what they may become; rather it must grow from an understanding of what they are and need as sixth formers who will shortly be facing all the complex problems of living in the modern world'.[12]

One of the perceived problems with education appears to be that the system has evolved in its own terms with little reference to what is occurring elsewhere,[13] and also that the education profession has for a long time shut itself off from the eyes of intruders.[14] Eggan suggests that educators have been so busy coping with immediate educational problems that they have had little time or opportunity to step outside their educational institutions and see them as a system in the society as a whole,[15] but Shanks would appear nearer the truth in commenting that 'it is . . . undeniable that the British educational tradition is essentially humanist, and that our technological development has suffered from the traditional undervaluation . . . of technology in our educational system and philosophy'.[16] The issue has been stated as being whether an education system should put the stress on individual development or on the claims of society,[17] but possibly what we should be doing is not stressing either, but thinking in terms of reconciling both national and individual interests, a problem of expanding and making more effective the national economy in manpower terms, whilst at the same time recognising the right of the individual to develop his ability.[18]

Increasingly it appears that the claims of society, or the economy, are being considered, and that an examination is taking place of what the education system is producing, our expectations of it, how it does relate to, and how it could closer relate to, the rest of society. It is probable that the situation that has existed – a split between the manpower supply and demand sectors – will improve. A major reason for this is put by Adams who suggests that if the current ferment in education does not demand it, the cost of new technological developments will force it.[19] If there is a new thread running through the patterns of relationship between educators and employers then it could be that the two principles of the indivisible society and the indivisible individual help considerably to explain; firstly, the growing interest of economic planners in schools and colleges, and of educational planners in industry and commerce, and secondly, to reflect the fact that 'a vigorous and progressive educational system and a vigorous progressive economy are in practice so closely intertwined that neither can be sensibly thought about or healthily developed without the other'.[20]

The problem of matching the supply characteristics of the labour force with the demand features of employment opportunities, a problem of improving the articulation between the world of work and the educational system, has been referred to by Ginzberg[21] as one of the more intractable manpower problems. A theoretical approach to this question of improving manpower utilisation has been formulated by Blaug and Preston[22] for the Industrial Manpower Project at the London School of Economics. What they are essentially attempting to do is to extend the concept of the production function to include education, so that the education of the labour force is linked in productivity terms to manpower planning in two ways: firstly, the derivation of education goals from the needs and demands of industry; and secondly, the analysis of the industrial consequences of particular educational policies. This approach implies that there is a general relationship between the occupational system and the educational system, but it makes clear that the connection between the two systems is likely to be extremely complex.

There are strong economic and social arguments in making the maximum use of people's abilities, and ensuring a flow of talent and skills to professions, occupations and jobs where they will best contribute to the national need.[23] This implies the need for an effective approach in three areas: the effective planning and utilisation of manpower by the employment system; adequate methods and procedures for guiding the flow of personnel from one system to the other; and a closer relationship between individual development and the manpower needs of the economy and the structure of employment opportunities. It should, perhaps, also be pointed out that this effective approach would need to cover the movement of personnel from the schools to the higher education institutions, for, as the Robbins Report illustrated, this is also an area where closer and more effective co-operation is needed.[24]

OCCUPATIONAL CHOICE – A PROBLEM OF INTERPRETATION

The subsequent chapters of this book will suggest that in all three of the above areas there are weaknesses and anomalies in the approaches and methods adopted at the present time. What this chapter is conerned with is to examine the approaches that have been developed to account for the process of occupational choice, and to develop an interpretation of this process which will provide a comprehensive framework for the analysis of the various elements involved in affecting the movement of individuals through the education system, into and through the employment system. It is suggested that theories which have been developed tend to reflect the orientations of particular disciplines, and that what is required is an approach to occupational choice that allows for the complexities of this whole process of movement, and which examines the different yet related effects of psychological, sociological, and economic influences.

Before examining in detail the major theoretical approaches to occupational choice, it is essential to examine fully the meaning of the term. Kuvlesky and Bealer[25] have drawn attention to the dangers involved in a lack of clarification in that the same term is often used for different ideas, and different terms for the same idea, and have further pointed out that erroneous implications can be drawn from such semantic confusion, implications which will impede both an understanding of the phenomena and efficient utilisation of knowledge concerning occupational placement in our society. The definition that Kuvlesky and Bealer adopt, that 'the job that one acquires is conditioned not only by the preferences and desires of the person for a particular occupational status, but also by many factors over which the individual has essentially no control' is broadly in line with the approach in this chapter, in that it acknowledges the importance of the structural aspects of the process as well as emphasising the individuals own desires and perceptions of the occupational structure.

Roe,[26] in arguing strongly that we need to define what is meant by choice, has pointed out that there are different meanings of the term. It could, for example, be taken as meaning what a person would most like to do (if, of course, he had the capacities, training and opportunity), or it could refer to what an individual is attempting to do, or even what the individual will actually come to do. The point made by Roe, has been taken up by Vroom[27] who has distinguished three meanings of the chosen occupation:

firstly, the occupation with the most positive valence (the preferred occupation); secondly, the occupation towards which there is the strongest positive force (the chosen occupation); and thirdly, the occupation in which a person is a member (the attained occupation). Occupational choice in this sense, therefore, is explained in terms of the relative strength of forces acting upon the person. Vroom does suggest that the term 'occupational choice process' can be used to cover all three factors and their determinants, and this emphasis on occupational choice as a process would seem sensible in the light of his differentiation between the preference, choice and attainment elements of occupations, and in view of the highlighted complexity of the experiences young people undergo in their last years at school and in their first years at work.[28]

Ford and Box[29] have tried to distinguish between the adventitious nature of occupational choice, and the purposive element of such choices. Adventitious choices are characterised as unique spontaneous behaviours with choices very often determined by situational contingencies, the implication being that often, in fact, no decision is made. Katz and Martin,[30] in their discussion of career choices of student nurses, illustrate this adventitious definition of choice when pointing out that the process of entry into employment may be looked on as the cumulative product of a series of specific acts which may or may not be directly focused on a deliberate career choice. The approach of Caplow,[31] which stresses the fortuitous nature of some choice behaviour is also indicative of an adventitious approach. For Ford and Box,[32] the purposive element in occupational choice is entirely different, and represents the culmination of a process in which hopes and desires come to terms with the realities of the occupational market situation, this distinction is made, for example, by Sherlock and Cohen in their study of recruitment to dentistry.[33]

It could be suggested that to talk in terms of a choice actually being made at all is misleading. Psathas,[34] for example, has asked the key question as to whether the individual actually chooses the occupational role he will subsequently perform. He argues that it is wrong to talk in terms of 'choice', and more appropriate to see occupational choice in terms of 'settings' which engender orientations to the occupational world. Reynolds[35] has shown that since people do not have sufficient information about the range of alternative opportunities to make deliberate rational choices, they simply 'drift' into jobs, and in line with this Blau et al.[36] have suggested that the conscious deliberation and weighing of alternatives is not necessarily a feature of occupational choice, that where people are entirely indifferent, no choice between occupations need in fact take place. On the other hand, Ford and Box[37] insist that choice does exist, and that it is objective and can be observed. the implication being that the movement from education to employment does occur, and that this should be the starting point for investigation.

Whilst accepting this point in general terms, it is essential to reiterate that this movement might involve any one, or all, of the processes of occupational preferences, occupational choice or occupational attainment, and it could be argued that what Ford and Box are discussing is in fact occupational attainment. If this is so, then it is necessary to point out that one's choice of occupation is not always followed by successful attainment of that occupation: a situation that might occur, for example, if an individual fails to meet any of the entry qualifications for that occupation. On the other hand, the situation will exist where an individual will successfully attain the occupation of his choice. However, in that situation, as Vroom[38] points out, the successful attainment of an occupation could well be the result of two sets of choices – a choice made by the individual and a choice made by social institutions – implying that people not only select occupations, but are selected for occupations. Certainly Merton's[39] suggestion that recruitment, occupational choice, and allocation to occupations, are but three aspects of the same process in that they are all concerned with the flow of personnel into the employment system, supports the view that occupational choice should not be looked upon solely as an individual's ideal choice of occupation.

The idea that the individuals choice of occupation should be seen in a wider context is present in the definition of the concept taken by Rottenberg,[40] who looks upon occupational choice as the mechanism by which the labour force responds to the demands of the labour market.This is essentially a view of occupational choice as an economic process, and certainly it is apparent that the classical economists saw men making occupational choices in terms of relative prices in different occupations. Adam Smith,[41] for example, had a simple approach to occupational choice – that every man will pursue his interest which will prompt him to seek the advantageous and shun the disadvantageous employment. Vroom,[42] too, has indicated that choices among occupations are a result not only of preferences among them, but also of the subjective probability and expected costs of their attainment; and Blau et al.[43] have referred to the importance of the individuals valuations of the rewards offered by different alternatives in the choice process. It could seem apparent, therefore, that economic concepts such as cost, price and reward, can have considerable utility in any analysis of the determinants of choice.[44]

It is obvious that there are many different interpretations of occupational choice, interpretations which emphasise particularly psychological, sociological or economic aspects of the process. It is possible, however, to draw together certain common elements of most of the definitions of occupational choice, and thus to put forward an interpretation of the term which will allow for a discussion of the various and wide-ranging theoretical approaches to the concept. It was said earlier that the approach of Kuvlesky and Bealer[45] was in line with the approach to be adopted in this chapter, since it emphasised the preferences and desires of a person for a particular occupational status, as well as the structural aspects of the process. There are, however, two important limitations to this interpretation: firstly, that there is no mention of the time scale in which the process is supposed to operate; and secondly, that it could be implied that since the structural aspects of the process they refer to cannot be influenced by the individual in the choice process, then they are static and are incapable of change either self initiated or a response to external pressure.

There should be no doubting the relevance of a time scale in the occupational choice process, and, in fact, most theoretical approaches to this subject do recognise the importance of this aspect. White,[46] for example, in her discussion of the occupational choice process makes the point that it is an extended process which can cover the period from childhood until well after the choice of a first job. It is certainly true that researchers in this area do tend to concentrate on what are regarded as certain key periods in this process – for example, the transition period from ordinary to advanced level at school, the movement from the sixth form to employment or higher education, or the movement from higher education to employment – but this concentration is generally conducted within a framework of the whole process. Thus, an important addition to the Kuvlesky and Bealer interpretation should perhaps be, that the preferences and desires of individuals do develop over a long period of time, starting from childhood and continuing throughout one's occupational life.

The second point is perhaps less a reservation than an extension of Kuvlesky and Bealer's definition, and refers to the fact that many of the structural processes which are generally accepted as being influential in the occupational choice process, are capable of being changed and manipulated, and that change will eventually come as a result of a greater awareness of the relative influence of the various structural factors. Individuals might not have the immediate power to control these factors, but investigation and clarification of the experiences of individuals involved in the occupational choice process, can indirectly lead to a change in the operation of many of these factors. For example, if it could be shown that subject teachers were more important than career teachers in terms of influencing future careers, then measures could be taken to expand the subject teachers' role in this direction.

One other key area which is often overlooked in discussions of occupational choice is that of *organisational* choice. Vroom,[47] who sees choice of organisations as essentially an extension of choice of occupations, argues strongly that any treatment of choice of work role involves both occupational and organisational choices. The logic behind this argument, of course, is that though choice of occupation comes first, ones choice of occupation can limit the choice of organisations available; and, in cases where an organisation is chosen before an occupation, then obviously ones choice of occupation could be considerably restricted. There is, therefore, a strong case for including the notion of organisational choice in any theoretical approach to occupational choice, since the two have an important relationship.

The difficulties involved in formulating a definition of occupational choice are considerable, and reflect the orientations of particular disciplines. The psychologist emphasises the motivational elements of the actual choice, and the aspirations and the goal seeking behaviour of individuals. The sociologists are concerned with the influences upon the perceptions and aspirations of individuals, and the way in which such structural influences shape expectations. Economists, on the other hand tend to emphasise the utility of certain economic concepts such as cost or price, as determinants of choice. All these disciplines have made substantial contributions to the study of occupational choice and can continue to do so, provided that occupational choice is not rigidly defined. If this occurs and too narrow a view is taken of the process this will possibly nullify the contribution of each discipline.

It is assumed here that occupational choice is a general concept accounting for the whole process of movement through the educational system and into the world of work. Most theories deal with what is viewed as the 'middle range' of the process, which account for the later years at school, moving into the higher education sector, and moving into and through the first years of employment. The research discussed in subsequent chapters is concerned with the middle areas of the process, and, thus, the following discussion of theoretical approaches to occupational choice is particularly relevant for the interanalysis. It is acknowledged that it is possible to take an extremely narrow and specialised view of occupational choice in relation to preferences and attainment, but it is suggested that by taking a wider view of the process and using it as a general concept to cover all the factors relevant to the movement from school to work the result is advantageous in practical and theoretical terms.

GENERAL THEORETICAL APPROACHES TO OCCUPATIONAL CHOICE

Psychological

White,[48] has recently attempted to outline the major theories of occupational choice, but significantly the theories she refers to are more psychological than sociological, theories which refer to 'the process of choice as part of the much wider process of personal growth and development'.[49] In this area therefore, studies of occupational choice have been characterised by an emphasis on the development nature of the process, and an analysis of the work of Ginzberg[50] and Super[51] illustrates this fact.

Ginzberg's approach to occupational choice, for example,[52] has emphasised the way in which decisions are made in a number of stages. These stages he sees as complementary to stages in the emotional and intellectual development of individuals. The focus in Ginzberg's work is essentially the psychological act of choosing a career, which occurs over a period of time in three phases: fantasy choice, tentative choice and realistic choice. The phases are differentiated by the manner in which the impulses and needs of individuals are translated into an occupational choice. It is suggested that within the fantasy period, which occurs before the age of ten or eleven, the child cannot assess either his capacities or the opportunities and limitations of the real life situation, and that the child's thoughts about occupations are seen as related to his wish to participate in adult life.

The recognition by the individual of the necessity of deciding on a future occupation marks the advent of the tentative choice period, a phase which is characterised by the subjective approach individuals take to the problem. The tentative period of choice is extremely complex, but it is possible to identify a number of stages which occur during the tentative stage. A tentative choice is initially made on the basis of the child's own *interests*, but in time this is modified by an increasing awareness of the *capacity* factor leading to an attempt by the child at self evaluation based on a greater understanding of his capacities and weaknesses. Interests can also be modified by the awareness of the early adolescent, that very often interests and *values* are incompatible. As Ginsberg says, 'the system of values as a means of resolving conflicts between incompatible objectives by establishing some kind of order among them'.[53] The final stage in the tentative phase is that of *transition* where the constraints of the adult world are becoming the focus of attention for the individual, and are, to some extent, taking the place of more subjective factors. The problem here is really one of a lack of experience and knowledge, which makes a commitment to a particular career extremely difficult.

The culminating period in Ginzberg's theory of occupational choice is that of realistic choice, which again involves the individual in passing through a number of stages: the stages of exploration, crystallisation, and specification. Though Ginzberg tries to relate the realistic choice period to a specific age range (from about seventeen to some time between nineteen and twenty-one, it is perhaps more relevant to comment that the time the individual takes to pass through these stages is much more related to specific elements of his personality, and to his various life experiences. The stage of exploration is closely linked with the final transition stage in the tentative choice period, in that it represents the attempt of the individual to associate his decision making with the real world. Thus, for Ginzberg the exploration stage is character-ised more by 'reality centred' behaviour, than the subjective behaviour of individuals involved in the final stages of the tenta-tive choice period, although, the important point should be made that in the exploration stage, the individual makes a final attempt to effectively link up his occupational choice with his interests and values. It could be said, in fact, that the ultimate aim of the exploration stage is for the individual to find a job from which he will derive a great deal of satisfaction. A useful point about this exploration stage, is made by White,[54] when she refers to it as a period of 'hesitation' and indicates that an effective hesitation period will result in a lessening of ultimate dissatisfaction since the individual will be better prepared for, and more aware of, the demands of his chosen career. The great problem here, of course, is the practical one of the inadequacies of the systems involved in preparing individuals for the world of work.

The acceptance of a job or career marks the emergence of a crystallisation stage, where individuals are committed to a vocational objective. It is suggested now, that though there is some uncertainty on the part of individuals about the exact details of their chosen career, they are now able to work towards furthering their choice, and in this sense, crystallisation is the culmination of the entire process.

There is, however, one final stage in the realistic period, that of specification, which allows for specialisation and planning within the area of choice. The individual in this stage is committed to a particular work area, and it is worth noting that specification will often be delayed until an individual has acquired some training or experience.

Ginzberg makes a number of additional points about the developmental process outlined above, which served in some ways to limit, and in others to expand his theory. Of the three main points – the continuity, irreversibility and compromise nature of the process – he says that 'occupational choice is a process which takes place over a minimum period of six or seven years', that 'since each decision during adolescence is related to one's experience up to that point and in turn has influence upon the future, the process of decision making is basically irreversible', and that 'the crystallisation of occupational choice inevitably has the quality of a compromise'.[55]

The work of Ginzberg and his associates at the Columbia University Human Resources Centre has made a major contribution to the study of occupational choice, their theory being invariably used as a base for other theories, and as Roberts[56] points out, much of the merit of Ginzberg's work is that it provides a plausible framework within which information about various aspects of the entry into employment can be co-ordinated. Yet, the developmental theory developed by Ginzberg has been criticised on a number of points. Roberts himself, whilst praising the theory overall, does highlight the important fact that Ginzberg's sample was drawn exclusively from the educationally privileged sectors of society, (a fact, incidentally, referred to by Ginzberg who did not, however, regard it as a destructive limitation). The fact that Ginzberg and also Burchinal,[57] have equated occupational choice as a developmental process has been criticised by Kuvlesky and Bealer,[58] who regard the terminology as too inclusive, and suggest that it fails to do justice to the important implications of such a process. White[59] makes two criticisms of the Ginzberg theory, arguing, firstly, that the three periods of choice are determined more by the life circumstances of the individual, rather than by development and increasing maturity; and, secondly, that occupational choice should be distinguished from childhood occupational preferences. The first criticism by White is an important and useful one, for its highlights the problem of an emphasis on what might be termed the personality development of the individual, without recourse to the great mass of outside factors which undoubtedly influence, to a considerable degree, his career perceptions and ultimate career choice.

The approach of Super[60] to occupational choice is in many ways similar to that of Ginzberg and his associates, particularly in their view of occupational choice as a developmental process. Super, in fact, extended the developmental approach of Ginzberg by focusing on the development of the individual's career, involving an examination of the sequence of occupations, jobs and positions in the life of the individual, rather than looking somewhat narrowly at the actual choice of occupations. Super did, however, have one major criticism of the work of Ginzberg which centred on the compromise process involved in occupational choice. Super envisaged the development of stages similar to those of Ginzberg in the process of occupational choice, but he placed much greater emphasis on the impetus of outside influences, or the individual's social environment, in moulding the individual's view of his own interests, activities, values and capacities, rather than on the individual's gradual awareness of his attributes and limitations. That Super's view of occupational choice is a great deal more realistic than Ginzberg's can be illustrated by reference to two further points: firstly, that he regarded it as false to say that the ambitions of individuals were firmly crystallised at the time of entering employment; and secondly, he disagreed with the implication that career development consisted simply of putting into practice one's previously formulated ambition. However, despite a greater acknowledgement of the realities of the work situation than Ginzberg, Super's approach remains psychological, emphasising the way in which the social environment can be manipulated and used by the individual, rather than a concern with the way in which the social environment structures and influences the situations open to the individual.

One of the key elements in the theory of occupational choice outlined by Super is the self concept; in fact, he regards the process of vocational development as essentially concerned with developing and implementing a self concept, a compromise process in which the self concept 'is the product of the interaction of inherited aptitudes, neutral and endocrine make up, opportunity to play various roles, and evaluations of the extent to which the results of role playing meet with the approval of superiors and fellows'.[61] The close relationship between the self concept and the occupational choice process, is emphasised by a number of psychologists in their discussions of occupational choice. Vroom[62] has drawn attention to the fact that we would expect individuals to prefer and to choose occupations in which they were of the opinion that they would have the opportunity to utilise those skills they thought they possessed. The self concept may affect occupational choice in another way, and Morrison,[63] for example, has suggested that either individuals choose occupations in line with their estimation of their similarity to the members of that occupation, or else that individuals project their particular characteristics on members of the chosen occupation. Occupational choice is also seen by both Holland,[64] and Roe,[65] as being at least in part due to a self evaluation, a recognition of a certain self evaluation, a recognition of a certain self image.

One's choice of occupation must inevitable play a crucial part in the final determination of one's identity, but it is important to stress that the formation of an individual's identity takes place over a long period of time, and is part of the process of individual development. It has been suggested[66] that children during various phases of their development identify with certain aspects of the behaviour of people with whom they are in close physical and mental proximity, and certainly final identity will be influenced by all the major identifications made by individuals during personal development. Discussing this question of identity formation in relation to occupational choice, White[67] makes several interesting points: that young people may seek to express their self conception in their choice of occupations; that negative influence in identification may be as important as positive influence (as for example in Sommers's[68] study which showed that vocational choice could be presented as a defensive struggle against identification with a parental figure); and that problems of occupational choice may be indicative of a problem of identification (Galinsky and Fast[69] in their discussion of vocational choice as a form of identity search have illustrated this latter point). It is possible that the idea of a self concept or the formation of an identity could be used to link up psychological and sociological approaches to occupational choice. The personal development of individuals at different stages will be characterised by the acquisition of a number of self concepts, determined both by the various stages of his development, as well as by various sources of identification, and it might well be fruitful to use the idea of a self concept to integrate sociological and psychological perspectives of the occupational choice process.

It could be fairly said that the main emphasis in Super's work is on the process of compromise involved in choosing an occupation; and indeed he criticises Ginzberg strongly for failing to place sufficient emphasis on the compromise involved in occupational choice; a compromise between the interests, values, abilities and capacity of individuals, and the limitations of the real life occupational world. This, too, is the position of Katz and Martin,[70] who, in their discussion of career choice processes, acknowledge the work of Ginzberg and his discussion of occupational choice as a developmental process which involves compromise, but diverge from Ginzberg in terms of the emphasis put on the elements of compromise. Thus, they suggest that career choices should be conceived as courses of action which are composites of adaptions to meet the exigencies of particular situations. They suggest on the basis of their work in the nursing profession, that the decisions which lie behind the choosing of the nursing profession by individuals have more to do with limited situational contingencies rather than the deliberate planning of nursing as a career. This point which underlines the importance of adapting to the demands of an immediate situation, is a useful one, but it should be emphasised that many people do have a commitment to a particular profession from an early age, and retain this commitment through the crucial period when an occupational choice must be made. Katz and Martin apparently recognise this, by qualifying their suggestions with the statement that reaction to situational contingencies applies to 'at least some people'.[71] One important point which follows on from the work of Katz and Martin is that if for 'at least some people' the demands of a particular immediate situation is the key factor in the movement into an occupation, then it is essential to identify the factors in that particular situation which are operating on the individual, and are producing the demand element whereby he does have to make an actual choice.

One of the most important areas in which a process of compromise is necessarily involved, relates to the distinction that must be drawn between the aspirations and expectations of individuals. The need to differentiate between the two is at the core of the conceptual framework of occupational choice developed by Blau et al.,[72] for they see occupational choice as being a process of compromise between the individual's preferences for, and his expectations of, being able to enter various occupations.

This framework is an important contribution to the subject of occupational choice for it discusses in some detail the constraints within which an individual has to choose an occupation.

Within Blau *et al.*'s framework it is possible to identify certain key elements: that occupational choice is a decision-making process; that it involves a compromise between preferences (aspirations) and expectations; that actual entry into an occupation depends considerably upon the amount of information an individual has about that occupation; and that choice of occupation is closely related to selection for it. An analysis of Blau *et al.*'s approach to occupational choice as both a developmental and a decision-making process, reveals an extremely enlightened theory which is readily supported by most studies of the educational development of individuals. Thus, the decision-making process is not seen as a simple choice between two alternatives, rather that the complicated and extended developmental process resulting in a choice of occupations must be considered as a whole series of interrelated decisions which gradually narrow the range of possibilities open to the individual. The end result of the series of decisions is seen as the presentation by the individual of himself to the prospective employer as a candidate for a number of more or less related occupations. This also illustrates quite clearly the close relationship between occupational choice and organisational choice. In addition, in stressing the relationship between why an individual chooses a particular occupation and why he is selected for it, the implication is brought out quite strongly, that, occupational choice is, like recruitment to, and selection for, occupations, simply one aspect of the whole process of personnel flow. Recognition of this fact by Blau *et al.,* leads them to comment that the occupational *selection* process is complementary to the occupational *choice* process, and involves the successive decisions of employers and other selectors about applicants for jobs. Recent research by the author supports this point, emphasising the importance of selectors' decisions in the process of graduate recruitment. In many ways the conceptual framework outlined above presents a bridge between psychological and sociological approaches to occupational choice, particularly in its emphasis on the compromise between aspirations and expectations, and on the importance of the amount of information as a limiting factor. Thus, occupational choice is seen as being restricted by lack of knowledge about existing opportunities, and variations in knowledge, in rationality, and in discrimination between alternatives are regarded as the major limiting conditions for occupational choice,

E

which is thus a compromise between preferences and expectations. Of course, simply listing information as a limiting factor on choice of occupation does not solve any problem, but it does illustrate that there is an important relationship between structural factors such as 'information', and motivational factors such as 'preferences', and that an examination of this relationship in theoretical terms is most necessary. Certainly there is much that could be done in examining further the concept of 'information' in terms of its quantity and quality, and in its effect on the subsequent behaviour of individuals.

The other important element in Blau et al.'s theory which could be served as a link between sociological and psychological approaches, is that of the compromise between aspirations and expectations. The interpretation here is that expectations are often the result of the way in which the individuals experiences (in the widest possible sense) affect his ideal preferences or aspirations. The sociological approaches of, for example, Ford and Box,[73] and Roberts,[74] both acknowledge the relationship between preferences and expectations. In Ford and Box's discussion of purposive approaches to occupational choice they examine the way in which occupational choice represents the culmination of a process in which hopes and desires come to terms with the realities of the occupational market situation. Roberts, on the other hand, discusses the interesting relationship between ambitions, aspirations and expectations, indicating that the ambitions of young people seem to be based on the occupations they expect to enter rather than on the vocations they would ideally choose to follow. Ambitions are thus seen as anticipations of the direction careers are going to take.

The need to differentiate between aspirations and expectations has been referred to by both Stephenson,[75] and Kuvlesky and Bealer.[76] The latter have pointed out that frequently there is a failure to discriminate fully between aspirations and expectations, and an examination of their 'classification' of the concept of occupational choice in terms of a differentiation of the two terms is important, for though their interpretation has certain weaknesses, it does highlight the usefulness of linking the factors which serve to limit attainment of an occupation, to the preferences of, and desires of, the individual. Thus they suggest that 'from a social psychological perspective, a minimal conceptual distinction is thus suggested between the individual's preferences for work statuses and that huge undifferentiated residual, consisting of all those factors in the persons situation which condition attainment but are not subsumable as preferences'.[77]

The interpretation by Kuvlesky and Bealer of the term 'aspiration' is essentially motivational; aspiration is usually seen as referring, to a person's orientation towards a goal area; and it is regarded as possible to classify aspirations on the basis of goal areas, and also to differentiate within the goal areas on quantitatively or qualitatively differentiated choices. (In line with this, Haller and Miller,[78] have advanced the term 'aspiration' to indicate that one or more persons are orientated towards a particular goal and have attempted to develop a scale for the measurement of occupational aspirations.) It is stressed by Kuvlesky and Bealer, that logically, aspirations and expectations are two completely different and separate aspects of the occupational choice process, but they do suggest that there is a relationship between them, and that an examination of the interaction between the two is an important future area of study. The relationship becomes apparent in the light of their definition of expectations, as 'the individual's estimation of his probable attainment in reference to a particular goal area'.[79] In other words, the individual expects to attain a particular occupational position, and an expectation is an anticipated occurrence. It is particularly here, in the discussion of expectations, that the approach of Kuvlesky and Bealer appears to recognise and encompass the true complexity of the process of occupational choice. Thus, the individual is seen as making a more or less accurate assessment of the limiting factors of both the external environment and his own abilities, capacities, and values.

Perhaps the major criticism that can be made of this work is that whilst it is an attempt to clarify the nature of the occupational choice process it does not go quite far enough. It is an important step to differentiate between aspirations and expectations, and they do make the point that occupational aspirations are distinct from occupational attainment, but they fail to develop the vital implication inherent in their discussion of expectations, namely that if one takes Vroom's distinction between occupational preferences, occupational choice and occupational attainment, then within the model advanced by Kuvlesky and Bealer it could be argued strongly that expectations correspond to occupational choice. For example, they distinguish quite clearly between aspirations and actual attainment, and argue that occupational aspirations are really occupational preferences. If this is so, it can surely be argued that since one's expectations represent a compromise and a rational assessment of the probability of entry into an occupation, then in the majority of cases one's choice of occupation will be loosely related to one's expectation of attaining entry.

The above examination of the difference between aspirations and expectations in goal seeking terms, is an important development in occupational choice theory, particularly since it does emphasise that individuals may hold a number of occupational goals at any one time, and also, because it draws attention to the key point about the strength of orientations towards particular goals. Thus in order for a complete explanation and a high level of prediction to be obtained, it is important to know how strongly a goal is held relative to others.

The need of individuals to set particular occupational goals has been commented on by Caro and Philblad[80] in their discussion of the two concepts of aspiration and expectation. They assume that people can and do rate possible goals on a desirability dimension, so that, for example, if an individual has what might be termed 'limited goal orientations', this could be interpreted either by the individual's preference hierarchy being at odds with the general concensus, or in terms of limitations in perceived accessibility. Occupational choice is again, therefore, seen as a compromise process, with occupational aspirations taken to represent a pure occupational value without regard for perceived limitations in accessibility and occupational expectations interpreted as a compromise, with aspirations based on some experience of the realities of the occupational world. As a result, it is concluded that the size of the difference between the levels of aspiration and expectation is a reflection of the individual's perception of access limitations.

The way in which occupational aspirations and expectations are linked is likely to be extremely complex, and certainly, as Caro and Philblad suggest, it could be argued that the two are not independent. Any attempt, therefore, to explain this important relationship, or to develop the compromise element in the choice process is useful, and one approach to this has been the introduction of 'balance' theory suggested by Heider,[81] and utilised by Cao and Philblad[82] in their attempt to assess the importance of perceived limitations in academic ability, as a factor affecting the access of students to high prestige occupations. In a situation where an individual has a strong commitment to an occupational goal, and where this is seen to be unattainable, he is likely to undergo considerable personal frustration. In terms of balance theory, the individual would attempt to bring about a reduction in this discognancy between what he wants, and what he thinks he can get in occupational terms, by lowering his aspirations. Similar concepts would include the 'homeostatic principle'[83] which involves the achievement of a state of equilibrium, and the theory of 'cognitive dissonance' developed by Festinger.[84] Certainly the introduction of such concepts as balance, theory, homeostasis, cognitive dissonance, as a means of interpreting the complex relationship between aspirations and expectations does illustrate the possibilities in developing an encompassing approach to the occupational choice process.

It was said earlier that interpretations of the term 'aspiration' are usually motivational in nature, and certainly there exist a number of attempts to theorise occupational choice in motivational terms. Davis and Moore,[85] for example, see occupational choice as a motivational process where individuals are in competitition with each other for occupational roles. They extend this further by breaking down and defining the particular characteristics of occupational roles which are thought to be the primary motivations for such individuals, namely the societal rewards of income, prestige and power.

At this stage it would be useful to clarify the concept of motivation, which, though extremely useful in psychological terms for an understanding of human behaviour, is characterised by a good deal of complexity. It has been suggested by Stagner and Rosen,[86] that one of the reasons why motivation is so difficult to discuss, is that it is an abstraction that cannot be seen or manipulated directly. However, it is suggested that motivation is based on two elements which are much more concrete; firstly, the *needs* which operate from within an individual; and secondly, the *goals* in the environment towards which or away from which the individual moves. Thus the term 'goal directed' behaviour combines the key elements of the concept of motivation, implying that the individual is constantly striving towards certain goals in order to bring about the fulfilment of certain needs. Implicit in the approach of Roe,[87] for example, is the idea that the individual has certain physiological and socio-psychological needs which are to varying degrees satisfied by the particular occupation he has entered.

An interesting attempt has been made by Zytowski[88] to link up individual needs and job satisfaction by the use of the concept of work values; which again is seen as motivational in character. Thus altruism, autonomy, and prestige would be examples of work values, and these terms which designate values, are seen as being descriptive either of the internal state of the person (needs), or of the kind of reward or satisfaction which is available to that internal need. A work value of prestige, for example, would imply that a person is internally disposed to obtain for himself those external attributes which are ordinarily terms of prestige. Zytowski, therefore, specifies that the term 'value' reflects the correspondence between need states and satisfactions. An important extension of this hypothesis could be provided by an examination of how the relationship between needs and job satisfaction relates to the prediction of occupational choice. If choice of occupation or job is looked upon as an attempt to bring about the greatest anticipated job satisfaction, then possibly, the concept of 'values' could be suitable for the prediction or explanation of both behaviours. In fact, the concept of work values has been used in studies concerned with factors thought by individuals to be important in planning a particular type of work, and various studies[89] conducted in this area appear to agree on the most important factors, and the suggestion is implicit that individuals planning to enter different occupations hold differing values preeminent.

One of the major motivational discussions of occupational choice is that by Vroom[90], who to a considerable degree does succeed in giving to his theory of occupational choice a social-psychological perspective. Vroom, though essentially a motivational theorist, does acknowledge the two-way nature of the motivation process, emphasising not only the effect of motivational variables on people's behaviour in obtaining and performing work roles, but also the effects of the entry process and the work role on motivational variables. In this respect, therefore, it is possible for occupational choice to be treated as a function of the relationship between the motives of persons, and the actual or cognised properties of work roles.

Vroom utilises his important distinction between occupational preferences, occupational choice and occupational attainment as a framework for an examination of the assumption that occupational choices are determined by the motives of individuals. He is, therefore, able to collect and analyse research findings which are relevant to each of the three categories in this framework. Thus, the work of McLelland,[91] who has shown that a high level of achievement motivation tends to be associated with a preference for business occupations, of Atkinson[92] who has stressed the importance of risk (probability of success) on the part of high need achievers, and of Burnstein[93] who has shown that high need achievers tend to choose occupations which they have a 'moderate probability of attaining, is taken to illustrate the high degree of correspondence between individual's motives and their occupational preferences.

Much of the work concerned with the relationship between occupational choice itself and motives, has concentrated on an analysis of the observed values or interests of individuals who have actually chosen an occupation (though not necessarily attained it). Thus, the work of Seashore[94], who analysed the differences in values of social science and physical education students, and Rosenberg,[95] who illustrated a positive relationship between the values of college students and their chosen occupations, is indicative of the fact that values and chosen occupation are closely linked, and on a wider plane, that motives are connected with occupational choices in a very similar way to the manner in which motives are connected to occupational preferences.

The great problem with any attempt to examine the relationship between motivation and the whole process of occupational choice, is that the tendency appears to be to examine the motives in isolation from the constraints of the occupational world. It is to some extent reassuring that Vroom's model allows that 'the probability that a person will choose an occupation is a function not only of its valence, but also of his expectancy that it can be attained, and of the amount of "cost" which he expects to be associated with its attainment,'[96] but in spite of his awareness of the 'reality' factors, many motivational studies appear solely concerned with the internal dynamics of the motivation process. Thus, when the relationship between motives and occupational arrangements is examined, the emphasis tends to be upon personality dynamics of the motivational process. Thus, when the relationship between motives and occupational attainments is examined, the emphasis tends to be upon personality dynamics and individual interests, rather than on aspects of the systems involved in the process of occupational attainment which might have been particularly influential. Vroom, for example, stresses the work of the psychoanalytic theorist to indicate that persons prefer, choose and enter vocations which have some symbolic relationship to their conflicts and unconscious impulses.[97] On similar lines, Forer[98] regards choice of occupation as a somewhat blind, impulsive, and automatic process, that is not always subject to practical and reasonable considerations.

Examinations of the relationship between motives and occupational attainment, have invariably been concerned with the personality differences and distinguishing characteristics of the individuals in different occupations and have indicated that need for achievement is related to status of occupation (Veroff *et al.*),[99] that there are differences in level of need achievement between managers and specialists in the same organisations (Meyer *et al.*),[100] and that certain types of scientist have particular distinguishing characteristics (McLelland).[101] The narrowness of such approaches can be illustrated by referring to the fact that McLelland, in attempting to provide a motivational explanation for such differences, suggested that there could be two approaches, one based on sexual motivations, the other on aggressive motivations. Vroom, in criticising this approach and the attempt to obtain a single motivational basis for any choice of occupation, makes a vital point by bringing in the concept of occupational role, and how this is attained, in suggesting that entry to an occupational role may well produce changes in psychological variables. This emphasis on the way in which structural aspects of the systems involved in personnel flow interact with, and can, and do, affect the psychological process is crucial if a wider understanding of the occupational choice process is to be obtained. In this respect, Vroom's model of the process represents a considerable advance on theories which are more narrowly based.

Another area which offers the opportunity of obtaining a wider approach to occupational choice, is that of the relationship between particular aptitudes and abilities and different occupational categories. It has been suggested, that much of the research into aptitudes and abilities can be related to the occupational choice process, to indicate, for example, that there is a rough correspondence between the intelligence of persons and the intellectual requirements of their preferred occupations; that there is a tendency for persons with abilities corresponding to an occupation to choose that occupation; and that there are considerable differences in abilities among people working in different occupations. On similar lines Roe[102] has found certain patterns of abilities and interests related to particular occupations.

Categorisations or descriptions of occupations in psychological terms appear to be characterised by their links with the psychological variables which are seen to influence the choice process. Thus, Holland,[103] has developed a taxonomy of occupations which he has attempted to relate to personality factors, and occupational choice is then seen as a move on the part of the individual to direct his particular interests towards one of a number of vocational areas; motoric, intellectual, supportive, conforming, persuasive and aesthetic. What is particularly interesting about Holland's approach is the way in which he specifies the fact that this is an 'ideal' process, and that, in practice, there are a variety of factors which will limit the working of the process, such as the amount of information available, and social, environmental and economic factors. This type of approach is a considerable advance on, for example, Roe's attempt to classify occupations on two dimensions, level of occupation and field of activity; or of Super, who simply adds a further dimension to Roe's classification, type of enterprise. It is essential that any approach to the process of occupational choice should relate the aspirations and interests of individuals to the realities of the occupational world, and Holland's approach appears to recognise this fact. The social psychological perspective which Vroom brings to the process of occupational choice allows for this two-way approach, and certainly, to talk in terms of the outcomes which occupations have for their members, allows for the possibility of the prediction of occupational preferences. Thus, 'a persons preferences amongst a set of occupations could be predicted quite accurately from measures of the amounts of money, autonomy, status, etc. which these occupations provide, and from measures of the valence of these outcomes to that person'.[104] Yet, the point should be made, that it is on the realism of the individual's conception of occupations that such predictions of preference will depend, and it is crucial for an understanding of the occupational choice process that more attention is given to the complex relationship between aspirations or preferences, and expectations (which are taken here to mean aspirations modified by exposure to the realities of the occupational situation).

Economic

One area which has been somewhat neglected in many theoretical discussions of occupational choice is the field of economics. Much discussion at present surrounds the relative importance of monetary factors in terms of 'job satisfaction' and 'motivation', and it is surprising that so little use has been made of economic concepts in attempts to explain the occupational choice process. Zytowski,[105] goes so far as to say that no theorist has so far made use of long existing constructs of choice behaviour developed by economists in an attempt to ascertain the determinants of a person's chosen or attained occupation. This claim by Zytowski is not strictly true, but does indicate that the economic area has been considerably neglected. Exceptions to Zytowski's claim would include the theoretical discussions of both Blau *et al.*[106] and Vroom.[107] Blau *et al.*'s use of economic concepts can be seen in their discussion of occupational choice in terms of differentiation between aspirations and expectations, so that a choice between various possible courses of action can be conceptualised as motivated by two interrelated sets of factors: the individual's valuation of the rewards offered by different alternatives and his appraisal of his chances of being able to realise each of the alternatives; this conceptualisation of the choice process is very much dependent on the individual's choice between alternatives in economic terms. Equally, Vroom had stressed in his theoretical discussion of occupational choice, the importance of 'cost' or 'investment' in one's chosen occupation, and if 'risk taking' is regarded as an economic construct then Atkinson's[108] theoretical model which accounts for the level of risk of high need achievers, could be said to utilise an economic construct in a discussion of occupational preferences.

In an attempt to rectify the inadequate emphasis on economic determinants of occupational choice, Kaldor and Zytowski[109] have represented occupational choice as an approximate case of economic choice behaviour in input-output terms. Thus, the person's characteristics which are helpful for obtaining preferred consequences can be viewed as inputs (or means), and when these inputs are applied to a given occupational alternative then certain outputs (or ends) follow, depending on the characteristics of the inputs and of the occupation. The aggregate of the values of the outputs may be attached to each alternative, and similarly inputs are priced by the individual in terms of the values of the things he foregoes in using them in a particular occupational alternative. This aggregate cost is then balanced against the aggregate value of output, and the net value is derived for each alternative; the chosen alternative is the one which offers the largest net value.

The implications of this approach could provide the means for linking together the concepts used by other disciplines in their approaches to occupational choice. Thus, if it is accepted, for example, that the individual's assessment of the outputs following a choice is determined by his system of values, then the degree to which the individual obtains the outputs he wants in the proportions he wants them, will equate with what the psychologist terms 'job satisfaction', and what Kaldor and Zytowski term 'occupational utility'. Similarly, the individual's value system is the result of what the sociologist would term his 'socialisation'.

It is important, too, to recognise that economic factors are but one element in what can be looked at as a complex motivational process. It could, therefore, be said that to perceive occupational choice as being made in terms of isolated economic concepts, such as relative wage, relative price, or relative cost, is not particularly useful, and that it is necessary to integrate these factors in a wider motivational framework. As Rottenberg indicates, 'it is clear that total net advantage and not price alone is the touchstone of occupational choice and change in the theory of the economists, and it is total net advantage and not price alone that is said to be equal in all employments',[110] and similarly, occupational choice in terms of relative wages can only be seen in the context of a larger framework in which all other job properties are given. Actual monetary reward, therefore, is only the determinant of choice when all other attributes are compared. The point to be made here, is that it is misleading to talk in terms of occupational choice resulting from a single motive; job choice is the end result of the interaction of a number of motives, reflecting the complexity of the motivational system, and often we find an individual who equates his choice with one particular motive is seeking to rationalise the complexity of the decision-making process by responding in single motivational terms. Clerk Kerr,[111] for example, makes the point that it may be misleading to talk in terms of wages being a single motivating factor, and suggests that wages are only one of several important considerations which repel workers from some jobs and attract them to others.

If the theory of total net advantage – which includes the concepts of relative price, relative cost, and relative wages – is to be useful, it is important to identify and understand the limitations of the theory. One such limitation would be the state of knowledge of the individual about the particular qualities attaching to jobs – economic and non-economic. We certainly know that the knowledge individuals have about overall employment conditions and terms in other organisations is often severely limited. The quality and quantity of information which is available to an individual, and the extent to which he can assimilate and utilise this information, is a vital consideration in occupational choice, and is something which must enter into all theoretical approaches to the subject. Associated with this 'knowledge' factor are conditions of certainty or uncertainty, within which the individual makes estimates about particular jobs; the economic assumption here being that if a choice is made in conditions which are more certain rather than less certain, then the choice is likely to be more successful. Rottenberg's[112] approach to this is that 'optimum resource distribution' is retarded by conditions of uncertainty for both firms and workers.

Other issues which are relevant to the total net advantage theory would include whether the worker is 'pushed' or forced into a choice or change, or whether he is 'pulled' or encouraged to join or move into an occupation; the role of security in relation to price in the making of job decisions; and the rationality of worker behaviour in labour markets. This latter point is especially crucial for the total net advantage theory, for if it could be shown that workers do not act rationally when making job decisions according to habit, then this could cast considerable doubt on the theory that workers make comparisons of net advantage in alternative employments.

In many ways the economic theories of occupational choice stand or fall on the assumption that people faced with a choice act rationally, or as Reynolds and Shuster[113] suggest when discussing job horizons, that the individual behaves like a scientist, carefully gathering all the relevant facts, and then choosing the job which promises the greatest net advantage. There is a good deal of evidence to show that many people do not act rationally, and that many people are often not in a position to make what might be termed a rational choice, but the fact remains that a choice is made, however limited the process of weighing up of all the factors involved. It is suggested, therefore, that it might be useful to think of the choice being made within a framework of different degrees of limitations, and that even in the most limiting framework to see the choice being made with some relevance to what the individual regards as his best interests. His interpretation of his best interests will reflect the interaction of such varied factors as his own ambitions, his present achievements and situation, his abilities, the information he has assimilated, and the limitations of what he regards as costs of attainment. The costs of attainment need not, necessarily be solely economic, but will also include psychological costs. In the attainment of a particular occupation, therefore, possible costs could include tuition fees and income not earned during additional years of schooling (economic costs), and the demands for time and subsequent loss of recreation (psychological costs).

The importance of decisions taken during the occupational choice process, should be seen in the context of the individual making a considerable investment in a particular career. Sofer,[114] for example, has pointed out that initial entry into an occupation starts an investment, that an irreplaceable amount of time has been committed, and that if the initial career decision is not followed through then the investment is very probably lost. Associated with the investment aspect of career choice, is the fact that decisions made during the career choice process are to a large extent irreversible. It is important to differentiate at this stage between those factors in the process over which the individual has no real control (for example, family circumstances, social class, initial schooling), and the decisions which the individual makes at different stages of the process, (although in practice they are closely related), since the educational and social experience of the individual represent the parameters within which the decision must be made. Within these parameters the decisions which an individual makes about his future are crucial and often irreversible. These decisions are initially educational in nature, and can have wide-ranging implications, particularly in a society where the occupational fate of an individual is linked closely to educational factors. Thus, the decision about the subjects to be taken in the latter years at secondary school can effectively close a number of occupational avenues, just as the decision which is made for the individual about which secondary school he will attend has the same effect. Roe,[115] has criticised the approach of writers such as Ginzberg who she feels overemphasise the irreversible nature of occupational decisions, and certainly many decisions are not totally irreversible. However, the fact remains that whilst it may be *possible* to reverse a previous decision the probabilities are extremely low, because of the many consequences that have flowed from the decision, and the multiplied difficulties of actually changing. Thus, if an individual decides not to enter university at the end of his secondary school career, this does not mean that if he changes his mind subsequently he will not be able to attend, but it does mean that he will find a great many barriers in his way.

Though it cannot be said that vocational choices are irreversible, it is apparent that the consequences of particular decisions can be far reaching, committing an individual to a type of work and even a style of life for much or all of his working life. Vroom[116] has made an interesting attempt to equate the stability of an occupational choice to the decision-making process, indicating that an occupation is greater than the 'strength of force' attracting him to other occupations. In this context, any revoking of an occupational choice will come as a result of the relationship between the decision-making process, and changes in what Vroom terms the 'force field'. Changes in the force field are seen as occurring as a consequence of the decision itself, as a consequence of actions taken to implement the decision, or as a consequence of the receipt of further information about the alternatives. This approach reflects the fact that once an individual makes a decision he will attempt to justify or rationalise it to himself. This justification is the basis of Festinger's[117] theory of cognitive dissonance, which indicates that once a choice has been made the attractions of the chosen alternative will tend to increase for the individual whilst the attraction of the other alternative(s) will decrease. The making of a decision, therefore, about entry or non-entry to a particular occupation, is not something which can be looked upon in isolation, rather as part of a process, the consequences of which can affect both motives and values.

Sociological
One of the most important elements in a decision-making process is the fact that decisions not only involve internal subjective processes, but that they are also based on objective social facts. Thus, during the decision-making process the individual is constantly being guided, affected and influenced by other individuals, social groups, and more formal influences. The role and importance of such social structural influences is stressed by most of the more sociologically orientated occupational choice theorists. Occupational choice is generally regarded by such theorists as a process of interaction between aspirations and expectations, self analysis and influence, and opportunities and experiences, and, as Sofer[118] has indicated the occupational decision itself will be affected by such factors as the amount of information available, the opinions and influence of key persons to whom the individual is exposed, formal vocational guidance, and the state of the labour market. The approach of Keil, Riddell and Green in their discussion of the transition from education into employment, conforms almost exactly to the above diagnosis of the nature of sociological approaches to occupational choice. They state that

'evidence from a wide variety of research suggested that family, neighbourhood, peer groups, education received, influences from the mass media, the extent of formal vocational guidance all need to be considered, and that experience from these sources, as well as the nature of the work undertaken, are relevant to the development of any particular reaction towards working life. . . . This implies that entering the world of work and adjusting to it is a process.'[119]

In particular the socialisation process is an integral part of most sociological theories in this area, drawing attention to the way in which the developing behaviour of individuals increasingly reflects the importance of taking account of the needs and demands of other people and institutions, as well as their own needs and demands. In this sense then, socialisation is a continuing process throughout life – although as Kelvin has pointed out there are important differences between its course in childhood and in maturity.[120]

The utilisation of the concept of socialisation in occupational choice reflects the importance of conceptualising the occupational choice process in sociological terms. Thus, though occupational choice tends to be seen by sociological theorists as a process (conforming to Ginzberg's view of it as a developmental process), it is the particular influences or structural elements which are the focus of attention, reflecting the essentially social nature of the process. Of course, this is not to say that an over simple view should be taken of the social structure, or of the social nature of the occupational choice process, a criticism which could possibly be aimed at the approach of Miller and Form[121] in their early attempt to conceptualise occupational choice in terms of socialisation. However, despite this criticism, the work of Miller and Form does represent an important contribution to the sociology of occupational choice, for they attempted to utilise and integrate concepts such as socialisation, and role, which formed the basis of later approaches. In another sense, too, their work was comprehensive, for they attempted to link up what they termed the 'preparatory work period' with later periods of work adjustment which they termed 'the lifework pattern'.

The preparatory work period formulated by Miller and Form contains two essential elements: socialisation within the home, and socialisation within the school. Within the home the child learns to take, and rehearse, a role based on the behaviour of a 'model', a person whose behaviour provides an example of learning; vocational goals are seen as being formed and developed essentially by this role-taking device. Also in the home situation, there is the importance of primary work models, that is parents, brothers, sisters, relatives, who bring in information about the outside world work. Within the atmosphere of the home Miller and Form suggest that attitudes are formed, aspirations found, and patterns of adjustment anticipated. The other main element in the preparatory work period, the process of socialisation within the school, takes account of two cultures which exist in symbolic relationship – the peer culture and the school culture, and the point is made that the school is, in fact, a limited work world.

The second element in the approach of Miller and Form is that of the lifework pattern, which is essentially an attempt to identify certain periods of work adjustment. These periods would include a preparatory period which would take into account the early experiences and adjustments in the home, school, and community; an *initial* period of job impermanence whilst the individual was still undergoing formal education; a *trial* period or period of job transition; a period of *stability* or job persistence; and finally a period of *retirement*. The significance feature of this approach is that it shows a realisation of the fact that the movement into, and through, the world of work is a continuous process, and that any attempt to conceptualise occupational choice must take account of this fact.

If the approach of Miller and Form is to be criticised it should be on the grounds that it oversimplifies the process of moving through the education system, into and through the employment system. As Keil, Riddell and Green[122] have pointed out, it is important to take account of the complexity of the experiences of young people in this process. It is much more difficult to criticise their approach on the grounds that it fails to provide a general framework, albeit a simple one, within which data on occupational choice can be examined. Thus, the argument of Musgrave[123] that there is a need for a general theory which would cover the whole process of first choice of occupation, take account of the continuing influences operating on individuals, and apply to job choices and changes made at later stages in the life cycle, is to a certain extent met by the approach of Miller and Form.

The relevance of the socialisation concept for occupational choice can be seen in terms of the possibilities for examining the various influences – and their relative importance – on the choice process. It would appear, however, that in the context of occupational choice, socialisation is used both normatively and empirically, and it is essential to distinguish between such approaches. With this in mind, it is useful to examine two sociological approaches to occupational choice both based on the concept of socialisation, yet differing in approach – one being basically normative, the other empirical.

In many ways the attempt by Musgrave[124] to move towards a sociological theory of occupational choice represents a considerable advance. It is a well-considered attempt to ground occupational choice within sociological theory, and more specifically using the concepts of socialisation and role theory. The two concepts are seen as being closely linked, in that central to the sociological analysis of socialisation is the availability of roles to the individual involved in the process. Musgrave's sociological theory, therefore, sees occupational choice as one of four major elements, the others being socialisation, economic socialisation and anticipatory socialisation. The individual chooses, or has chosen for him a number of different roles that are available during the life cycle, and each choice that is made governs future choices. This is important for, throughout life, and particularly during the educational process, decisions which one takes or are taken on one's behalf, can have far-reaching consequences: examples would be choice of school, choice of subjects whilst at school, parent's attitude to continuance of education into the sixth form, and eventual choice between undertaking a higher education course or entering employment. Of course, many of the more important roles which are available are economic in character, and economic socialisation, which involves the learning of consumer and producer roles, is seen as covering the cluster of roles relating to the economic institutions of society. In particular the learning of the producer's role has particular relevance for occupational choice, for it concerns the behaviour, values, and attitudes relating to particular occupational categories. Finally, Musgrave stresses the importance of 'prior role rehearsal' or anticipatory socialisation in moving through the socialisation process.

Within this context of socialisation and role theory, occupational choice is examined and is seen as involving four stages: pre-work socialisation, entry to the labour force, socialisation into the labour force, and job changes. The period of pre-work socialisation – which one assumes is meant to cover the development of the individual right up to the time he comes to enter the labour force – operates to narrow the possible roles available for an individual, as a result of his experiences with three key agents of socialisation, the family, the school, and the peer group. Thus, within the family, the individual learns both family roles and economic roles, governed by the behaviour, values, and attitudes of his parents; as a result in the educational system the range of future available roles is shaped; and the peer groups are seen as providing alternative values to those learnt within the home and school. At entry to the labour force, i.e. where occupational preferences become occupational choices, it is argued that such choice should match the selection processes of, for example, industry and commerce, and that the role of vocational guidance is to arrange for such a perfect fit. The final stages cover the periods after entry to employment – initial socialisation into the job and subsequent job changes, and are based on the assumption that the systems controlling movement from education to employment are inadequate, and that people will subsequently change jobs. The stage of socialisation into the job, is therefore, a vital part of any theory, in that the initial choice is unlikely to be the final choice for most people. Similarly, subsequent job changes for any reason will involve the learning of new roles which could be termed 'resocialisation'.

Musgrave's attempt to construct a sociological theory of occupational choice has been strongly criticised on a number of counts, but mainly because of the idealised picture he presents of the process. Coulson, Keil, Riddell and Struthers,[125] in fact, have presented a critique of Musgrave's theory which makes three major points: that his assumption that the social structure within which individuals play out roles is unified and cohesive is a major theoretical weakness; that the process of socialisation is much more complex than Musgrave would have it; and that far from individuals being able to learn the stereotypes of different occupations in the labour force before making a choice, research has shown that young people lack any clearly formed ideas about the world of work. All these points are to varying degrees justified, illustrating that it is not enough to formulate a theory of what ought to happen, but necessary to take account of the realities of the situation. The interaction of the psychological variables involved and the various social and structural influences is extremely complex, and it is misleading to oversimplify this process, by suggesting that all such influences are operating in the direction of making it easier for individuals to enter the employment system.

This failure to appreciate the extent of the complexity of the occupational choice process is perhaps the most valid criticism of Musgrave's work, yet in many respects his work represents a useful advance. The merit of his work lies in the attempt to construct a theory which takes account of subsequent job movements, on the grounds that there are factors common to both the process of initial choice and of later choices. It is the shift in emphasis from a narrow view of entry into employment, to a far wider view of the process of movement which provides a framework of considerable significance.

If it is accepted that Musgrave's approach suffers from a rather simplified view of the workings of the social structure, and an apparent lack of awareness of the complexity of the process of personnel flow – and this would appear to be justified in view, for example, of his treatment of the supposed role of the Youth Employment Service – it could be argued that what is needed is a sociological theory of occupational choice which is more empirically based. It is of interest, in this respect, to contrast Musgrave's attempt to locate a theory of occupational choice in sociological theory with the work of Keil, Riddell and Green[126] who have attempted to provide a coherent framework for the literature available on the transition from school to work (which they suggest is inadequate).

Keil, Riddell and Green are primarily concerned with the influences upon individuals during the school years, at the point of job entry, and during the period of adjustment to working life. However, they do attempt to locate these factors or influences within a sociological framework, utilising particularly the concept of socialisation. The process of movement involved in occupational choice is seen in terms of the socialisation of the young person to the employment systems, which, together with previous work experience and wider social influences, leads to the formulation of a set of attitudes towards, and expectations about, work. All these factors are seen as explaining the actual job entry, and following from this, experience in the employment system leads to the individual's adjustment or non-adjustment (expressed as satisfaction, new attitudes and expectations, ritualised dissatisfaction, or possibly subsequent job change).

This attempt to explain the process of occupational choice has the merit of at least attempting to reconcile the individuals perception of the occupational world in the form of attitudes and expectations, with the factors which influence these perceptions. Admittedly, it is only recognition of psychological variables at a fairly superficial level, the approach being essentially sociological, with the attention focused on the role of the social influences, but it does indicate that for a general theory of occupational choice to be viable it is necessary to consider both psychological and social variables.

The limitation of the work of Keil et al., would appear to be in the scope of their discussion, which primarily concentrates on movement through the education system, actual job entry and early adjustment to work. Yet their work has considerable value in that the analysis of the influences on occupational choice is firmly based on empirical studies, enabling them to highlight the fact that although the system available for coping with the occupational choice does operate in practice as it is supposed to do in theory in some areas, equally there are many discrepancies between what ought to happen and what does, in fact, happen.

The assumption that most sociological discussions have converged to view occupational choice as part of a rational process where desired ends are judged against the perceived probability of attainment, is implicit in the approach of Ford and Box.[127] On this basis they formulate two major propositions: firstly, that when an individual chooses between two alternative occupations he will rank the occupations in terms of the relation between his values and the perceived characteristics of the occupation; and secondly, that the higher an individual perceives the probability that he will obtain employment in the higher ranked occupation, the more likely he is to choose that occupation. The obvious problem here is that the theory rests on the assumption of a rational choice being made, and there must be some doubt as to whether this in fact happens. Almost in anticipation of such a question being raised, Ford and Box formulate, and answer, the question of whether a theory of rational choice is viable for school leavers, say of fifteen. They argue that it is viable because however the school leaver has acquired his particular values, however inadequate his perception of the available jobs and the conditions within them, and however faulty his perception of his own chance of attaining employment in any of these jobs, it is still possible to determine the extent to which he attempts to gain employment in that job which he considers both available to him and consistent with his particular values. This approach is not dissimilar to the economically orientated approaches of Kaldor and Zytowski[128] who utilise the concept of work values, and Rottenberg[129] who discusses occupational choice in terms of total net advantage. However, whilst movement does occur in that the individual moves from the education system to the employment system, if this is termed rational choice then the implication is that this is a positive action, when the evidence surely shows that all too often this process of movement is extremely negative and haphazard. In fact some writers argue that to talk of choice in many cases is to give a false impression of the process: Psathas,[130] for example, suggests 'orientations to particular settings', and Reynolds[131] suggests that the process refers to 'drift'. This is not to argue that the theoretical formulation of Ford and Box is wrongly based, simply to suggest that the emphasis on the choice being a positive act is possibly misplaced. On the contrary their approach is significant for the way it allows for integration of the approaches

of various disciplines; it is firmly based on the process of socialisation in that the values of individuals will reflect their socialisation experiences; it accounts to some extent for the total net
advantage theories of the economists; and the process which they
refer to involves the interaction of psychological variables.
Certainly the ideas suggested by Ford and Box could usefully be
examined in further detail, preferably in the context of other more
general theories and the available empirical evidence.

The concepts of socialisation, and role, are relevant to the
sociological model of the occupational choice process developed
by Ashley, Cohen, McIntyre and Slatter.[132] Their particular work
refers to the teaching profession, and involves the construction of a
model of an occupational system as a sub-system, within the
overall social system. In this respect they then attempt to develop
a classification system for choice of occupation (in this instance,
teaching). The basis of this work is the Parsonian model of the
social system, in which, for effective operation a system was seen
as having to come to terms with four functional problems, which
resulted from a consideration of the external and internal aspects
of the system, as well as the distinction between goal oriented and
means oriented action of actors in the system. Thus, the functional
problems are adaption – goal attainment, and pattern maintenance – integration. The argument of Ashley et al., is that this model
of a social system also holds for the operation of a sub-system,
and that it is more meaningful to categorise an individuals motivation in terms of his orientation towards a particular occupational
system. They then suggest that individuals have certain expectations about the roles which they will perform in an occupational
system, and will tend to view their roles in relation to their functions
within the system. On this basis, it is suggested that a classification
can be obtained of an individual's reasons for entering an occupation, which is based on the structure of the situation, and the
frame of reference of the student.

The approach to choice of occupation outlined above is very
narrowly based. It could be argued that a sociological analysis of
choice of occupation must take into account the fact that the
individual's frame of reference, his definition of the situation,
reflects his socialisation – by the home, the school, peer groups
and other more formal influences. Thus, for Ashley et al. to say
that in their research they are not directly concerned with the
personality structure, nor the historical past of the individual
student but rather with the manner in which he perceives and
evaluates the teaching system, is to nullify much of the value of

their work. The way in which an individual will perceive and evaluate an occupational system will obviously depend on his prior socialisation experience. This example of a rather fragmented approach to choice of occupation, illustrates the need for an overall framework which would enable such specific studies as this to be integrated into a more comprehensible view of the social processes involved in occupational choice. It is significant, that when they utilise the concept of role, thereby placing their work firmly in sociological theory, it becomes altogether more meaningful. Thus by use of the role concept which is what Parsons and Shils have called the 'conceptual unit of the Social system',[133] they provide a reference point for other studies in the occupational choice field.

The utilisation of role theory is, in fact, central to the approach of Psathas[134] who makes two key points. Firstly, whilst it is established that most people, at some generally observable stage in life, are expected to perform an occupational role, it is far from being established whether individuals actually choose this role, and if they do, what factors condition such choice. Secondly, that in view of available evidence an adaptive sociological theory of occupational choice must be grounded on the assumption that prospective occupational role performers have only partial knowledge, both of the number and type of occupational roles available and of the appropriate means of training and entry. It is essential that such factors are realistically considered, before attempts are made to conceptualise the occupational choice process.

In this respect, the framework developed by Roberts[135] for the process of entry into employment is extremely realistic, and the basis of his work, which is firmly grounded in sociological theory, is the *limited* nature of the choice process. His argument is well worth considering in further detail, since it is concerned with the way in which the socialisation process affects the so-called occupational choice of individuals. His theory is simply stated, 'that the momentum and direction of school leavers' careers are derived from the way in which their job opportunities become cumulatively structured, and young people are placed in varying degrees of social proximity with different ease of access to different types of employment. The ambitions of school leavers adapt to the direction that their careers take and are not major determinants of the occupations that young people enter.'[136] This is essentially a model of the structure of opportunities which become available to individuals, and is important in that it takes account of the fact that the movement of individuals through the social and educational system is determined by the operation of certain structural influences, and the way in which the individual's aspirations (ambitions) adapt to this. Thus, whilst focusing attention primarily on the socialisation process, and its relationship with future occupational role allocation, Roberts, does attempt to examine the psychological processes involved, in an essentially sociological framework.

Given the fact that individuals do adapt readily to available occupational roles, it is then possible to examine the major factors operating in the social structure, in an attempt to explain this work orientation. For Roberts, there are three key factors in existence which help to explain this. Initially, there is the ideology of free occupational choice, implying that people genuinely believe that they do choose an occupational role. Secondly, he suggests that performing an occupational role has a great significance for the formation of an identity, and finally, there is the limited nature of the knowledge of school leavers about occupations, which it is suggested, helps explain why the ambitions of young people should adapt so readily to the occupations they happen to enter. In his identification of these factors, it is contended that Roberts has succeeded in advancing the understanding of occupational choice in a number of ways. By utilising the psychological concepts of ambition and identity formation, he is integrating at least some of the psychological processes involved with the sociological concepts of socialisation and occupational role allocation, which in themselves ensure that the opportunity structure theory is grounded in sociological theory. In addition, the question of whether or not choice does take place is at least considered as a first step, and his suggestion that individuals *believe* that choice takes place, is a starting point for his model, and also for others concerned with the choice process. Further, the consideration of the knowledge and experience of young people faced with choosing an occupational role, is a key element in any approach to occupational choice, for it reflects the working and inadequacies of the socialisation process, and the acceptance of this as a key factor does allow for the availability of a reference point for future studies of various aspects of the process.

Certainly, Roberts's attempts to develop a framework for entry into employment, marks an important step, but perhaps the major limitation again is the concentration on entry into employment. True, he does specify the parameters of his interest, but it is surely of importance to consider whether the framework is viable for subsequent job choice or change? It could be that it would not hold for later choice (although most of the factors would appear to be applicable), but to illustrate this fact would be a considerable advance, suggesting perhaps the possibility that a number of theories might have to be advanced to explain choice at different levels. Roberts, in fact, hints at this when suggesting that despite the widespread prevalence of the ideology of free occupational choice, different groups of school leavers do possess differential ease of access to various types of employment, but fails either to differentiate clearly between these different groups in his discussion of orientation to work, or to mention the problems of the large group of young people who complete a higher education course before entering employment. This inability to adequately account for people in different situations is a fault of most occupational choice theoreticians, and whilst Roberts does emphasise initially the importance of educational factors in structuring the occupational opportunities open to individuals, his attempt to relate this to the way individuals adapt to the work situation is weakened by classifying all young people about to enter employment as 'school leavers'.

The above discussion highlights the fact that most sociological approaches to occupational choice are based heavily on the concepts of socialisation and role allocation. It is, therefore, of considerable importance to analyse in depth the socialisation process, as related to future occupational role allocation, in order to identify the major influences – and their relative importance – on individuals at different stages of the occupational choice process. Of course, the difficulty with attempting such an analysis is that many of the factors influencing career choice, or career decisions, are interrelated. Veness[137] for example, in her attempt to construct a typology of different reasons for job choice (tradition directed, inner directed, and other directed) acknowledges the fact that such categories are not mutually exclusive. However, given the difficulties involved in such analysis. it is possible to identify several major influences on career choice. In fact, there would appear to be reasonable agreement by writers in this field as to the nature of such areas of influence, and accordingly we shall examine the influence of the family (and social class), the influence of the education system, peer group influences, and other more formal influences. It is important at this stage to note that these influences are not necessarily working for the advantage of the system of personnel flow, or for the advantage of the individuals concerned. We are not primarily concerned at this stage with the inadequacies or detrimental effects of such influences – the later empirical work will enable such drawbacks to be discussed – rather to look objectively at their operation.

There is a good deal of evidence available to show that the influence of the family, and related social class, can be far reaching in its effect on the operation of the occupational choice process. Home background is an important factor in the socialisation process, and future occupational choice is closely related to the family situation of individuals. In theoretical terms, it can be seen in terms of the father (and often the mother) as transmitting the values, attitudes and behaviour of a particular economic role to the child; the parents here are seen as the bridge between the family and the economy, since they perform roles within both systems.

There would appear to be some relationship between the occupation of the father and the occupational choice of the son. Rosenberg,[138] for example, has shown that there is a marked relationship between the economic position of the family and the occupational choice of the student, whilst Kelsall[139] had illustrated the way in which the sons of men in traditional professions, tend to enter their father's profession, or at least enter one of the other professions. Similarly, Bendix, Lipset and Malm have produced evidence that sons tend to enter, and remain in occupations which are similar to their fathers.[140]

Empirical evidence is also available to link aspiration level to socio-economic status. Sewell, Haller and Stauss,[141] for example, in a study where measured intelligence was controlled, found that despite this control, a status position was an important influence on the level of educational and occupational aspiration, and in a similar study, Liversedge,[142] too, acknowledged the importance of status factors in occupational choice decisions. White,[143] has pointed out that there is very little evidence to show whether social class has any effect upon the extent to which parents try to influence their children's choice, indicating that though parents from higher socio-economic levels may well have a greater knowledge of the occupational structure, and thus be better able to advise, there is no information about what actually happens in this respect. She also makes the point that there may well be strong parent pressure for the child to move up the social scale, in both the working-class and the lower middle-class situations, and that in middle-class families there may well be negative pressure from parents manifesting itself in them making clear to the child that there are certain occupations of which they disapprove.

There are a number of ways in which home background influences the occupational choice process. It is accepted that social class background is related to success in the 11+ examination; secondary modern leavers have been shown to place most importance on parental influence in career choice;[144] the Crowther Report[145] highlighted the way in which associated economic and cultural factors in working-class backgrounds exert pressure on individuals to leave school; and parental occupational expectations for their children, represent a strong influence which can result in later parent-child conflict.[146] However, in this context, certainly the most important relationship is that between home background and the educational system.

It has been pointed out,[147] that the emphasis of studies in the sociology of education in Britain has been on class chances in education, and certainly the Robbins Report,[148] showed that in terms of achievement grammar school pupils whose fathers worked in non-manual occupations had better examination results than those pupils whose fathers worked in manual occupations. It is certainly apparent from the results of a number of studies (for example, Floud, Halsey and Martin,[149] Kelsall,[150] Bernstein,[151] and Douglas[152]) that social class is closely related to education, particularly in the way that the social class of parents affects the type of education the child received (and also the length of time spent in the educational system). Given this relationship, it has been argued[153] that since education and occupation are linked such characteristics as social class and economic level of the family will have a marked influence on the attitudes to and expectations about work, as well as on the type of job entered. Certainly, the way in which the British educational system operated at least until 1944 reflected the importance of the relationship between social class and education, and the manner in which different social class groupings perceived the structure of employment opportunities. Thus, before the 1902 Education Act there was a distinct class division between the great majority using the very limited state elementary school system, and what might be termed an elitist group, with the means to afford a separate private system. With the establishment of state secondary schools in 1902 (to some extent modelled on the private schools), further opportunities did become available, particularly to the middle-class groups, but Banks[154] has argued that both middle and working-class parents saw these opportunities in terms of white-collar occupations (professions or offices), and not in terms of industrial careers. In this respect, it is interesting to note that Banks has related the introduction of the 1896 Technical Education Act to the introduction of state secondary education 1902, in order to highlight a number of interrelated factors, in particular the low status of technical careers, the desire of parents for white-collar jobs for their children, and the fact that greater social status was given to grammar schools and their pupils because they compared most favourably with the private schools.

Subsequently events in education, such as the 1944 Education Act; the up-grading of technical education, representing an acknowledgement of the need to establish technology on a new basis (and not least in the provision of more technologists and technicians); the considerable expansion of higher education generally; and the trends towards comprehensive education, could all be indicative of a desire to lessen class chances in education. However, as Crichton[155] has pointed out, sociological research in the last fifteen years has demonstrated the waste of talent which occurs under our present educational system, but it has also demonstrated that it is not only the fault of the system but of the child's home background. An example would be Carter's[156] study of school leavers in Sheffield, in which he related the attitudes found in the areas from which the schools drew their pupils. It is certainly apparent that simply to make structural changes in a system such as education, and expect the influence of family background to be immediately lessened, represents an over-simplistic view of the socialisation process. Structural changes in the educational system aimed at increasing opportunity and equality for all, will, *in time*, effect improvement in this area, though one suspects, not in isolation; rather such improvements will depend, as much as anything else, on the effect of such changes on the family system. This is not to say that the influence of the family and associated social class factors is not lessening, and the influence of the educational system increasing, in occupational choice terms. In fact, there is evidence to show that this is happening, and Liversedge,[157] in a comparative study of the aspirations of schoolchildren in grammar and secondary modern schools, concluded that whilst previous experience may be of great importance in shaping the school-child's expectations of the future, the most potent force operating is undoubtedly the experience through which the child passes during his involvement in that part of the educational system to which he has been assigned.

The importance of the education process as a socialisation agent cannot be over-emphasised. King[158] has suggested that the educational system has a major socialising function and acts as a bridge between the family and the world of work, and that the child is introduced into the role of pupil and then into an occupational role, Durkheim's[159] early definition of education as the 'systematic socialisation of the young generation' also emphasised the social nature of the process. The process of socialisation within the educational system can best be looked at as a training, perhaps in the form of role playing, for the performing of future occupational roles, implying that ones experience in the educational system – the type of school one attends, the subjects available and studied, the relationship of particular schools to particular occupations – is very closely connected to the occupational roles available. Education plays a vital part in governing the occupational roles people will perform, and hence the level of the occupational hierarchy they will reach, and it is apparent, that in addition to the manifest socialising function of education, it also performs a number of latent functions. Thus, the educational system also performs an important selective function (deriving from the occupational structure), in that it allows for differentiation between occupations, and it operates as a channel of social mobility. The fact that the structure of occupational roles is reflected to a large extent in the educational system, has led Blackstone[160] to comment that the sociology of education is concerned with the study of the processes of selection involved. It is about ascription and the extent to which achievement is ascribed.

It is possible, and for analytical purposes, useful, to differentiate between the types of experience an individual will undergo within the educational system. The above discussion of the socialising function of education and its relationship with the occupational structure, represents an analysis of the role of education in general terms, a synthesis of the different elements involved in the educational process. To adequately differentiate, it is necessary to look at the educational process as spanning a period of time during which the child grows to youth, adolescence and adulthood, and during which he is influenced not only by elements within his family situation, and by the formal nature of the education system (for example, type of school), but also by the dynamics of the education process which refers to his relationships with, for example, subject teachers, careers teachers, and, of course, peer groups, and by the outside formal vocational influences such as the youth employment service and vacation work.

A number of studies have shown the importance of occupational advice of an informal and personal nature to people progressing through the education system. It would seem probable that subject teachers, for example, would represent an important source of influence on pupils, particularly where the need for specialisation has greatly restricted the number of subjects a student takes. In this situation it is likely that the pupil will develop a fairly close relationship with a subject teacher and will obviously be influenced by the attitudes, norms and advice of the teacher concerned. Of course, there could well be certain consequences of this in that the act of taking advice might be seen as constituting a form of commitment, and the student might feel obliged to conform to expectation and to take the given advice; equally fear of this commitment could deter a student from seeking such advice. This is not to say that advice which is given by subject teachers is necessarily good advice, but there can be little doubt that teachers who have a fairly close relationship with students are likely to be an important influence (good or bad) on their pupils.

It is possible for peer groups to exert influence both from within and without the educational institution. The peer group, which again can be regarded as a primary agent of socialisation, can operate from without the institution (and the family situation) as an alternative to the values of the family and the educational institution. In this context, students whose friends have started work or have gone into higher education can be influenced to act in similar fashions. Within the particular educational institution, the formation of informal social groups is of particular importance for any discussion of occupational choice, in that the culture of such groups will quite likely involve the formation of attitudes to work and particular kinds of work; examples of this could be the philosophy that work is a necessary evil or sheer drudgery, or the disinclination of individuals to work in certain industries for ethical reasons. Certainly, any attempt to examine occupational choice, must take into account the role of the peer group, and informal social groups in the choice process, especially since such groups are highly relevant to later job choice and change; the peer group in this respect constantly provides a source of reference for individuals throughout their careers.

In addition to the more dynamic or informal influences on occupational choice, there exist many formal or institutional influences reflecting, perhaps, an awareness of the need to provide vocational education. This provision covers the career teacher role, the Youth Employment Service, Vocational Guidance Centres, careers conferences, works visits, Appointments Boards, sandwich courses and numerous other ways of providing vocational instruction or guidance. In a theoretical approach to the process of occupational choice the tendency is to offer an idealised picture of the role these formal influences should play, rather than to acknowledge the fact that in practice they often operate inadequately.

Formal institutions such as the Youth Employment Service and the University Appointments Boards, set up with the aim of improving the transition from education to employment have also been shown to have deficiencies – primarily deficiencies of scale. The Youth Employment Service, for example, has come under considerable criticism for failing in its role of vocational guidance and placement. Yet, as has often been pointed out[161] it is essentially a question of inadequate resources, and as a result the youth employment officer does too little and he does it too late.[162] Thus the ten or twenty minutes given to children by youth employment officers, which is in itself inadequate, often only applies to the secondary modern or technical schools, and as Maizels[163] has indicated, the Youth Employment Service is often more involved in subsequent job placement than in initial job placement. Similarly, the Appointments Boards have been criticised for failing to provide a really effective link between the universities and the world of employment.[164]

The question of the inadequacies of the formal agencies in career guidance and job placement raises two fundamental issues: whether such agencies are ineffective because they are inadequately provided for and badly run; or whether a formal approach to guidance and placement is correct. Evidence suggests that the job information possessed by school leavers and graduates is minimal, but that informal sources are more effective than formal sources. Yet the informal sources are usually ill informed (e.g. parents, subject teachers) and the informaion they provide and advice they give will be in terms of their own narrow experience. There are instances where information from formal sources is important – for example, university prospectuses, literature from firms, but it could be argued that the importance of such sources is due to the fact that the key informal influences lack this necessary information.

The answer would appear to lie in greater co-ordination between formal and informal influences. Formal sources are obviously necessary to provide the correct information, but information passed in a formal way is much less effective than information interpreted in an informal manner. It is obvious that the guidance function is absolutely vital and that individuals with career problems will seek such guidance from relatives, friends and sub-ject teachers, rather than make a formal approach to supposed guidance experts. If such professionals are to be effective in their guidance role the guidance must surely be continuous over a long period of time, so that changes in an individual's personal growth and development can be monitored and examined against a background of the widest range of employment opportunities. Allied to this, and given the importance of certain key figures of personal influence, it is essential that more thought is given to the education of parents, subject teachers, and career teachers in the area of vocational guidance. In Sweden the system exists where special courses are run for parents on vocational guidance, and where careers teachers can earn more than head teachers; there vocational education is raised to the level it deserves. In this country we firstly have to ascertain what are the major sources of influences in career decisions, and when that has been done to decide how to ensure that guidance and information is being effectively provided, in terms of both quality and quantity.

Extending the career choice process to encompass subsequent career decision, it is significant that there has been increasing attention given by employing organisations to the career guidance role, and allied to this a growth in the numbers of external guid-ance experts or consultants (usually focused on recruitment and selection). It is apparent that career decisions taken throughout the employment system are subjected to the same structural influences (in theoretical terms) that affect pre-employment entry decisions.

A SUMMARY AND IMPLICATIONS FOR MANPOWER PLANNING

It is suggested that for a theory of occupational choice to be of relevance to the manpower planning process, progress is required in two major areas: firstly in terms of an adequate definition of occupational choice; and secondly, in terms of the integration of the contributions of researchers representing the various disciplines.

It has been shown that the term 'occupational choice' is often interpreted in different ways, and that it has been taken to mean preferences or aspirations, expectations, the choice itself, and actual attainment of an occupational role. In this context, the term 'occupational choice process' is considered more meaningful, reflecting the fact that it covers the whole process of movement of individuals through the education system, into and through the employment system, and allows for analysis of the facts which influence the rate and direction of this movement. Thus the concept of occupational choice is not restricted, as it often is, to the immediate events, and period of time, surrounding the initial entry into employment, rather does it refer to career decisions and patterns throughout the life cycle.

In discussing the contributions of psychologists, economists and sociologists to the concept of occupational choice, the point was made that the main differences between these contributions was one of orientation, or concentration on particular aspects of the process. In this respect, the psychological approaches were shown to concentrate on the developmental nature of the process (emphasising the personal growth of individuals in emotional and intellectual terms), and the motivational nature of occupational choice (emphasising individual needs, desires, hopes and aspirations). The approach of the economists to occupational choice was discussed in relation to the utilisation of such concepts as cost and price, and in terms of the theory of total net advantage. The contribution of sociologists reflected the importance of the processes of socialisation and of the allocation of occupational roles, and emphasising those aspects of the social structure which represented both influences and constraints on the occupational choice process (for example, the family, the education system, the peer group, and formal guidance agencies).

Perhaps the most significant thing, though, about the various contributions outlined above is the way in which they are all interrelated. Thus to talk solely in terms of the aspirations of individuals without reference to the structural limitations upon them, is to ignore the realities of the social structure. Similarly, it is surely not possible to talk in terms of total net advantage without relating this to theories of motivation, just as it is not possible to concentrate on the structural aspects of the process without relating this to the extent of individual freedom of action. What would seem to be required, and what is attempted in the subsequent empirical work in this thesis is an approach which integrates the above orientations.

However, at this stage the observation must be made that the choices available to individuals over time generally become restricted, and that the philosophy of freedom of occupational choice is limited in practice. As Taylor has pointed out, 'the occupational organisation and the social organisation of the society provide few, if any, mechanistic norms for equating and understanding of the range of occupations with one's abilities and interests. Accordingly one's occupational aspiration and one's choice are narrowly limited'.[165]

Accepting that individuals are increasingly being channelled towards occupational areas at an earlier age, and because of other factors, it is perhaps more relevant to talk specifically of individual freedom of action in terms of *job* choice and change, and *organisational* choice and change once an individual has actually entered the employment system. A theory of occupational choice, it is argued, would account for such movement (proposed, considered or actual). In terms of manpower planning which is essentially concerned with both the movement and stability of personnel, if it is proposed to alter vocational decisions, which would obviously affect both movement and stability, it is essential that we understand the dynamics of the process by which decisions are made.

As Vroom[166] has pointed out occupational choice has significance for both individuals and for society. For the individual such choices have considerable implications for later satisfaction and adjustment, whilst for society, social systems are dependent on the vocational decisions of individuals. Given the importance of such decisions, it is surprising that more attention has been given to normative approaches to occupational choice than to empirical study. Thus, formal vocation systems such as the Youth Employment Service tend to be based on what might happen rather than on the realities of the situation. Given this lack of empirical study, it is contended that what is required is: firstly, an examination of those factors in a career which individuals regard as important, so that attempts can be made to match their expectations; secondly, an analysis of the needs and characteristics of occupations, and organisations so that these can be effectively conveyed to individuals faced with a career or job decision, as well as to individuals and institutions concerned with career advice and information; and thirdly, an examination of the way in which the process of occupational choice, occupational selection and occupational recruitment takes place, and which factors in these processes are of importance, Given such analysis it should then be possible to make manpower planning decisions which bear some relation to the realities of the situation.

CHAPTER 3

A Study of the Career Choice and Recruitment Process in Higher Education

If manpower planning is perceived in terms of matching the supply and demand characteristics of the labour force, then obviously a key factor in the external supply of manpower available to any organisation in the future is the educational system.[1] The reciprocal relationship between industry and education has already been noted,[2] as has the fact that education has emerged as a productive investment;[3] but the significance in this context of the relationship between the education and employment systems is the way in which educational institutions function as agencies for the selection, training and occupational placement of individuals.[4] It could, however, be suggested that the educational system does not perform such latent functions effectively, and that in any case, as Drucker has indicated 'schools and universities were not designed for the selection processes thrust upon them in a modern economy by the tightening band of schooling with occupation . . . nor were they designed to act as agencies of social justice, distributing life chances'.[5] The manifest function of educational institutions may be to educate, but the fact remains that selection is one of a number of latent functions[6] performed by educational institutions, and any analysis of the *actual* relationship between education and employment must account for such factors.

The empirical research presented in this book is concerned with the high talent manpower sector, defined by Harbison and Myers[7] as the stock of high-level manpower in a country as measured by the total number of persons with secondary education or above in the population. In terms of this definition, it is possible to identify two key stages where occupational choice decisions take effect, and where individuals move either from the education system into the employment system, or from one educational level to another; these stages have been identified as the school fifth and sixth forms, and the final year undergraduate or postgraduate level. In a study of the career choice process at sixth form level, conducted by the author,[8] it was found that the majority of leavers at this level aspire to enter the educational system. Despite the fact that not all of these leavers would have their aspirations met, the likelihood is that a large proportion of those students wishing to enter the higher education system will do so, implying that for many such students the process of career choice will be delayed.

It has been suggested that occupational aspirations and choice are narrowly limited, and that the multiplicity of the organised society affords little support for the ideological freedom of individual occupational choice.[9] This is, in many ways, the basis of sociological approaches to occupational choice, indicating that as one passes through the educational system opportunities available become increasingly structured. Yet, it could also be argued that though an individual, in his educational experience from the sixth form into the higher education sphere is in one sense possibly restricting the occupational roles open to him, in another sense he is widening those same opportunities in terms of the freedom and flexibility the higher level of entry will give him. It is, therefore, possible for the higher educational system to perform simultaneously, two functions which superficially might appear to be contradictory. The aspirations of sixth formers to enter the higher educational system must certainly be considered in the light of their perceptions of the functions of universities or colleges, but it is important to highlight the fact that such institutions perform other important functions, some of which are particularly relevant to the process of personnel flow.

It is the vocational functions of higher education institutions with which this chapter is primarily concerned, and in this context a most useful discussion of the vocational implications of degree courses is provided in a general survey by the Careers Research and Advisory Centre.[10] They suggest that the vocational value of a degree can be of four kinds: where the degree can simply educate students to a level where they are able to enter a particular career at a graduate rather than a school leaver level; where the degree can provide the student with a grounding which is relevant to a particular career though not essential for entry; here the degree provides a grounding which is not only relevant to a particular career but is essential for entry into it, even though it does not provide a vocational training; and finally where the degree actually trains the student for entry into a particular career. The significant point is that given such evidence as is provided by research into the aspirations and expectations of sixth form leavers – particularly the fact that only a relatively small proportion of sixth formers are able to be highly specific about future careers – the majority of students are for a variety of reasons going to find themselves within one of these four categories and will accordingly have differential ease of access to various occupational categories. Thus, choice of degree course at sixth form level is likely to be made in educational rather than vocational terms, yet in practice the vocational considerations in higher education increase as the degree course progresses, culminating in a vocational decision in the final year which has been considerably influenced by the original choice of degree at sixth form level, made largely in educational terms.

The career choice process in the higher education system has implications for both recruiting organisations, and for the individuals making career decisions, and at this stage it is useful to make some general points in relation to these two different standpoints.* The demand for graduates by employing organisations does, of course, vary, depending largely on economic circumstances (and especially in certain employment areas), but given the fact that an increasing number of the ablest sixth formers are entering higher education, and that the total output of graduates in 1970 was 55,600, as compared with an output of 21,700 in 1960,[11] then the output of the higher education system is likely to remain a very important recruitment source. Rogers and Williams, for example, comment that industry and commerce has been and will continue to be the growth area for graduate employment with some 11,000 graduates entering this area in 1967–8,[12] whilst the Careers Research and Advisory Centre point out that over the past few years there have been several important additions to the list of employers who are specifically interested in employing graduates – such as banks, insurance companies and local authorities.[13] The reason for this has much to do with the expansion of the higher education sector and the decline (both in terms of numbers and perceived quality) of individuals wishing to enter employment from the traditional recruitment sector, i.e. the sixth form. Thus, increasingly as the CRAC point out, employers are being driven to look to the higher education institutions simply because such a high proportion of the country's identified ablest talent is located there. It would appear, however, that the response of more traditional organisations tends to be reactive rather than proactive and that once a decision has been taken to employ graduates this is followed through with scant regard for the

* Appendix 1 presents some of the major trends in the graduate employment situation in the UK

consequences of welding a new set of expectations and attitudes on to a system solidly based on the values of the sixth form leaver whose values are likely to be rather different. This is the extent of the problem facing organisations where the personnel policies tend to emphasise such features as low age of recruitment, a gradual career progression, and age related salary scales.

To return, however, to the recruitment of graduates by employing organisations; there are two further points which are particularly relevant to the process of movement from higher education into employment. The first refers to the fact that many graduates will not enter employment of any kind after first graduation – the University Grants Committee returns in fact, show that only 45% of arts and social studies graduates entered employment in 1968, and 61% of pure and applied science graduates. Prospective employers are therefore faced with a situation where about half of the potential recruits are thinking largely in terms of extending their time in the educational system in one form or another. Added to this, of course, is the fact that there will be variations in employment patterns according to class of degree, and that it is likely to be those with better degrees who are accepted for further academic training. Given this situation it is then possible to realise the competitive and difficult situation which faces recruiting organisations, and it highlights the significance of the recruitment and selection procedures employed by these organisations. The experiences of undergraduates and post-graduates in work situations during their university courses, and their experience of the recruitment and selection procedures of recruiting organisations are therefore likely to be of considerable importance for the career and job choices of final year students. The responsibility of the recruiting organisation in this respect has been strongly emphasised by Plumbley in commenting on the need for 'a clear definition by employers of their needs – the jobs to be done; the candidate market; the training to be given, so that we may get a maximum return from this country's vast investment in its future human resources'.[14]

The second point to be made at this stage refers to the formalising of the process of movement both from the higher education system, and from the first degree level within educational institutions into more advanced courses or research areas. The subject of degree and class (or likely class) of degree will structure the future occupational situation for individuals, and in addition the actual mechanisms which cater for career advice and choices are structured and formalised. Processes for occupational entry and re-entry are specified and formalised for organisational purposes, and as Taylor has pointed out, given an increasing number of occupational opportunities together with a large increasingly well qualified population, potential employees and employers are unable to identify the full range of employment opportunities and employee potential; thus 'the development of increasingly formal mechanisms for entering occupations is consistent with the complexities of social organisation and with the multiplicity of occupations'.[15] It is possible to look at the University Appointments Boards, and the recruitment and selection procedures of recruiting organisations (of all kinds) in these terms, indicating the impersonal and formal nature of the process of career flow at the higher educational level.

The other major aspect of the career choice process in the higher education system consists of the aspirations, expectations, and perceptions of the students involved with this process. Daws[16] has commented on an important distinction between psychological and sociological approaches to the work situation, illustrating psychological concern with the rational matching of people's abilities and inclinations with the known requirements of jobs, and the increasing occupational analysis undertaken by sociologists which have underlined the extensive influence of the job on an individual's life, and the influence of the ethos of the organisation within which working life is spent. The significance, therefore, for individuals of choice of job does not lessen the longer the choice is delayed nor does such choice become less difficult; although it could be suggested that choice might be easier at undergraduate level rather than sixth form level as the capacity of the individual to appraise himself will have improved to the point where individuals can think of themselves in fairly mature and sophisticated terms. However, this kind of interpretation adds little to our understanding of the career choice process since it fails to identify those elements in the situation which greatly influence the nature and quality of a career decision; a greater capacity for self evaluation is of little use to someone faced with a career choice decision if the structural elements in the process of personnel flow are inadequate.

In the theoretical framework of the occupational choice process presented in the second chapter, it was argued that for a meaningful analysis to take place it was necessary to take into account the complexity of the process and the interaction of all the factors bearing on career decisions. It was suggested that an integrated approach to occupational choice was required which considered the motivational nature of choice (emphasising individual needs, desires, aspirations and expectations), in terms of the processes of socialisation and occupational role allocation, i.e. emphasising the way in which elements of the social structure acted as influences and constraints on the occupational choice process. Research into the career choice process as applied to final year university students would therefore need to examine not only the perceptions and expectations of such students, but also their experience of those parts of the social structure relevant to their career perceptions, and career choice. As Monk[17] had indicated, there has been little attempt at this level to determine how the undergraduate perceives his approaching employment, or to ascertain what needs such students possess. It could be suggested, therefore, that there is a need both to examine the way in which such prospective employees perceive their career situation, and to examine the dimensions relevant to such perceptions.

A STUDY OF THE CAREER CHOICE PROCESS IN HIGHER EDUCATION

The aim of the research presented here was to attempt to highlight the major social structural features of the career process as applied to final year university students at Liverpool University, and to discover the significance of the students' experiences of such features for their career perceptions. The particular concern was with the industrial and commercial sectors, but the results are related to the other major employment sectors. The major areas of interest in the enquiry were types of work experience and the effects of such experiences in career terms, the numbers and types of job applications, the current job situation of the students (for example, whether jobs had been accepted, offered and not accepted, jobs applied for but not offered, or jobs not applied for), attitudes to industrial and commercial recruiting techniques based on experience of such procedures, career perceptions in terms of job progression and time progression, and factors in the work situation held to be personally important as compared with the perceived extent of their provision in an industrial or commercial work situation. In addition, relevant information was obtained on such factors as age, sex, marital status, nationality, university courses being taken and home and school background.

In Easter 1970, questionnaires were sent out to four out of every five of the final year students registered with the Appointments Board at the University of Liverpool. A total of 430 replies were received (330 undergraduates, 100 post-graduates) representing a response rate of just over 47%. It is, perhaps important to point out that the results relate specifically to students registering with the Appointments Board and, as a consequence, the result exclude those students who had made their own contacts directly with employers and those who by Easter 1970 had taken no action in terms of finding a job.[18]

TYPE OF UNIVERSITY COURSE ATTENDED

The distribution of respondents by type of university course is shown in Table 3.1.

Table 3.1

DISTRIBUTION OF RESPONDENTS BY TYPE OF UNIVERSITY COURSE ATTENDED

Department	Undergraduates		Post-graduates	
	No.	%	No.	%
Engineering	89	27	11	
Science	122	37	35	
Business studies			34	
Commerce	23	7		
Arts	43	12·9	14	
Social science	51	15·5	5	
Building science				
Law	2	0·6	1	
Total	330	100	100	

It is interesting to note that the distribution compares very favourably with the actual total distribution of all graduating students in 1970 in terms of university course undertaken. Thus, the total number of students graduating in engineering and science in 1970 was 951 out of a total of 1,723 representing about 55% which compares with a combined total of post-graduate and undergraduate respondents undertaking engineering and science of 257 or 59% of the total. The profile, therefore, of the respondents is very similar to that of the total distribution of final year students in 1970. The relatively high proportion of post-graduate respondents undertaking business studies courses reflects the fact that the study was conducted from this department. However, given the orientation of these students to an industrial/commercial career this is taken as being a useful feature.

SEX, MARITAL STATUS, AGE AND NATIONALITY

In both the undergraduate and post-graduate samples the majority of the respondents were unmarried males, but there were differences in the size of this majority as can be seen in Tables 3.2 and 3.3.

Table 3.2

THE NUMBER OF RESPONDENTS BY SEX DISTRIBUTION

| | Undergraduates | | Post-graduates | |
	No.	%	No.	%
Male	255	77	90	90
Female	75	23	10	10
Total	330	100	100	100

Table 3.3

THE NUMBER OF RESPONDENTS BY MARITAL STATUS DISTRIBUTION

| | Undergraduates | | Post-graduates | |
	No.	%	No.	%
Married	13	4	31	31
Single	317	96	69	69
Total	330	100	100	100

In comparison with the actual sex distribution of the graduating students of 1970 the sex distribution of respondents is biased overall towards the male side. The actual ratio of male to female students graduates in 1970 was approximately 65%:35% (undergraduate), and about 85%:15% (post-graduate), whereas in the respondent sample the ratios were 77%:23% and 90%:10% respectively. This slight bias, however, is possibly useful given the particular concern of the research with those considering employment in the industrial and commercial sectors. In addition, the large majority of women graduates appear to enter two or three easily identifiable areas of employment, teacher training or secretarial training, actual teaching or local government. There are no comparable official figures for marital status to ascertain the representativeness of the sample in this respect, but it would appear logical that a greater proportion of the post-graduate students were married given the fact that they were generally older than the undergraduates and were also more secure (i.e. in terms of having achieved a First degree).

The age distribution of the respondents illustrated the fact that all except three of the undergraduates were under 25 on the 1 June 1970, with a large majority of these under the age of 23. In comparison, the post-graduates were distributed as follows: 25% between the ages of 20 and 22, 68% between 23 and 26, and 6% between 27 and 34. Thus generally, we are dealing with the 20–26 age group which is of significance in career terms. The nationalities of respondents again showed small differences within the undergraduate and post-graduate areas. All except one, in fact, of the undergraduates were British, whilst 86% of the post-graduates were British.

HOME AND SCHOOL BACKGROUND

The significance for occupational choice decisions of family and social-class background, and type of education received, has been emphasised by most occupational choice theorists. It was suggested in Chapter 2 that the career aspirations and expectations of individuals were related to and influenced by such factors as social class, type of school, and other educational experiences, and the research into the career perceptions of sixth form leavers referred to earlier[19] illustrated this fact. Accordingly, it was thought necessary to include in this study of the career perceptions of final year university students an examination of the socio-economic background, type of secondary school attended, and advanced level subjects taken. The distribution of respondents according to social-class background is shown in Table 3.4.

Table 3.4

NUMBER OF RESPONDENTS BY SOCIAL-CLASS BACKGROUND DISTRIBUTION

Social-class Background	Undergraduates		Post-graduates	
	No.	%	No.	%
Professional	55	17	6	
Intermediate	112	33	41	
Skilled	111	33	27	
Partly skilled	18	6	9	
Unskilled	5	2	2	
Deceased or retired	29	9	15	
Total	330	100	100	

The students were asked the job performed by their fathers or guardians, and the occupational sector in which he worked. The results showed that 15% of the post-graduates and 9% of the undergraduates reported deceased or retired fathers – the higher ages of a small proportion of the post-graduate respondents could possibly account for this. Most of the students appeared to come from the intermediate and skilled classes, but rather more post-graduates than undergraduates came from the intermediate class; however, proportionately three times as many undergraduates came from professional homes as post-graduates. The differences in skilled and partly skilled class derivation were not significant.

It was suggested earlier that although social class factors do represent an influence on career choice, the education system can be a great 'leveller'. Most of the evidence for this view relates to the secondary school level,[20] but research by Musgrave[21] indicates that the process might be extended and class factors decrease as educational experience increases. It would certainly appear reasonable to suggest that if education is serving to some extent as an antidote to class factors at secondary level then it is likely to be even more important at the higher educational level.

Educational background does play a significant role in the occupational choice process, and sociological approaches in particular[22] have highlighted the way in which decisions taken by one or for one at various stages in the education process will structure the opportunities available. Examples of such decisions would be type of secondary school attended, and choice of specialist subjects. It was, therefore, thought useful to collect information about these factors in this study, and results are shown in tables 3.5 and 3.6.

The largest proportion by far of both post-graduates and

Table 3.5

DISTRIBUTION OF RESPONDENTS BY TYPE OF SECONDARY
SCHOOL ATTENDED

Type of Secondary School	Undergraduates		Post-graduates	
	No.	%	No.	%
Grammar	255	78	66	
Modern	4	1	5	
Technical	8	3	3	
Public	31	9	13	
Others	32	9	13	
Total	330	100	100	

undergraduates came from grammar schools, but interestingly post-graduates appeared slightly less likely to have attended grammar school. In addition, there was a greater but not significant chance of post-graduates coming from modern or public schools. The major impression is of a more varied school background on the part of the post-graduate respondents.

The subjects taken at advanced level in the secondary school effectively structures the range of university courses open to students, and in this respect represents a major influence on the career choice process. Such decisions also have implications for various occupational groupings, since, given the philosophy of freedom of occupational choice, each occupational sector is dependent for its future supply of manpower on all aspects of the career decisions of individuals – of which choice of advanced level subject is a vital early decision.

Table 3.6

DISTRIBUTION OF RESPONDENTS BY GCE ADVANCED LEVEL PASSES

Advanced Level Subjects	*Undergraduates*		*Post-graduates*	
	No.	%	No.	%
Science	247	75	60	
General and practical	1	0	0	
Languages	39	12	12	
General Arts	33	10	20	
Others	10	3	8	
Total	330	100	100	

The information obtained from the respondents about advanced level subjects becomes extremely meaningful when examined in conjunction with the distribution of respondents by university courses being taken. Perhaps the major point of interest is the fact that although 75% and 60% of undergraduates and post-graduates respectively had taken science subjects at advanced level, only 64% and 46% respectively were taking degrees in the science and engineering faculties. This apparent loss of scientific manpower between the school and the university highlights what has been acknowledged to be a serious problem in high talent manpower supply nationally in recent years. Various government working parties – in particular the Swann Report,[23] the Dainton Report,[24] and the Jones Report[25] – have reported on various aspects of the shortage of manpower resources in science and technology;

although the methods of forecasting used by such committees has been criticised with apparent justification by Gannicott and Blaug.[26] There appears to be an awareness now that the graduate supply question is rather more complex than has previously been made out, and certainly the choice decisions of individuals in this respect are of vital importance. One final point about the distribution of post-graduate respondents by advanced level subject area refers to the fact that the large proportion of post-graduates who took general arts subjects at advanced level may be accounted for by business studies and social science post-graduates.

THE NATURE AND SIGNIFICANCE OF STUDENTS' WORK EXPERIENCE

There is an increasing amount of attention being given to the whole question of vocational education, and one suggestion which is often put forward is to give students experience in work situations whilst they are still involved in the education system. Of course, many students do obtain such experience in an informal way, primarily through vacation work, but information on the nature and extent of such experience is limited, and there appears to be little awareness of the effect of such experience in influencing – either positively or negatively – future career decisions.[27] But it is an assumption, and it is argued here that before any further schemes are developed for formalising 'prior work experience', there should be some detailed research conducted into the effect of informal work experience.[28]

An important part of this study was to examine the nature and significance of such factors amongst the undergraduates and post-graduate respondents. The emphasis was particularly on the work experiences of students in the fields of industry and commerce, and information was obtained about work experience before entering university, during university, and the importance of such experience in influencing career decisions. The results are shown in Tables 3.7, 3.8, and 3.9.

It can be seen that 37% of the undergraduate and 40% of the post-graduate respondents had obtained industrial or commercial work experience before entering university, which, if it is representative is a surprisingly low figure, and raises questions about the narrowness of the experience of most older secondary school leavers. The inference is that nearly two-thirds of the respondents had not experienced a work situation at the age of university entrance which generally would be about eighteen; at such an age

Table 3.7

TYPE OF INDUSTRIAL/COMMERCIAL EXPERIENCE BEFORE
ENTERING UNIVERSITY

Total Number with Work Experience	Undergraduates 123 (37%)		Post-graduates 40 (40%)	
Type of Experience	*No.*	*% (of 123)*	*No.*	*% (of 40)*
a Temporary employment	107	87	26	65
Permanent employment	16	13	14	35
Total for *a*	123	100	40	100
b Shop floor/manual work	66	54	15	36
Office/scientific/managerial work	26	21	12	31
Manual and non-manual work	31	25	13	33
Total for *b*	123	100	40	100
c Experience in one organisation	70	57	15	37
Experience in two organisations	28	23	17	42
Experience in three or more organisations	25	20	8	21
Total for *c*	123	100	40	100

most of their peers would have been working for three years. Certainly the results indicate the fact that career decisions at the later school-leaving age are not likely to be based on adequate experience or information, and this perhaps suggests an inadequate base for career choices at this level.

Of the undergraduates who had obtained industrial or commercial experience before starting their university careers, the great majority (87%) had obtained this experience in temporary employment; for over half of the students this experience had been of a shop floor or manual nature, whilst 25% of the undergraduates had obtained work experience of a manual and non-manual nature. One other interesting point related to the numbers of organisations worked in; over half (57%) of the undergraduates had only worked in one organisation – which backs up even further the earlier point about the narrowness of the experience of school leavers – whilst 20% had work experience in three or more organisations.

The work experience before entering university of the post-graduates was different in a number of ways. Proportionately more of the post-graduates had experienced permanent employment, and possibly related to this was the fact that a greater proportion of post-graduates than undergraduates had work experience of an office, scientific or managerial nature. In addition, the post-graduate students appeared more likely to have had experience of working in more than one organisation.

The work experience of both undergraduate and post-graduate *during* their university career shown in Table 3.8 reveals a number of interesting points.

Table 3.8

TYPE OF INDUSTRIAL/COMMERCIAL EXPERIENCE DURING UNIVERSITY CAREER

Total Number with Work Experience	Undergraduates 207 (63%)		Post-graduates 50 (50%)	
Type of Experience	No.	% (of 207)	No.	% (of 50)
a Temporary/vacation employment	200	95	44	88
Part of university course	7	5	6	12
Total for a	207	100	50	100
b Shop floor/manual work	82	40	18	36
Office/scientific/managerial work	63	30	15	30
Manual and non-manual work	62	30	17	34
Total for b	207	100	50	100
c Experience in one organisation	81	39	18	36
Experience in two organisations	73	36	17	34
Experience in three or more organisations	53	25	15	30
Total for c	207	100	50	100

A total of 207 (63%) of the undergraduate and 50 (50%) of the post-graduate respondents had obtained industrial experience during their university careers, a significantly higher proportion, particularly in the case of the undergraduates, then the numbers obtaining such experience before entering university. The reasons for this increase would appear to have a great deal to do with age and the changing financial situation of students – vacation work becomes increasingly necessary for financial reasons. In addition, the long summer vacation at university leaves a large amount of time available for employment, whilst school vacations are generally much shorter.

The 207 undergraduates who had obtained industrial or commercial work experience during their course had obtained this experience slightly more on the shop floor (manual) side (40%) than the white-collar side (30%), but nearly a third of all these students had experience of both manual and non-manual work. The great majority of this experience had come from vacation employment, with only 5% of the undergraduates obtaining work experience as part of a university course. In terms of the number of organisations in which this work experience had been obtained, although 39% of the students had worked in only one organisation the numbers working in two or more organisations had significantly increased compared with the work experience of students before entering university. There was, therefore, a tendency on the part of the undergraduates to work in more organisations as they progressed through the education system.

There did not appear to be a marked increase in the numbers of post-graduates obtaining industrial or commercial experience during their university careers as compared with the numbers gaining such experience before entering university. Of the fifty post-graduates obtaining such experience, a large proportion (88%) were involved in vacation work as opposed to working as part of a university course. As with the undergraduates, there was a slight tendency for this work experience to be of a shop floor nature (36%) as opposed to white-collar work (30%), but again there were over a third (34%) who had experience of both types of emloyment. Again, as with the undergraduates although 36% obtained their work experience in one organisation only, this indicates that 64% (nearly two thirds), obtained experience in two or more organisations.

Given the nature of the work experience of the respondents, which provides interesting information in itself of the activities of students in vacation periods, the major concern in the study was the perceived importance of such experience by the students.

A total of 233 of the undergraduate respondents and 76 of the post-graduate respondents had obtained work experience of an industrial or commercial nature before the survey was conducted.

Table 3.9

THE PERCEIVED IMPORTANCE OF WORK EXPERIENCE FOR
THE CAREER DECISIONS OF RESPONDENTS

Response	Undergraduates		Post-graduates	
	No.	%	No.	%
Experience the major factor in influencing me to enter industry commerce	13	6	9	12
Experience of some importance in influencing me to enter industry/commerce	72	31	19	25
Experience of minimal importance or irrelevant in my consideration of industrial/commercial career	116	49	35	47
Experience of some importance in deterring me from entering industry/commerce	16	7	5	6
Experience the major factor in deterring me from entering industry/commerce	2	1	3	4
I have not considered a career in industry/commerce	14	6	5	6
Total	233	100	76	100

The figures for both groups were remarkably similar, and although just under half of both undergraduates and post-graduates felt that their experience had been of minimal importance or irrelevent in considering an industrial or commercial career, a significant proportion (37% in each group) thought their experience had been either of some importance, or the major factor, in influencing them to enter industry or commerce. If this latter figure (37%) is examined in relation to the proportions of both groups who felt that their experience had been either of some importance (7% and 6% respectively) or else the major factor (1% and 4% respectively) in *deterring* them from an industrial or commercial career, then the proportions of both undergraduates and post-graduates whose experience had influenced them either *positively* or *negatively* when considering an industrial or commercial career was about the same as those whose experience had not influenced them in any way.

The fact that for nearly half of both groups their experience was

H

a factor in influencing a career decision raises a number of interesting points, and has implications for both vocational education and for the recruitment policies of organisations. The obvious importance of industrial and commercial experience gained either before entering university or during university for career decisions relates strongly to the approaches of most sociological discussions of occupational choice, with their emphasis on the concepts of role and socialisation. Musgrave[29] has utilised both concepts in his discussion of occupational choice; in introducing stages in a sociological theory he suggests that a stage of 'anticipatory socialisation' is a vital analytical tool, and that adequate anticipatory socialisation will ease the later taking of an occupational role. Prior role rehearsal, therefore, a prior knowledge of what is involved in filling occupational roles, is seen as an important element in preparing for the taking of such roles. In addition, both Roberts[30] and Blau et al.[31] have stressed the importance for career decisions of information about occupational areas, and Vroom[32] has referred to the limited nature of occupational choices as a consequence of the restricted range of information which people have about the world of work.

The sociological interpretations of the significance of work experience are not very explicit, however, and the type of experience obtained by students in this study was largely of a temporary kind. It is suggested, therefore, that a useful contribution to a sociological theory of occupational choice would include some analysis of the type of information students obtain and the type of work experience obtained before entering an occupation.

The fact that 37% of the undergraduates and 37% of the postgraduates with work experience thought it influenced them to some extent or to a major extent to enter industry and commerce would appear to be extremely significant considering the fact that this experience was likely to be of a temporary kind, i.e. during the vacation periods. If what is essentially informal experience – albeit of a varied kind (certainly more varied than usual assumptions about the predominantly manual nature of university students' vacation work experience) – is an important factor in influencing students to enter industry and commerce, then it is pertinent to ask what would be the likely effect of formalising such work experience. In other words, if students work anyway in their vacation periods (and most would appear to do so) and if such experience is useful and influential for their subsequent career decisions it would seem logical for prospective employers to attempt to formalise such work experience, and possibly liaise with the higher education sector in arranging programmes of a more meaningful nature. There would certainly appear to be considerable benefits for prospective employers, and for universities, too, if they are concerned at all about the vocational aspects of education.

One final point might relate to the finding that out of 233 undergraduates who had obtained work experiences before the survey date, only fourteen had not considered a career in industry and commerce, a similar low proportion of post-graduates (five out of seventy-six) had not considered an industrial or commercial career. If this is reasonably representative then it also points to the lack of success of industry and commerce in their recruitment of graduates.

JOB APPLICATION EXPERIENCES OF FINAL YEAR STUDENTS

The importance of job application experiences for career decisions needs little stressing. To apply for a job is a positive act which comes at a vital stage for the student when he or she is making a career choice which can in some ways be looked upon as a 'delayed choice'. The experience a student has of applying for jobs and of the recruiting procedures used by organisations is something about which not a great deal is known, yet is a necessary prerequisite for a greater understanding of the career choice process.

This study set out to examine aspects of the nature of the job application experiences of final year students. The major areas of interest are desired occupational area, number of jobs applied for, number of rejections, reasons for non application for jobs, nature of job offers, and the number of job offers in 'desirable' areas.

The occupational areas in which the students desired to work can be seen in terms of their aspirations. In the study of the career choices of sixth form leavers referred to earlier, the aspirations of the sixth formers to work in particular occupational or economic sectors were compared with their expectations of actually entering the area of their choice; the results showed that the more glamorous occupational areas suffered in terms of students' expectations of entering these areas, and that industry and commerce whilst not accounting for the aspirations of students to any considerable degree rated highly in terms of students' expectations of entry. In the present study it is possible to take this comparison a stage further, and compare the aspirations of final year university students with actual entry in order to discuss the relationship between aspirations and reality. The areas in which students desired to work are shown in Table 3.10 and figures are given for both undergraduates and post-graduates; it should also be noted that in this case, the students were allowed to specify an unlimited number of occupational/economic areas in their replies which means that the response total may be more than the actual number of students responding.

Table 3.10

THE PROPORTION OF RESPONDENTS FINDING EACH
OCCUPATIONAL CATEGORY DESIRABLE

Occupational Category	*Undergraduates* (350)		*Post-graduates* (123)	
	No.	% (of 350)	No.	% (of 123)
a Agriculture	2	0·5	0	0
b Industrial/commercial management	93	26·5	40	32
c Industrial research, design, engineering	118	34	36	29
d Professional practice	30	8·5	8	7
e Teaching	25	7	11	9
f Government service	24	7	7	6
g Academic life	14	4	16	13
h Journalism, arts etc.	16	4·5	2	1·5
i Others	28	8	3	2·5
Total	350	100	123	100

Given the concern with the recruitment problems of industrial and commercial organisations, it would be fair to say that the above results provide useful information for these sectors. It would be inaccurate simply to combine the percentage figures for those students attracted to industrial and commercial management *and* to industrial research, design and engineering for it is highly likely that many of the same respondents are attracted to both areas; it is therefore realistic to suggest that the proportion of respondents attracted to an industrial or commercial career would be between 34% and 60·5% (undergraduates) and 32% and 61% post-graduates. These figures to compare with the results from a survey of undergraduate career choice conducted at Cambridge University in 1969[33] when it was found using exactly the same categories as this study that 47% of undergraduates (of all years) were attracted to a career in industrial or commercial management and 34% to a career in industrial research, design and engineering. Again, taking the higher figure as being indicative of the minimum proportion attracted to the industrial and commercial sectors this would give a range of 47% to 81%, compared with the 34% to 60·5% in the present study which, of course, deals with *final year* students only. Taking the proportions in the present study this illustrates the potential source of recruitment for industrial and commercial organisations concerned with recruiting at this level. An examination of the actual proportion of students recruited into industry and commerce in 1970 from Liverpool University however, reveals a disparity between the level of attraction shown above and actual entry. Thus of the 1969–70 total output there were 1,165 undergraduates known to have entered employment (including post-graduate work), and of these 26% had entered the industrial or commercial sectors in one form or another, 18% had continued with post-graduate work, and 27% had either entered teacher training or gone directly into school or technical college teaching. The *actual* distribution of graduating students at Liverpool in 1970 is shown in Table 3.11.

Table 3.11

ACTUAL PERCENTAGE DISTRIBUTION OF 1970 LIVERPOOL GRADUATES IN EMPLOYMENT BY MAJOR EMPLOYMENT SECTOR

Employment Sector	(*Total 1165*) *Undergraduates* %	(*Total 187*) *Post-graduates* %
Industrial/commercial employment	26	29
Post-graduate study	18	—
Academic career	—	25
Teacher training/teaching	27	8
Government service	8	18
Other areas	21	20
Total	100	100

Source: University of Liverpool Appointments Board Annual Report 1969–70.

Of the post-graduate students who actually entered employment in 1970 it can be seen that a slightly greater proportion entered industry and commerce but the major differences occurred in the areas of post-graduate study and academic posts. The figures for the two groups (undergraduates and post-graduates) are similar in this context – 18% of the former entering post-graduate work

and 25% of the latter taking up an academic post – almost
certainly indicating that for an academic career further post-
graduate study is an essential prerequisite; this can be seen as an
attempt by an occupational grouping to restrict entry and to
control the conditions thought to be generally acceptable to
members of that profession. Other interesting features of the
results refer to the large proportion of undergraduates entering
teacher training or entering teaching directly, and the tendency for
proportionately more post-graduates to enter government service.

Of course, these results are for both sexes, and if a breakdown is
made of the sex differences in terms of occupational categories
entered the picture becomes clearer (see Table 3.12).

Table 3.12

THE SEX DISTRIBUTION OF 1970 GRADUATES IN
EMPLOYMENT BY MAJOR EMPLOYMENT SECTOR

Employment Sector	*Undergraduates*		*Post-graduates*	
	Male (750) %	*Female* (407) %	*Male* (172) %	*Female* (15) %
Industrial/commercial employment	31	11	30	20
Postgraduate study	25	13	—	—
Academic career	—	—	26	20
Teacher training/teaching	16	28	11	26
Government service	7	12	20	6
Other areas	21	36	13	28
Total	100	100	100	100

Source: University of Liverpool Appointments Board Annual Report
1969–70.

Almost one third (31%) of male undergraduates and a similar
proportion of male post-graduates enter industry and commerce,
whilst the proportion of female undergraduates entering these
areas is considerably lower (11% and 20% respectively). Even so,
when compared with the fact that at least 36% of the respondents
in the study were attracted to a career in industry and commerce
(as well as the fact that 77% of the respondents were male), there
is an important disparity between those attracted to a career in
industry and commerce, and possibly aspiring to such a career,
and the actual numbers entering the sectors. The disparity could
be due to a number of factors: the quality (or lack of it) of the
students, the failure of industry and commerce to recruit effectively,

or more complex changes in the situation; but it would appear that the information relating to this disparity could be used as a starting point for further investigation into the reasons why aspirations or attractions are not being fulfilled.

Other features of the sex breakdown illustrate the large proportion of undergraduates, especially males, who go on to postgraduate study, the large proportion of female undergraduates (28%) and post-graduates who enter teaching or teacher training, and the recruitment by government or local government of large numbers of undergraduates and post-graduates.

The number of job applications by the respondents provides factual information of a kind which is not readily available. Results are shown in Table 3.13.

Table 3.13

THE NUMBERS OF JOBS APPLIED FOR BY RESPONDENTS

Number of Jobs	Undergraduates		Post-graduates	
	No.	% (of 271)	No.	% (of 72)
0–5	98	36	28	40
6–10	119	44	28	40
11–15	35	13	10	15
16–20	10	4	—	—
21–25	3	15	2	5
26–30	3	15	—	—
Total	271	100	72	100

It is important to point out that not all of the total number of respondents had actually applied for jobs so that the two figures of 271 and 72 respectively apply to those students who had actually applied for jobs. The majority of both undergraduates and postgraduates (80% of each) had applied for less than ten jobs, but equally the majority of both groups (64% and 60% respectively) had applied for more than six jobs which illustrates the extent of job application experiences, and the degree to which students 'shop around' when job hunting. The exact reasons for this number of job applications was not investigated, but could illustrate the lack of information which students have about careers and hence a tendency to apply for a large number of jobs, equally it could show a carefully planned exercise to obtain the best possible employment, or it could illustrate the inadequacy of formal guidance systems at this level which do not channel student applications effectively enough. The career choice literature would tend to indicate that the middle suggestion is the one out of sympathy with the realities of situation.

Allied to the number of job applications made by students is the number of rejections and these are shown in Table 3.14.

Table 3.14

THE JOB REJECTIONS RECEIVED BY RESPONDENTS

| *Number of Rejections* | *Undergraduates* | | *Post-graduates* | |
	No.	% (of 271)	No.	% (of 72)
0–5	196	72	54	75
6–10	55	20	15	21
11–15	14	6	3	4
16–20	5	2	—	—
21–25	1	—	—	—
Total	271	100	72	100

The vast majority of the respondents had had rejections but 72% of the undergraduates and 75% of the post-graduates had received less than five rejections. This still means, though, that more than six rejections were received by 28% of the undergraduates and by 25% of the post-graduates, a situation which must surely be unsatisfactory from a number of standpoints. It certainly highlights a situation where the movement from higher education into employment is a haphazard process, and where formal guidance is possibly deficient. Obviously certain students are difficult to place and the rejection will undoubtedly have much to do with personal deficiencies but the proportion of such students simply cannot be anywhere near as large as the 28% and 25% respectively of students who have received more than six refusals. This would tend to indicate that the whole process of personnel flow in this area is characterised by a lack of awareness on the part of the student (for which there may well be a variety of reasons) and a system of guidance and recruitment on the part of guidance agencies and prospective employers which is clearly lacking in a number of respects. The problems of the University Appointments Boards remain those highlighted by the Heyworth Report,[34] overloading of work, and inadequate supporting services of staff and accommodation, and employers have long attempted to find ways round the now familiar and often depressing recruiting tours of universities, yet the problem remains, and as the recent CBI Working Party Report on careers guidance indicated the process of personnel flow and career choice at this level is 'by any standards, an inefficient way of preparing the talent of the nation to take its proper place in the community which expects much of it, and to which it should, in the end, have much to give'.[35]

A large proportion of the respondents had, of course, applied for jobs with varying degrees of success, but it is relevant at this stage to point out that of the fifty-nine undergraduates and twenty-eight post-graduates who had not by Easter 1970 applied for any job, the great majority (74%) had decided to wait for their examination results before doing anything about future careers – most of these were hoping for either a post-graduate place or an academic job.

From those students who had applied for jobs, and had been offered jobs which they had either accepted or were still deciding whether or not to accept, an attempt was made to ascertain the numbers of job offers they had received, the nature of the job offers they had received, and the job offers received in a desired occupational area. The total number of job offers received by both these categories of respondent are shown in Table 3.15.

Table 3.15

THE TOTAL NUMBER OF JOB OFFERS RECEIVED

Number of Job Offers	Undergraduates (175)		Post-graduates (40)	
	No.	% (of 175)	No.	% (of 40)
1	60	34	20	50
2	53	30	11	28
3	24	14	6	15
4	22	13	1	2
5	16	9	2	5
Total	175	100	40	100

It is interesting that 76% of the undergraduate respondents who had received job offers by Easter 1970 had received two or more offers, which would tend to indicate that these particular groups of students had been identified as potentially good by more than one firm. The post-graduates in the same position totalled 50%. This would appear to lend support to the argument that in graduate recruitment there exists the position of too many firms chasing too few graduates (in terms of identified potential).

Again, using the same groups of respondents, i.e. those who had been offered jobs and had either accepted a job or were still deciding, an examination was made of the nature of the job offers they had received. Results appear in Table 3.16.

Table 3.16

THE NATURE OF JOB OFFERS RECEIVED

Type of Job Offer	Undergraduates (175)		Post-graduates (40)	
	No.	% (of 175)	No.	% (of 40)
Direct appointment	60	34	31	77·5
Traineeship	115	66	9	22·5
Total	175	100	40	100

The contrast between the undergraduate and post-graduate respondents is quite marked, with a large proportion of undergraduate job offers being traineeships (66%), and a large proportion of the post-graduate job offers being direct appointments. This would appear to reflect the recognition by employing organisations of the fact that some undergraduate courses and more post-graduate courses provide, far better than other types of course, a background which can be used almost immediately in a direct appointment.

It does not necessarily follow that the job one eventually takes will be in a desired area, but the assumption could be that those who obtained job offers before others would; firstly, be the students identified by employers as having potential; and secondly, that they would have been likely to apply in the first instance to organisations within their desired occupational area, and therefore, if they were offered jobs in response to initial applications these would be likely to be in desired areas. These assumptions were examined in this study, and results are shown below in Table 3.17.

Table 3.17

THE JOB OFFERS RECEIVED IN DESIRED OCCUPATIONAL
AREA BY RESPONDENTS

Offers Received	Undergraduates (175)		Post-graduates (40)	
	No.	% (of 175)	No.	% (of 40)
Desired area	158	91	37	92·5
Not in desired area	17	9	3	7·5
Total	175	100	40	100

The results would appear to support further the thesis outlined above that there exists a proportion of students who are in demand from employers and who are able to choose more easily than others the jobs they would like in the economic sectors they would like. It could certainly indicate that recruitment activities of firms are concentrated on these particular students, and that it is only after the 'allocation' of these students that the remainder of the student population is distributed.

One part of job application procedures which is often criticised by students generally is the effectiveness (or lack of it) of the feedback procedure from organisations they have applied to. The students in this study were therefore asked about the number of firms to whom they had applied but from whom they had not heard after a reasonable period of time. Results are shown in Table 3.18.

Table 3.18

THE NUMBERS OF FIRMS APPLIED TO AND NO REPLIES RECEIVED

Firms Not Replying	Undergratuates (271)		Post-graduates (72)	
	No.	% (of 271)	No.	% (of 72)
0	175	65	42	59
1	52	19	14	18
2	25	9	6	9
3	17	6	1	1
4	2	1	4	6
5 and over	—	—	5	7
Total	271	100	72	100

It can be seen that of the 271 undergraduates who had applied for jobs, 65% had received replies from all the firms; of the seventy-two post-graduates, the comparable proportion was 59% This means that 35 per cent of all undergraduate respondents who had applied for jobs, and 41% of post-graduates, had not received a reply from firms they had applied to within what they considered to be a reasonable period of time. Even allowing for the fact that most of these had not received a reply from only one organisation, and for the fact that there will inevitably have been different interpretations of 'a reasonable period of time', it would seem to indicate an inadequacy in the recruitment procedures of organisations. In a sense, the students interpretation of a reasonable period of time will be based on what directly or indirectly he has been told by the organisation, which would tend to indicate that some recruiting organisations are either not responding to job applications effectively or are promising a feedback service which they are not equipped for. Whatever the reason it is apparent that the onus is on organisations to make absolutely sure that if people apply for jobs – and if they are really interested in recruiting – that information is fed back to applicants as early and as efficiently as possible. An applicant by the very act of applying has made a positive decision and a commitment, and expects his application to be dealt with in the same way.

It is also worth commenting that the feedback system of recruiting organisations to applicants has implications for theories of occupational choice. Most occupational choice theorists emphasise the importance of information for career decisions,[36] and given the significance of information and its sources for occupational choice, it is apparent that recruiting organisations at the higher education level have a major role to play in career choice decisions by virtue of their role as givers and receivers of information. One final point which relates to the process of information flow in general is that if firms are ineffective in their recruitment procedures, then one would imagine that this 'information' would spread through the student's own (and probably extremely effective!) information system with what could be serious consequences for the quality of applicants to these firms.

The process of personnel flow from the higher education system into the employment system assumes that the majority of final year students will apply for jobs during their last year. However, there are students who do not apply for jobs before their final examinations, and in this case fifty-nine of the undergraduate respondents and twenty-eight of the post-graduate respondents had not applied for jobs at the time of the study. The majority of these students (74% of the undergraduates and 50% of the post-graduates) were intended to wait for their examination results in the hope of staying on for post-graduate study to obtain an academic post. This is of some significance in career choice terms, for it illustrates that 18% of all the undergraduate respondents and 28% of the post-graduate respondents were prepared to ignore any other job area and hence to obtain something as a standby, and to stake everything on obtaining good examination results and hence continue in the academic sphere. It is likely that these students will also be the most able (in academic terms) in that it is fair to assume that they have a reasonable expectation of good results, which in turn might indicate that effectively the highest quality of graduate is not available to other sectors and thinks largely in terms of a specific goal – continuing in academic life.

EXPERIENCE OF, AND ATTITUDES TOWARDS, RECRUITING PROCEDURES

The experience of students of the recruiting procedures of organisations is, of course, reflected in the attitudes of these students towards such procedures (and towards the particular organisation). Such procedures represent the bridging point between the world of employment and the academic world, and also represent the first contact of the applicant with the organisation, and vice versa. The recruitment (and selection) situation, therefore, is a vital one for both parties, and in this study as a follow up to the job application experiences of students it was decided to examine the recruitment and selection experiences of students and their subsequent attitudes towards the effectiveness of the procedures. Questions were initially asked as to the quantity of information received from organisations, the quality of information in relation to its relevance to career decisions, and the general effectiveness of industrial and commercial recruiting procedures in indicating what is involved in an industrial or commercial career. It transpired that 236 of the undergraduate respondents had experienced such procedures and sixty-eight of the post-graduate respondents, and the results are shown below in Table 3.19.

The amount of information received on all aspects of employment within the organisation was judged as more adequate by undergraduates than by post-graduates, which perhaps reflects the fact that better provision is generally made for recruitment at undergraduate level in universities. Thus, whilst only 54% of the post-graduates thought that the quantity of information received was adequate or better, 71% of the undergraduates were satisfied with its adequacy.* It is of concern, however, that 29% of the undergraduates, and 46% of the post-graduates thought that the quantity of information received was barely adequate or worse. Clearly even if recruitment procedures of organisations at university level have become well established there would appear to be some perceived gaps in the information presented to students.

In terms of the quality of information received from organisations as related to the needs of students in deciding on a particular job, there appeared to be slightly more dissatisfaction. Thus, although 63% of the undergraduates and 43% of the post-graduates thought the quality of information quite relevant or better, there still remained sizeable proportions of both groupings (37%

* $X^2 = 5.45$, $p = 0.02$. The difference is significant.

Table 3.19

ATTITUDES TOWARDS INDUSTRIAL/COMMERCIAL
RECRUITING PROCEDURES

Quantity of Information Received on Employment in Organisation

	More than adequate	*Adequate*	*Barely adequate*	*Totally inadequate*
Undergraduates 236	9 (4%)	157 (67%)	66 (27%)	4 (2%)
Post-graduates 68	2 (3%)	35 (51%)	28 (40%)	4 (6%)

Quality of Information Received as Relevant to Career Decision

	Extremely relevant	*Quite relevant*	*Not very relevant*	*Irrelevant*
Undergraduates 236	13 (5%)	137 (58%)	81 (35%)	5 (2%)
Post-graduates 68	—	30 (43%)	35 (52%)	3 (5%)

Effectiveness of Procedures in Illustrating what a Career Would Involve

	Very effective	*Quite effective*	*Not very effective*	*Ineffective*
Undergraduates 236	15 (6%)	105 (44%)	94 (40%)	22 (10%)
Post-graduates 68	1 (1%)	25 (37%)	39 (57%)	3 (5%)

and 57% respectively) who thought the quality of information not very relevant or irrelevant. Again the post-graduates were more dissatisfied,* but the implication again was that the information giving process by firms to students is not all it might be.

This is certainly borne out by the responses to the general question on the effectiveness of industrial and commercial recruiting procedures in illustrating to students what such a career would involve, where 50% of the undergraduates and 62% of the post-graduates indicated that they thought such procedures either not very effective or ineffective. This is disturbing on two main counts: firstly, that given the acknowledged importance of amount and quality of information for career decisions the conclusions must be from the above results that this is so in many cases; and, secondly, that if organisations are concerned with recruiting at this level then despite the fact that they might believe their recruitment is effective it would appear that this is in many cases not so. The ineffective nature of the recruitment and career choice process revealed above whilst not necessarily surprising, does highlight a major problem area, with implications for the recruitment policies of organisations and the role of formal careers guidance.

* $X^2 = 7.2$, $p = 0.01$. The difference is significant.

One further set of open ended questions allowed the respondents the opportunity to enter into detail about particular features of the recruiting procedures of firms, namely the worst and best features of industrial and commercial recruiting procedures and the ways in which such procedures might be improved. Not all of the respondents chose to complete this section, but from the replies of those that did a definite pattern emerged, and it was possible to identify features showing both the best and worst aspects of recruiting procedures; the results are shown below in Tables 3.20 and 3.21.

Table 3.20

THE WORST FEATURES OF INDUSTRIAL/COMMERCIAL RECRUITING PROCEDURES

Features	Undergraduates (169)		Post-graduates (64)	
	No.	%	No.	%
Lack of information on actual jobs	33	19	17	27
Poor interviewing techniques	22	13	9	14
Mass processing of Appointments Board	29	17	8	13
Formal interviewers	20	12	3	5
Delays in communication	22	13	7	11
Others	43	26	20	30
Total	169	100	64	109

Of those features perceived by the respondents as poor or ineffective, it would appear that lack of information about the nature of the job or type of job the applicant would be recruited for, is a major deficiency. Plumbley[37] certainly regards this as an area in which recruiting organisations are deficient, and he strongly emphasises the need for such organisations to define the job the new graduate will do to a far greater extent than is done at present. The criticism by 19% of the undergraduate respondents and 27% of the post-graduates supports the earlier results which illustrates some dissatisfaction with the quality and quantity of information received by students. The other major features of recruiting procedure (embracing both the ignorance of interviewers and the poverty of interviewing techniques), the delays in communication, and the mass processing system manifested by the University Appointment Board. Taking criticisms of poor interviewing techniques and of interviewer ignorance together as reflecting dissatisfaction with the whole interviewing process, there are two relevant points here. Firstly, the actual system of recruitment at this level, due to the large numbers of students involved, allows for only a short period of time for each first interview (twenty minutes is an average period); this means that both students and interviewer are to a large extent under a significant time constraint, which inevitably affects the performance of both parties. To be fair to organisations, this system is often imposed on them by Appointments Boards but nonetheless a poor performance by an interviewer reflects not on the Appointments Board but on the interviewer's organisation. The second point relating to criticism of the interviewing process concerns the way in which interviewers are selected or instructed by recruiting organisations; the first interview at university, despite all its faults, is perceived as important by the student in that it gives him his first introduction to the organisation he has applied to. It is important to examine the expectations of the student with regard to the interview, for it is on this basis that he will judge initially (and perhaps finally) the organisation; he will expect to be told about the jobs available and relevant to him in some detail, he will expect to hear of career progression possibilities; he will expect answers, in other words, to all his questions, which could cover a wide range of issues. If his expectations are not met then it could be said that the interview has failed, and that the recruitment activities of the organisation have been ineffective. The important thing for organisations, however, is that they do have the means to meet the students' expectations, by careful recruitment and by careful selection and training of interviewers. Despite all the drawbacks of the first interview system, organisations can be effective in recruiting at this level, but it is clear that many are failing because of inadequate attention to the interviewing process.

The shortage of time for first interviews is a reflection of the Appointments Board system, and this 'mass processing' was a major criticism. It is true the Appointments Board do have considerable difficulties,[38] and that because of the large numbers being dealt with a standardised system is inevitable, but the impersonality of such a system is obviously dispiriting. It is to be hoped that the vocational guidance role of the Appointments Boards is not to be sacrificed even more so that it becomes merely a processing function. The final major criticism of delays in communicating with students after the first interviews is again a reflection of the lack of importance attached by some recruiting organisations to the relatively simple matter of distributing information. Again it is within the power of organisations to control this, and again it is worth stressing that failure to communicate effectively could mean the loss of good quality recruits in the first instance and could lead to an eventual shortage of good quality applicants.

The perceived best features of industrial and commercial recruiting procedures shown in Table 3.21, illustrate the areas on which recruiting organisations could further concentrate.

Table 3.21

THE PERCEIVED BEST FEATURES OF INDUSTRIAL/
COMMERCIAL RECRUITING PROCEDURES

Features	Undergraduates (158)		Post-graduates (51)	
	No.	%	No.	%
Informal interviewing procedures with opportunities for meeting similar people already working	42	28	19	37
Visits to place of work	25	16	4	8
Good interviewers and interviewing techniques	31	19	6	12
Expenses	13	8	2	4
Appointments Board System	16	10	2	4
Others	31	19	18	35
Total	158	100	51	100

Interestingly, two of the features which were mentioned as representing the worst features of recruitment procedures are mentioned as providing the best features – interviews and interviewing techniques, and the Appointment Board System. With regard to the former, this would seem to highlight the considerable disparity between firms which achieve a high standard of interviewing performance and those which perform badly in this respect; it could in fact be suggested that these latter firms could suffer even more, in terms of recruitment, as a result of this comparative element. The other feature which appears significantly as a best and worst feature, the Appointments Board System, reflects the nature of individual difference of students, some preferring the impersonality and mass processing (10% of undergraduate respondents and 4% of post-graduates) whilst others – a large proportion (17% and 13% respectively) – are unhappy with such a system. The fact, too, that 10% (undergraduates) and 4% (post-graduates) regard it as the best feature could be taken as a relatively poor response to the Appointments Board system.

I

The features rated highly as the best features of recruiting procedures, reflect a distinct pattern, which lends support to the argument that a personal approach in recruiting is regarded favourably by students. Thus the features rated highly are informal interviews which also provide the opportunity to meet people employed on similar jobs to the one the applicant would be performing if recruited, visits to the organisation, and good interviewers and interviewing techniques. The listing of 'expenses' as a factor can be interpreted as understandable or disgraceful depending on ones frame of reference! However, the most highly rated feature from both the undergraduate and post-graduate respondents (28% and 37% respectively) was the informal interviewing situation which combined discussions with people with similar backgrounds doing the kind of work the applicant would be performing if recruited. If this is looked at in conjunction with the high rating given to visits to the work organisation (15% and 8%) then the implication is quite clear that nearly half of the respondents regard the extended informal recruitment and selection procedure as highly desirable and beneficial. It illustrates a desire on the part of the students for a more detailed procedure which allows them full opportunity for seeing and hearing for themselves the nature of the prospective job and the prospective firm. This procedure is obviously more costly and more time consuming for the firm, but it is surely desirable from their standpoint, too, reflecting the fact that a longer and deeper examination of the applicant is preferable to the relatively short formal interview; certainly it is in line with the often stated standard objective of most interview situations namely that the interview is essentially a two-way process. It is argued here, that although some early selection may be necessary, the crucial importance of any selection decision – with its far-reaching implications for future organisational growth – alone should necessitate a rethinking of recruitment and selection policy on the lines indicated here.

Inadequacies in this area are certainly shown by the response to the final open ended recruitment question which allowed respondents to suggest what might be done to improve the recruitment system. The suggestions reflect most of the comments made in the preceding paragraphs with the three major suggestions being more and better information (40% of undergraduates and 30% of post-graduates), more opportunities to visit the organisations and discuss informally the job to be done (20% and 8%), and better interviewing techniques and interviewers (15% and 25%). The pattern emerging from this section is clear, and there can be no question as to the responsibility of recruiting organisations in this respect. If they are concerned with recruiting at this level, recruiting the better graduates, and keeping them, then the desires and expectations of students are important and attempts perhaps could be made to adapt recruitment and selection procedures to such expectations.

Employment of graduates is costly, and the justification for such adaption is essentially economic.

AN ANALYSIS OF CAREER PERCEPTIONS

The final part of this particular study involved an attempt to identify factors in a career thought by students to be important, and to show the relationship between these aspirational factors and the extent to which students expected such factors to be provided. Specifically, questions were asked about career perceptions in terms of both job and time progressions, and also factors within the work situation; firstly, as related to their personal importance to students; and secondly, as related to the perceived extent of their provision by industry and commerce.

To ascertain the career perceptions of students in respect of time and job progression, they were asked; firstly to indicate which of a number of statements about job progression corresponded most closely to their own feelings; and secondly, the length of time they anticipated staying in their first job. The results are shown in Tables 3.22 and 3.23.

Table 3.22

THE PERCEIVED JOB PROGRESSION OF RESPONDENTS

My Ideal Career	*Undergraduates* (300)		*Post-graduates* (100)	
	No.	%	No.	%
One specialist activity in one organisation	35	11	10	
Several different activities in one organisation	83	28	22	
One specialist activity with a number of organisations	46	16	14	
Several different activities with different organisations	38	13	25	
An opportunistic job progression	63	21	19	
Not considered	35	11	10	
Total	300	100	100	

The information produced by the job progression question becomes more meaningful when examined in conjunction with the information produced on perceptions of time progression in Table 3.23.

Table 3.23

THE PERCEIVED TIME PROGRESSION OF RESPONDENTS

Perceived Time in First Job	Undergraduates (300)		Post-graduates (100)	
	No.	%	No.	%
Up to 2 years	25	8	16	
2 years to 5 years	60	20	14	
Over 5 years	12	4	3	
Depends on opportunities	197	66	62	
Not considered	6	2	5	
Total	300	100	100	

What is termed a 'high level of graduate turnover' is often regarded as a serious manpower problem in industry and commerce, yet little information is available to indicate the nature of the criteria by which high turnover is assessed. The above two factors, perceived job and time progression are, it is suggested here, two of the most important factors on which such judgements should be based. One other major assumption on which a firm's graduate recruitment policies are based is that graduates will stay with the organisation – it is recognised, of course, that wastage occurs, but an organisation when selecting a graduate must inevitably be selecting him for the future and assume that they are recruiting him for a reasonably long period of time. It is suggested, therefore, that it is important for organisations to understand the way in which final year students perceive their careers in terms of jobs and time.

It is shown from the results of the job progression questions that 39% of the 300 undergraduate respondents see themselves as working with one organisation, 29% see themselves working in several organisations, and a further 21% will respond to opportunities. It is suggested, therefore, that graduate recruitment policies might reasonably account for the fact that something like 39% of the undergraduates are reasonably committed to a one organisation career, and that a further 21% could stay in one organisation if their career expectations are met – this will depend to some extent on the success of the organisation in integrating its personnel policies so as to provide adequate opportunities for these graduates. However, 29% of the undergraduates would initially only see their first employing organisation as a first step in a career which would take them to a number of organisations. The results from the 100 post-graduate respondents are even more biased towards working in several organisations (39% as compared with 32% wanting to work in one organisation, and 19% who will respond to available opportunities.

Regarding the alternatives of specialisation, or of performing a number of activities, it is interesting to note that the greatest proportion of the 300 undergraduates (28%) wished to perform several activities in one organisation; if this is added to the proportion (13%) wishing to undertake several activities in several organisations it can be seen that 41% of the undergraduates do not wish a specialist career, but would prefer mobility in terms of job functions. The comparative proportion from the 100 post-graduates is 47%. Further analysis reveals that 27% of the undergraduates and 24% of the post-graduates wish to specialise, which would indicate an apparent flexibility on the part of most job applicants at this level with regard to the actual jobs they wish to do. The criticism, therefore, sometimes levelled at graduates about their fixed employment ideas would not appear justified in the light of such results. This does not, of course, mean that graduates do not have fixed ideas about other features of employment. But it does appear that organisations have little to complain about in relation to the initial flexibility of graduates with regard to specific jobs, and that the onus is very much on them to provide jobs which satisfy the graduate's expectations about the nature of tasks (shown in Table 3.24).

Before discussing those features of the work situation which are related to the expectations of graduates, the other aspect of graduate career perception to be high-lighted is the question of the length of time students expect to spend in their first job. As can be seen from Table 3.23, the great majority of both undergraduate and post-graduate respondents anticipate responding to opportunities, which supports the point made earlier about the initial flexibility of students, and again helps emphasise the responsibility of organisations for structuring job and organisational conditions, and developing personnel policies related to the expectations of students. Of the students who were able to be specific about the period of time they wished to spend in their first job, 20% of the undergraduates, and 14% of the post-graduates, specified a period of between two and five years, and a further 8% and 16% respectively specified a period of less than two years. Interestingly these figures would appear to reflect the fact that much of the graduate turnover in organisations occurs after two to three years, which might indicate that a proportion of graduates are committed to a well formulated career plan, and that there may be little an organisation can do to prevent this; however, identification of such individuals at an early stage is a problem in itself, and in the absence of such information it could be suggested that organisational policies should be geared towards providing meaningful careers for all its graduate intake. In this context, too, it is important to mention that the interpretation of what constitutes a meaningful career will vary from graduate to graduate. Daws,[39] for example, has pointed out some of the psychological reasons for individuals desiring particular careers and has related this to the basis of an individual's self-esteem and the ways in which individuals measure their own worth, whilst Turner[40] in a sociological analysis of career mobility suggests that the degree of predictability of career structure is a key factor in differentiating between occupational choices. Certainly, both these interpretations are relevant to the analysis of career perceptions presented here.

One of the major aspects of any analysis of the career choice process is the relationship between aspirations and expectations. At the graduate level this relationship becomes especially important since progression through the higher education system will have increased the aspirations of students. In order to examine the exact nature of this relationship – referred to by Super as a 'compromise' process – a list of work situation features was drawn up and two different sets of ratings were obtained from students; the first set referred to the importance or each factor in a work situation to each student personally, and the second, to the perceived extent of the provision of each factor in industry and commerce. The factors were rated on a five point scale from 'very important' (5), to 'unimportant' (1), the scores for each factor added, and a ranking obtained for each set of ratings. Results are shown in Table 3.24 in rank order.

It is noticeable that of the five factors rated as most important in the personal work situation of undergraduate respondents – opportunity for initiative, intellectual challenge, career and promotion opportunities, competent management, and the opportunity to plan ones own work – all were rated lower in terms of the perceived extent of their provision by industry and commerce except for career and promotion opportunities which in the

Table 3.24

THE RELEVANCE OF WORK SITUATION FACTORS

Factors in the work situation	Importance in personal work situation		Degree of provision by industry and commerce	
	Under-graduate	Post-graduate	Under-graduate	Post-graduate
Career and promotion opportunities	3	2	1	1
High slaary prospects	9	6	2	2
Regular appraisal	13	16	5	3
Job security	10	13	10	4=
Intellectual challenge	2	1	4	4=
Opportunity for initiative	1	3	6	6
Authority for decision making	7	4	7	7
Social status	18	18	9	8
Varying job locations	17	19	8	9
Use of academic training	15	12	14	10=
Opportunity to plan one's work	5	5	11	10=
Holiday entitlement	12	14	13	12
Reputation of the organisation	19	15	12	13
Freedom from supervision	11	9=	17	14
Interesting environment	6	7	3	15
Competent management	4	9=	15	16
Opportunity for creativity	8	8	16	17
Access to information	16	17	18	18
Acceptable ethical environment	14	11	19	19

N.B. Correlation between undergraduate scores $= r = 0.426$; post-graduates $r = 0.440$.

case of both undergraduates and post-graduates was rated as an important feature in their personal work situation and as the factor best provided for by industry and commerce. This is an important finding in a number of ways: it initially reflects creditably on the industrial and commercial sector for projecting an image of the provision of career and promotion opportunity, yet also increases the pressure on such organisations to provide in practice such opportunities. If individuals aspire to career and promotion opportunities, and also expect, or have been led to expect, such opportunities to be available, then the consequences of their aspirations and expectations not being met can be far reaching. Young[41] has indicated what can happen when expectations of promotion are not met, and the above results appear to bear out his suggestion that a decline in expected promotion opportunities can lead to severe wastage with consequential recruitment and succession problems.

The five factors perceived as being best provided for by industry and commerce – career and promotion opportunities, high salary prospects, an interesting environment, intellectual challenge, and regular appraisal – relate quite closely to the factors perceived by undergraduates in the Cambridge University study as being provided for by industry. In that study, responsibility, high salary prospects, and promotion opportunities were rated as major factors. It is interesting to note the relatively low rating of high salary prospects in the personal work situation of students in the present study, as related to the perceived importance of this factor by industry and commerce, a point which would tend to support current approaches in the field of motivation[42] It is apparent that the more important factors in the personal work situation of the respondents relate to work which is challenging and interesting, in which there are opportunities for exercising initiative and creativity, and where scope in terms of both the nature of the job, and in terms of career and promotion prospects is considerable. In the case of nearly all these factors, the degree to which they are perceived as being provided by industry and commerce does not meet the aspirations of students; students do not expect their aspirations to be met in the industrial or commercial situation. Yet it is of some significance that the difference between aspirations and expectations do exist, and the implication would appear to be that the career choices of students are reasonably realistic in nature. Liversedge[43] highlighted the realistic appraisal of life chances by secondary school children, and the above results would tend to indicate that this process is continued at the higher education level.

The least important features in the personal work situation of the respondents – social status, location, organisational reputation, access to information – are in many ways just as important in their implications as the most important features, particularly when compared with the perceived extent of their provision by industry and commerce. All of these factors are seen as being much more important to the industrial and commercial sector than they are to the respondents. Again the Cambridge study[44] provides similar results, highlighting social status, a sense of public service, freedom from supervision, and high salary prospects as features thought relatively unimportant in career choice. The major implication here, of course, is for the recruitment policies of organisations and in particular, the assumptions on which such policies are based

As the author has pointed out in another context[45] it is disturbing to find statements made about the career and job attitudes of undergraduates which are assumed to be true; thus Rogers's and Williams's statement that 'our youth is endowed with a strong sense of social purpose and idealism'[46] is no more than an assumption, and would appear to be a wrong one in the light of the evidence. Organisations when recruiting should, it is argued, at the very least be aware of the needs, aspirations and expectations of the people recruited, and recruitment procedures and policies account for this accordingly. Of course, the implications go far deeper than this; it would be pointless to direct recruitment towards the aspirations and expectations of applicants if the organisation could not possibly hope to fulfill some of these. It is important for recruitment and selection to reflect all organisational policies and practices – if they do not then the results of recruitment on a false basis will obviously be detrimental; however, if organisations are too honest in this respect it may well be that they will fail to recruit the best personnel who could achieve change for them. A fine balance is perhaps needed in recruitment between reflecting the organisation in terms of its policies and practices and in taking account of the needs and expectations of applicants. Certainly what would appear to be absolutely necessary is an analysis of the basis of recruitment – the assumptions on which it is based and the degree which it reflects the organisation's policies in general – and an analysis of the aspirations and expectations of the segment of the labour market towards which recruitment is being directed. It could be argued that only with such a knowledge and understanding can effective recruitment and selection take place.

A SUMMARY

This chapter has been concerned with an analysis of the career choice process in higher education, in the light of the discussions of the theory of occupational choice presented in Chapter 2. It was suggested there that an integrated approach to occupational choice was required, in which both psychological, sociological and economic features of the process were highlighted. Given the nature of this framework, the examination of the career choice process at the higher education level attempted in this chapter was concerned with investigating the nature of and relationship between the career perceptions (aspirations and expectations) of final year students at Liverpool University, and the vocational experiences of the students (recruitment, guidance and actual work experience).

The research initially identified the major features in the home and school background of the 430 respondents (330 under-graduates and 100 post-graduates), and then examined four major areas: the nature and significance of the students work experience; their job application experiences and aspirations; their experience of and attitudes towards recruiting procedures; and finally career perceptions.

The work experience of students was shown to be largely of a temporary nature, with a significantly larger proportion of respondents obtaining work experience during their university career than before entering university. The influence of such experience in influencing students' career decisions – either positively or negatively – was important, with nearly half of the respondents thinking the experience of some or of considerable importance in affecting their career decisions.

The aspirations of students with respect to careers illustrated a surprisingly high proportion aspiring to an industrial or com-mercial career which when compared with the figures for those actually entering this sector reveals that at least 10% of the students will not have these aspirations realised. It seems reason-able to suppose that the experience of individuals with job applications has a good deal to do with this and these were in-vestigated. What was clearly shown was not necessarily that job application experiences in themselves were responsible for this situation, but that job applications reflected the lack of informa-tion, lack of guidance and generally haphazard nature of the application process, which in turn reflected back on the aspira-tions of students.

Job applications are, of course, part of the total recruitment process, and experience of an attitude towards recruiting pro-cedures represented the third major area of interest. The analysis of the quantity, quality and effectiveness of information from recruiting organisations revealed a number of inadequacies, a situation which becomes even more meaningful given the known importance of information for career decisions. In a more detailed investigation of the best and worst features of recruiting pro-cedures it was shown that the features rated badly were the information process, interviewing procedures and techniques, and the mass processing of the Appointments Board System. The best features referred to more detailed and more informal interviewing procedures with an emphasis on discussions with people already of a similar age and background and working, visits to the actual work situation, and more sophisticated interviewers. Significantly the identification of such features puts the onus on organisations to improve the nature of their recruitment, and it is suggested that improvements are well within the capabilities of all organisations. Certainly this remains one area where organisations can control the attitudes and behaviour of its members. The other feature which causes some concern – the Appointments Board System – highlights a possible inadequacy of vocational guidance at this level, and the perceived failure of the Appointments Board System could well be a reflection of the inadequate resources allocated to this area.

The final area with which the research was concerned – the career perceptions of students in terms of jobs and time progression and in terms of work situation features – provided information which could be of considerable use to organisations concerned with graduate recruitment. It was shown that though over a third of respondents saw themselves working on one organisation only, the majority of students were more flexible and were obviously going to respond more to available opportunities. Similarly, most of the respondents wished a flexible work career rather than a specialist career. The results for perceived time progression within a first organisation also indicated that a majority would respond to opportunities, although 28% were more definite in indicating they would leave in under five years. The analysis of the factors in a work situation thought important by students and factors in a work situation which were perceived as being thought important by industry and commerce revealed some significant differences between the two. Of the major factors thought important by the students all were perceived of as not being rated as highly by industry and commerce. Similarly, of the factors the students thought relatively unimportant, industry and commerce were perceived as rating them more highly. Such disparities highlight the need for organisations to question the assumptions on which not only their recruitment policy, but all their personnel policies are based. As Monk has suggested,[47] there is a need to provide a map of the way in which careers are perceived by possible employees, and an explanation of the dimensions are important in such perceptions.

It is argued that the results of the research discussed in this chapter support; firstly, the need for a comprehensive analysis of the occupational choice process which takes account of the perceptions and motivations of individuals as well as the nature and effect of the structural features in the process; and secondly, the hypothesis that organisations do have the means at their disposal to improve the quality and effectiveness of their personnel control – this chapter has been specifically concerned with the recruitment and guidance process and the deficiencies of current recruitment procedures have been illustrated. Given the importance of managing and utilising human resources effectively and of improving the articulation between the education and employment systems it is surely necessary for such deficiencies in recruitment and guidance to be at least reduced.

CHAPTER 4

The Graduate in Employment – An Analysis

It was argued in the first chapter that manpower planning could be examined in terms of two distinct yet related elements: forecasting and prediction, and influence or control. It is the second aspect with which this book has been primarily concerned, and the subsequent research findings have been related to the hypothesis put forward in Chapter 1, namely that organisations do have the means at their disposal to influence and control – to an extent that needs to be determined – the attitudes, behaviour, size, and nature of their populations. The extent and nature of such influence or control is related to an understanding of the complex behavioural processes existing in organisations, and an attempt has been made in this book to examine such processes in terms of occupational and career choice.

It is, at this stage, necessary to point out that there are important differences between the concept of 'career' and the concept of 'work', in behavioural terms, and Taylor has placed great importance on such differences in suggesting that in work an individual accepts a job, the primary purpose of which is to obtain the means to non work ends ... (whereas) the notion of career implies a greater number of future expectations which extend through the lifetime of the individual'.[1] The difficulty with Taylor's distinction, however, is its emphasis on the differences between jobs or work, and careers, which tends to detract from the important relationship between them; in this context, both Wilensky,[2] and Dubin,[3] have regarded careers as a succession of related jobs. Taylor's definition of work and discussion of its significance in terms of providing means to non work ends, is also indicative of a rather narrow interpretation of the meaning of work, representing what is essentially a 'social action' approach.[4] The assumption that people have prior orientations to work has been shown to be valid in certain situations,[5] but the research discussed here, which has been primarily concerned with the high talent manpower sector does cast doubts on the amount of influence exercised by prior orientations with regard to career, and to various aspects of the work situation. It is suggested, therefore, that a social action perspective tends to underemphasise the role which structural features, or organisational policies and practices, can play in shaping attitudes and influencing behaviour.

The relationship between the concepts of work and career is an extremely complex one, but it is important to understand the nature of this relationship before an attempt is made to discuss the career and job attitudes of graduates in industry and commerce. It is suggested that a useful framework can be developed by utilising three major dimensions of employment situations: the career dimension, the work situation dimension, and the job dimension. Taylor's definition of career with its emphasis on future expectations extending through the lifetime of individuals is useful, particularly when considered in relation to Wilensky's more specific interpretation of career as a number of related jobs. Yet both interpretations appear rigid, implying that careers are well thought out, and that career progression is relatively stable, whereas the research in the previous chapter illustrated that undergraduates at least, tend to emphasise the opportunistic aspects of career progression. It is argued here that career plans (like manpower plans) adapt to changing circumstances, and that such changes will be brought about largely through an individual's experience in the overall work situation, or in the more specific job situation. By job I am referring to the specific role one is performing (and this, of course, could be further broken down into actual tasks), and the work situation can be seen in terms of organisational conditions and policies (and could perhaps be extended to include the wider work situation including the policies of other organisations, and the work situation of peers or perhaps fellow professionals). There has been difficulty in the past over the rather loose definitions given to the concepts of job and work, as Child[6] and Parker[7] have indicated, but it is suggested that the above definitions do clarify the interrelationship between the different dimensions. Thus, it is possible to suggest that dissatisfaction with either elements of the work situation, or with the characteristics of a particular job, may lead to an individual deciding to change his job despite his original career interests – in this situation he could be seen as adapting his career perceptions to the new circumstances. Alternatively, a change in career plan might occur as a result of further experience in a job or work situation, or perhaps, as a result of external influences – here, for example, experience in a particular job might have opened up new areas of interest. Similarly, where an individual might have had a fairly fixed career plan before entering an organisation, which entailed spending two or three years in that organisation, his experience in the overall work situation (and hence his experience of the range of organisational personnel policies) might well lead to a change in his career plans.

An understanding of the relationship between career, job and work situation is also useful for a consideration of the behaviour and attitudes or organisation members in terms of the integrated theory of occupational choice developed earlier. It was suggested that such a theory should adequately account for the job choices and job changes of individuals at different stages in the life cycle, and for the factors involved in the process leading up to such decisions. Thus, in the present context – the career and job attitudes of graduates in industry and commerce – we are primarily concerned with the relationship between the graduates' experiences in his work role and in the overall work situation, and his wider career perceptions. This can then be seen in terms of the socialisation of the graduate into the organisation, his allocation to a particular work role as a result of his educational background, and his contact with the various structural features of organisational life. This sociological perspective would be particularly concerned with the role of personnel policies and practices, and other organisational features, in influencing career and job attitudes and behaviour. In addition, it is important to examine the relationship between the career and job aspirations of graduates, and their view of an 'ideal' career progression, work situation and work role, in the context of their actual organisational experiences. An examination of the interrelationship between sociological and psychological factors, together with an awareness of the role of economic considerations, is regarded as a prerequisite for any attempt to understand the working of the career choice processes after first choice of job, and it is also suggested that a differentiation between careers, jobs and the overall work situation, and the attitudes and behaviour related to such dimensions, is of equal importance for such an understanding.

It is suggested that the above theoretical perspective provides an important base for any discussion of the practical implications of graduate employment, and that it is important for organisational personnel policies to be based on an understanding of the dynamics of the process by which career and job attitudes are formed and crystallised. In this context, Hall[8] has indicated, that at the present time it is difficult to determine the relative importance of motivational and structural considerations in terms of their impact on mobility, and the nature of the problem has been succintly put by Child, who suggests that 'there is still every reason to investigate the limits which may be imposed upon social action by the economic, technological and organisational arrangements which happen to operate at any given time, and to assess the consequences for the quality of people's work experience'.[9] The problem as posed above by both Hall and Child is essentially a problem of understanding the relative importance of factors in given situations, and the necessary requirements for such an understanding are, it is suggested, firstly, an adequate definition of concepts (in this case career, job and work situation), and secondly a co-ordination of the major theoretical approaches to work attitudes and behaviour. Although, therefore, the approach adopted here is primarily an open systems approach, it is argued that, when examining the impact and influence of the needs of the organisational system (and the manifestations of such needs in the form of organisational conditions and policies) on the attitudes and behaviour of organisational members, it is also necessary to examine the role of external factors as influences on choice behaviour.

The above comments are not meant to imply that the relationship between organisational policies and practices on the one hand and, the attitudes and behaviour of organisational members on the other, is a deterministic one. On the contrary, organisational policies often, of necessity, adapt to the aspirations, expectations and behaviour of individuals, in the same way that individuals have to adapt to existing policies and practices. Sofer[10] has referred to this two-way relationship in suggesting that, though it is possible when formulating such policies and procedures to identify a pressure for objective rationality, in practice such rationality is modified by more realistic assessments of human situations.

The 'realistic assessment of human situation' referred to above by Sofer is dependent on information relating to the factors in the job and work situation which represent significant influences. An analysis of attitudes towards organisational conditions and policies, together with an analysis of actual behaviour (turnover, for example), can then be examined within a wider framework of career perceptions. An understanding of this three-way relationship is necessary for any realistic assessment of human situations and for the formulation of realistic personnel policies. A useful attempt to describe this complex relationship has been made by Thompson, Avery and Carlson,[11] who, although primarily concerned with the career concept, do recognise the importance of the other dimensions. In their discussion, they suggest that the three key elements in a career – the competence of the individual, his level of aspiration, and the perceived structure of opportunities – are modified by the orientation of the individual towards his career. The individual is then seen as adopting one of four career strategies: firstly, a 'heuristic' strategy orientated towards personal advancement; secondly, an 'occupational' strategy utilising a primarily occupational frame of reference; thirdly, an organisational strategy, concerned, largely with opportunities within the employing organisation; and fourthly, a stability strategy where considerations of other jobs are irrelevant for the individual. It should be pointed out that this attempt to categorise career strategies does not suggest that adoption of one strategy excludes the possibility of future change – on the contrary, such strategies are seen as changing over time. Perhaps the most important element in Thompson *et al.*'s analysis, is the way in which they see careers as very much affected by the source of the occupational role definition, which, in most cases, is the organisation. Such an analysis enables forms of career progression to be related to organisational policies and organisational work roles.

THE CAREER AND JOB ATTITUDES OF GRADUATES IN THE EMPLOYMENT SYSTEM

The relationship between career, work situation and job factors, examined above, provides an important base for the empirical research in this chapter, an examination of the attitudes of recent graduates towards particular features of their jobs and work situation. The other major base is the theoretical framework of the occupational process developed earlier in the thesis, which argued for an integration of psychological, sociological and economic approaches. In many ways a theoretical framework based on occupational choice decisions represents a useful tool for examining the attitudes and behaviour of individuals or groups in an organisational context – with particular relevance to staff categories where the notion of career is seen as a major feature of an individual's life style and primarily in terms of upward mobility. The relationship of such a framework with organisational behaviour models at this level can be close; Campbell *et al.*,[12] for example, have developed a model of manager behaviour which considers such behaviour as a function of individual characteristics, volitions,

K

social and organisational characteristics, and cost and utility considerations. Woodward[13] and Kynston Reeves[14] amongst others, have developed related models.

The two studies referred to in earlier chapters look at the occupational choice process at the first choice level, i.e. for the education system. This present study seeks to assess the applicability of the above occupational framework for the choice process *subsequent* to first choice of job. It is important to stress that the study investigates attitudes towards a wide variety of employment features, any or all of which might be relevant to the choice decisions of individuals. It is suggested that the background to such decisions is of major significance since this will reflect both the experience of individuals within the organisation, and hence their work related and career attitudes, and also the interrelationship of such experience-based attitudes with general career and job aspirations. The study was primarily concerned with attitudes towards appraisals, promotion, grading, salary, security, supervision and information sources, based on the organisational experiences of graduates, and with comparing such experiences with what graduates would regard as an ideal situation. An attempt was also made to examine overall personal satisfaction with the job situation in career terms.

The hypothesis to be examined, as postulated in the first chapter, was that organisations are able to influence and control the rate and direction of staff movement by the manipulation of personnel policies and practices. This influence or control would, it is suggested, initially be concentrated in the sphere of employee attitudes which in turn could be examined in relation to negative or positive mobility behaviour.[15]

The study took place in 1970, when questionnaires were circulated to eight organisations in the North of England. The final questionnaire had been developed after a pilot investigation in another organisation. The questionnaires were distributed by the organisations concerned to all graduates employed by them who had obtained their university degrees in the five years prior to 1970. The questionnaires were then returned directly to source by the respondents, to ensure confidentiality. A 40% sample of the respondents was then drawn up and interviews were subsequently conducted with individuals in this sample at their organisation. A total of 186 questionnaires were returned from the eight organisations, which represented a 60% response rate. The distribution of respondents was, of course, heavily weighted towards those organisations employing large numbers of graduates, and, in fact, three of the eight organisations provided between them, 150 respondents. This emphasis on three of the organisations will be used in the subsequent discussions of the research results for comparative purposes; the combined results for the total respondents will be used as the basis of the discussion, but it was thought useful to compare key parts of the overall results with the breakdown for individual organisations in order to examine any differences that occur, and this has been done for the more detailed questions. The distribution of respondents is shown in Table 4.1.

Table 4.1

THE DISTRIBUTION OF RESPONDENTS BY ORGANISATION

Organisation	Number of Respondents
Company A	70
Company B	50
Company C	30
Others (5)	36
Total	186

THE IMPORTANCE OF EDUCATIONAL BACKGROUND

The experience of individuals in various parts of the educational and employment systems, together with the information they receive about the organisations they wish to enter, and the job they wish to do, will considerably affect their aspirations and expectations. It can be postulated, that the aspirations and expectations of final year students will be subsequently modified when they have graduated and entered employment. This particular hypothesis was examined with particular reference to the utilisation of knowledge and skills and abilities, obtained at university, as well as in relation to the perceived importance of qualifications in the light of subsequent industrial experience.

The graduates were asked the extent to which they used; firstly, the factual knowledge gained in their degree course; and, secondly, the extent to which they used the skills and methods learnt on their degree course. Before discussion of these results, it is of interest to examine answers to the same questions given by the final year undergraduates and post-graduates in the study discussed in the previous chapter. These results are shown in Table 4.2.

These questions were only asked of students who had actually accepted a job, which limited the respondents to 112 undergraduates and 30 post-graduates. The evidence from the above results illustrates quite clearly that the major proportion of both

Table 4.2

THE PERCEPTIONS OF POTENTIAL KNOWLEDGE AND SKILLS
USAGE BY FINAL YEAR UNIVERSITY STUDENTS

Degree of Perceived Usage	Knowledge (%)		Skills and Abilities (%)	
	Under-graduates (112)	Post-graduates (30)	Under-graduates (112)	Post-graduates (30)
Extensively	30	46	37	45
Quite a lot	36	30	35	39
Little	24	16	23	12
Not at all	10	8	5	4
Total	100	100	100	100

undergraduates and post-graduates think that they will use the
knowledge, and skills and abilities gained during their university
course, at least quite a lot (66% and 76% respectively of undergraduates and post-graduates in terms of factual knowledge, and
72% and 84% respectively in terms of skills and abilities).

These results become particularly meaningful when compared
with the graduate results shown in Table 4.3.

Table 4.3

THE PERCEPTIONS OF ACTUAL KNOWLEDGE AND SKILL USE
BY GRADUATES IN THE EMPLOYMENT SYSTEM

Degree of Perceived Usage	Knowledge (%)				Skills and Abilities (%)			
	All (186)	A (70)	B (50)	C (30)	All (186)	A (70)	B (50)	C (30)
Extensively	5	4	8	3	11	10	18	13
Quite a lot	17	10	32	13	44	45	46	73
Little	57	60	54	60	34	30	34	10
Not at all	21	26	6	24	11	15	2	4
Total	100	100	100	100	100	100	100	100

The most important point relates to the disparity between expectations of utilising university training by final year students, and
the extent to which such training is thought intrinsically relevant
by graduates working in industry. Thus, 22% only of the total
percentage of graduate respondents thought that they used at
least quite a lot the factual knowledge gained on their degree course,
and 55% thought they used the skills and methods learnt on their
degree course. This disparity, or reduction, is further emphasised

when an examination is made of the proportion of final year students thinking that they would use their knowledge and skills and abilities *extensively*. In both cases the percentage for 'extensively' and 'quite a lot' were similar, indicating a very positive response, whereas in comparison a large proportion of the responses of the graduates were concentrated in the 'quite a lot' category, indicating a more negative response. The implications, therefore, are twofold: firstly that the expectations of final year students with regard to utilising their university training are unrealistic; and, secondly, that the usage by graduates of their university training is limited, raising interesting questions about the realism of the work perceptions of Final year students, the relationship between education and employment, and the personnel policies of organisations with respect to graduate utilisation. Certainly the point made by Rogers and Williams,[16] that in relation to the recruitment and training of graduates, there are grounds for challenging some of the university systems, appears relevant, and Pym,[17] in fact, goes further by suggesting that educational institutions through their processes of specialisation are contributing to one important aspect of misuse of manpower, namely the inability of many professionals to apply their skills to a wider range of industrial tasks. The above results make it possible to suggest that the relationship between education and employment – of which some of the difficulties have been discussed earlier – has particular inadequacies in this area.

In general, the results from the graduate respondents in each of the three major companies reflected the overall results, yet there were two interesting differences. In company B for example, there was a higher proportion of respondents then in companies A and C, who thought they used the knowledge gained from university training, and with respect to the utilisation of skills and abilities company C contained a very large proportion of graduates who thought they did utilise such skills and abilities. The reasons for this would appear to be that company B tended to recruit for specific jobs – mainly scientific – which likewise required specific knowledge, and, in fact, this company provided the largest number of Ph.D. employees. In the case of the utilisation of skills and abilities, company C was reported to make the maximum possible use of its investment in graduates.

The other area of interest in the analysis of the link between a graduate's university training and his subsequent organisational experience was in the relative importance of experience or qualifications (i.e. a formal manifestation of a graduate's university training) as factors affecting promotion chances. Graduates were asked what importance they thought the company attached to (*a*) qualifications and (*b*) experience in assessing whether they were to be promoted; results are shown in Table 4.4.

Table 4.4

THE PERCEIVED RELATIVE IMPORTANCE OF QUALIFICATIONS AND EXPERIENCE IN PROMOTION DECISIONS

Degree of Importance	Qualifications (%)				Experience (%)			
	All (186)	A (70)	B (50)	C (30)	All (186)	A (70)	B (50)	C (30)
Considerable importance	13	10	16	13	55	60	66	58
Some importance	52	65	52	60	38	36	30	36
Little importance	27	22	22	22	5	3	2	3
No importance	8	3	8	5	2	1	0	4
Total	100	100	100	100	100	100	100	100

The results indicate fairly conclusively that experience is regarded as a more important factor than qualifications in promotion, with 55% of all respondents thinking it of considerable importance, and a further 38% of some importance; this compares with 13% and 52% respectively in respect of qualifications. With regard to the individual companies, there was a similar response from graduates in all three companies relating to their perception of greater importance of experience as opposed to qualifications as a factor in promotion. However, it is interesting to note that though experience is seen as the more important factor, some 52% of all respondents regarded qualifications as being of some importance in promotion, which when looked at in terms of a further 13% who thought it of considerable importance, implies that organisational promotion policies are not based solely on performance related factors. This would seem to indicate a weakness in promotion policy (at least as perceived by the respondents); it certainly implies that organisations are seen as placing a good deal of faith on performance within the educational system, and in the degree classification system of universities. It could be suggested that performance in degree examinations, whilst useful for selection purposes, bears little relation to subsequent performance within the organisation, and further, that organisations accepting such differences maintain an extremely static view of the behavioural process, paying insufficient attention to the influence of different environments and different situations. It is interesting to note that it is usually graduates who are accused by industry of unrealistic expectations arising out of their degree qualifications, yet to judge by the above results it would appear to be industry which depends excessively on the nature and significance of qualifications. Certainly one suspects that the initial selection decisions of organisations in respect of fairly homogenous groups such as graduates, are the key ones and any differentiation made at this stage – even a small salary difference related to degree class for instance – could well prove a source of difference for some time to come. Highly structured organisations one might expect to conform to this view to a greater extent.

THE SIGNIFICANCE OF APPRAISAL SYSTEMS

The existence of appraisal systems in organisations reflects, as Sofer has indicated, the continued necessity for organisations to identify talent, and he has presented a most useful discussion of the problems involved in conducting appraisals, and the effects of appraisal procedures.[18] The main emphasis in the present study is on the latter issue, that is the reaction of employees (in this case graduates) to such procedures. It is the perceptions by the graduates of appraisal systems, and their effects, which is of particular importance, for no matter how administratively sound a scheme is, in the last resort it is how employees view the scheme which matters. In this respect, studies by Kay, Meyer and French,[19] and Thompson and Dalton,[20] among others, have illustrated the disparity between original intentions and desired results. As Thompson and Dalton have illustrated, what management perceived as fair and optimal, often leads to widespread discouragement, cynicism and alienation.[21]

All the organisations in the study had appraisal schemes in existence, and the first set of questions asked of graduates referred to various aspects of their perception of the operation of the scheme, covering the graduate's awareness of the existence of scheme, and the perceived regularity and nature of the scheme. Though formal appraisal schemes were in existence in all the organisations concerned, it is interesting to find that 8% of all respondents did not know of the existence of such a scheme; there were, in addition, some differences between the three major organisations in this respect, for though all the respondents in company B were fully aware of the existence of a scheme, 25% of company C and 26% of company A were not. There were also

differences between the three organisations in relation to graduates' responses to the question of whether the appraisal was
carried out regularly or sporadically, for whereas 88% of all
respondents thought appraisals were conducted on a regular
basis, the figures for companies A, B, and C were 75%, 98% and
90% respectively. It would appear that particularly in company C
there was a fair amount of confusion about the existence of an
appraisal scheme, and whether it was carried out regularly or
sporadically. Given the view that it is important for procedures,
if they exist, to be understood, it would appear to suggest some
inadequacy particularly in company C. A similar degree of confusion appeared to characterise the graduates in both company C
and company A in relation to the question of whether the appraisal
was discussed with them at any time, with only 80% in company C
and 84% in company A thinking it was discussed with them,
compared with 98% in company B and 91% overall. Though the
majority (and generally a large majority), were agreed on the
nature of the appraisal schemes in existence, it is still surprising
that a certain proportion of graduates were either unaware of the
scheme or confused about the nature of the scheme. The fact that
there was almost complete unanimity in the views of graduates in
company B and an approximately 3:1 disparity in company C
does tend to bear out the point that reactions to personnel policies
and practices will vary according to their effectiveness, and the
way in which the features of such policies and practices are communicated.

Regardless of the nature of the appraisal scheme, the success or
otherwise of such a scheme will depend on its effectiveness – which
implies that organisations must not only take action on the basis
of the appraisals but be seen to take action. Even given such a
situation it is open to question whether a positive link between
appraisals and subsequent organisational action, assists in rein-
forcing or modifying behaviour, but it is suggested here that there
is more likelihood of appraisals leading to action on the part of the
individual being appraised if he can perceive that such an appraisal
does have a differential effect on various aspects of his job, work
situation or career. This hypotheses was examined in the present
study, and questions were asked about the degree of importance of
appraisals in affecting three distinct features – job performance,
salary and promotion prospects. Results are shown in Table 4·5.
What these results show is that generally, appraisal is seen as
having most influence on promotion prospects, and least influence
on job performance. This might on the surface imply that the

Table 4.5

THE PERCEIVED IMPORTANCE OF APPRAISAL IN AFFECTING
JOB AND CAREER FEATURES

Degree of Importance	Job Performance (%)				Salary (%)				Promotion Prospects (%)			
	All	A	B	C	All	A	B	C	All	A	B	C
Considerable importance	35	30	52	40	41	35	40	400	55	42	68	40
Some importance	42	34	30	50	37	32	42	52	32	37	24	35
Little importance	15	26	10	8	16	25	14	8	10	14	4	15
No importance	8	10	0	2	6	8	0	2	3	7	0	10
Total	100	100	100	100	100	100	100	100	100	100	100	100

evidence quoted above that appraisals do not change job behaviour is supported; yet it is important to note that even though appraisals were seen as affecting job performance less than salary or promotion prospects, 77% of the respondents thought that it was at least of some importance in affecting their job performance. Thus, the perceived effect of appraisals was that they were important for job performance, salary, and promotion prospects. A clear relationship is seen between the appraisal and subsequent job behaviour, and although this does not necessarily mean that actual job behaviour will change as a result of appraisals, the important thing in this context is that it is seen as changing by the respondents. The relationship between appraisals and salary, which is perceived as being even more important than the job performance/appraisal relationship reflects the practice in the organisations studied of salary increases being given for performance during the year, and that this official assessment of performance is seen as resulting from the appraisal interview. Again this relationship is not necessarily based on a perfect or even effective system; in many of the interviews graduates expressed opinions that appraisals really only looked at recent performance, or personality. However, salary rises are seen as related to the formal appraisal, regardless of the weaknesses of the system. The final and apparently most important relationship, that between appraisal and promotion prospects, reflects the significance of career factors for graduates. The fact that the graduates regarded appraisals as affecting promotion prospects could be interpreted in two ways; either the graduates actually had a great deal of confidence in the promotion policies of their organisations, or else they hoped that promotion policies were based on appraisals. The fact that there was a distinct difference between the views of graduates in company B (who reported a significant relationship between appraisal and promotion) and in companies A and C (who were less certain) would indicate that the relationship was actually perceived as being important. The results, finally, do indicate that there are differences between the responses of graduates in different organisations. This is particularly so in the case of company C, whose appraisal procedure appeared to be rather ill-defined. Also with company C, the order of importance of factors seen to be affected by appraisals was completely opposite to the results from the other organisations, and for the overall respondents. Thus, the overall pattern indicated that appraisals were seen to influence, in order of importance, promotion prospects, salary and job performance; at company C the order of importance was reversed, and appraisals were seen to have more impact on job performance than promotion or salary.

Three further general points, in addition to the more specific factors discussed above, can be made at this stage. Firstly, the response to the appraisal questions indicates that an appraisal system can be looked at as a personnel institution and as such can affect the attitudes, and possibly the behaviour, of the individuals being appraised. The positive nature of the responses with regard to the importance of appraisals in affecting different employment factors, the fact that there were differences in perceived relative importance of appraisals on such factors between organisations, and the obvious differences in the perceived nature of such schemes, all help to suggest that different systems of appraisal (in all aspects) will produce different attitudinal and behavioural reactions. The second point to be made relates to the framework for analysis of employment features suggested earlier in the chapter, namely that any discussion of attitudes and behaviour in work organisations should be considered in terms of the inter-relationship of job factors, work situation factors and career factors. Thus, in the present context it can be observed that appraisals are perceived as being at least of some importance for job performance (a job related factor), salary (also relevant to job situation but of more relevance to the wider work situation), and promotion prospects (largely a career factor). It is necessary to consider the implications of appraisals, therefore, in terms of these distinct yet interrelated factors, and the indications are that there exists an important relationship between appraisals and job, work situation and career attitudes and behaviour. The final point relates to the significance for organisations in developing appraisal systems which are soundly based. As Vetter,[22] has pointed out, there is a need for qualitative information on the current performance of managers and on their future potential, in planning for the staffing of the future management structure, and it is important that before such a procedure is initiated or modified, information is obtained about the problems and likely effects of different types of appraisal.

FACTORS AFFECTING PROMOTION OPPORTUNITIES

The evident importance of the relationship between appraisals and promotion highlights the significance of promotion from both an organisational and individual standpoint. This study is primarily concerned with the perceived relative importance of a number of factors in promotional decisions, but it is necessary to clarify the various implications of promotion as an organisational policy.

A useful definition of promotion is presented by Pigors and Myers who refer to it as 'the advancement of an employee to a better job',[23] – in this sense the characteristics of a 'better' job are seen in terms of exercising greater skill or responsibility, and of higher pay. There are, of course, various types of promotion decisions which involve policy choices, and perhaps the most significant of all such choices in promotion is the relative weighting to be given to seniority and ability\. In this sense, though, as Hall[24] has pointed out, promotion is most meaningful in terms of mobility within the executive/professional hierarchy of organisations. From an organisational standpoint, promotional policies affect both present and future manpower situations, and Vetter[25] has suggested that given the aim of promotion programmes to provide a pattern of the mobility of management manpower, then such programmes should relate to broad organisational manpower goals and to individual manager career patterns. In similar vein, McLelland[26] has discussed the problem as one of matching organisational necessities with individual needs. The actual working of the promotion system within an organisation will, as Sofer[27] has indicated, involve two sets of norms; firstly, the existence of stable sets of expectations as to how a person must act to secure promotion; and secondly how those responsible for promotion should bestow it. It is, therefore, possible to look at a promotion system as a structural feature of organisations involving procedures, and norms, and in the light of this to examine individuals' expectations of, and reactions to, the system. In this context, Caplow[28] has discussed the social and personal effects of promotion procedures and decisions, and the subsequent discussion will deal largely with similar issues. The final point of relevance to the individual effects of promotional policies, refers to the relationship between opportunities for promotion and advancement, and motivational factors, particularly as manifested by measures of job satisfaction and need satisfaction. Herzberg,[29] for example, has argued that opportunities for advancement and associated factors relate positively to motivation and contribute to job satisfaction, Dill, Hilton and Reitman,[30] have indicated that a strong desire for upward mobility is characteristic of managers and executives, whilst Hill[31] in a study of the job attitudes of Shell graduates highlighted the importance of 'intrinsic' job features of which career and promotion opportunities was a major one.

It is argued here that it is the perceived nature of promotion policies which is important, and it is further suggested that such perceptions become relevant and meaningful for attitudes and behaviour when compared with the individual's view of what an ideal system should be. If there are disparities between the actual system and the desired system then the criteria by which individuals would wish to be evaluated would not appear to be adopted in practice. If promotion is looked at in terms of status assignment, then there would be a lack of congruence between actual status assignment and desired status assignment.

In line with this argument, the graduates in the study were asked to rate each of a number of factors in terms of their perceived importance in determining promotion within the organisation. In addition, they were also asked to rate the same factors in terms of the importance they would like to see assigned to them in an ideal system. Finally, they were asked about their overall satisfaction with promotional opportunities in their organisation. It is, perhaps, most useful to discuss the overall satisfaction with promotional opportunities first of all, in order to establish a base for discussion of the relationship between the actual promotion system and an ideal promotion system, and thus results relating to satisfaction with promotion are presented in Table 4.6.

It is interesting that of all the respondents almost one third were dissatisfied in some way with promotional opportunities, and that only 9% were completely satisfied. This becomes especially meaningful when compared with the career perceptions of final year students discussed in the preceding chapter. There the final year

Table 4.6

THE REPORTED SATISFACTION WITH PROMOTION
OPPORTUNITIES

Degree of Satisfaction	All (186) %	A (70) %	B (50) %	C (30) %
Completely satisfied	9	8	10	10
Fairly satisfied	58	43	68	52
Some dissatisfaction	29	43	8	28
Very dissatisfied	4	6	4	10
Total	100	100	100	100

students rated career and promotional prospects very highly in terms of personal importance, and also were of the opinion that this feature was provided for above all others by industry and commerce. Comparing those results with the above results, it is apparent that expectations of graduates are to some extent not being met, and that there is a disparity between the expectations and aspirations of graduates about to enter industry and commerce with reference to promotion prospects, and the actual degree of provision (or perceived degree of provision) of promotional opportunities. This could be an indictment of the manpower planning situation in a number of organisations. It was argued in the first chapter that organisations could influence the attitudes and behaviour of staff in a positive way by developing realistically based personnel policies, and it was further suggested that personnel policies should be closely co-ordinated. In this instance, it is apparent that the recruitment policies of some of the organisations in this study are not related to promotion policies. Evidence which illustrates that organisations can be effective in this area is readily available in these results, for company B appears to be significantly more successful than the other organisations in the provision of promotion opportunities. In fact, only 12% of the respondents in company B have experienced any dissatisfaction in this respect, compared with 38% in company C, 49% in company A, and 31% overall. Given the fact that graduate turnover, like that of other occupational groups, tends to rise to a peak early in service, and given the accepted relationship between turnover and lack of 'job satisfaction' and the importance of advancement prospects for 'job satisfaction', the results would appear to cast some light on the wastage of graduates in their early years of employment, an issue which some organisations regard as a major problem.

There are obviously certain perceived deficiencies in the provision of promotional opportunities, but given the actual promotion situation in existence in the particular organisations, it is important to understand the attitudes of graduates to the working of such a system, and, as suggested above, necessary to compare attitudes to the existing system with attitudes to what would be regarded as a desirable system. Graduates were, therefore, asked to rate each of nine given factors in terms of their perceived actual importance in determining promotion in their organisation; secondly, to rate each factor in terms of the importance they would ideally like each factor to be given in determining promotion. Scores were then calculated for each factor, with four points given for the most positive response and one point for the least positive, and the factors arranged in order of relative importance. Results are shown in Table 4.7.

Table 4.7

THE PERCEIVED RELATIVE IMPORTANCE OF FACTORS
AFFECTING PROMOTION

Factor	Ideal System				Company System			
	All	A	B	C	All	A	B	C
Ability in performing job	1	1	1	1	1	1	1	1
Ability in managing subordinates	2	2	2	3	5	7=	3	4
Hard work	3	3	3	2	2	2	4=	3
Experience in own field	4	4	4	4	4	3	4=	5
Training in own field	5	5	5	5	8	7=	9	6
Formal education	6	6	7	6	7	6	7	7
Good relations with superiors	7	7	6	7	6	5	4=	8
Length of service	8	8	8	8	9	9	8	9
Being in right place at right time	9	9	9	9	3	4	2	2

In terms of the combined totals, there appears to be a fair correlation ($r = 0.517$) between the importance of factors in the actual company systems and their desired importance in an ideal system. Similar correlations were obtained for company A ($r = 0.596$), B ($r = 0.441$), and C ($r = 0.466$), though it is apparent that the correlation for company A is more positive than both other organisations, and is also greater than the overall average. However, though the overall impression is of a fair relationship between actual and desired promotion systems, there are some important disparities which centre on the three factors, ability in managing subordinates, training in ones own field, and being in the right place at the right time. The first two factors are both rated more highly in an ideal system than in the company system, whilst the third factor represents the lowest rating in an ideal system, yet is given a fairly high rating in all company systems.

The high rating given by graduates to the question of ability in managing subordinates, as compared with the importance organisations are perceived as giving to such ability, has much to do with the fact that in managerial roles performed early in service, the managing of subordinates is a relatively new aspect of the individual's experience, is probably the most important feature of the managerial role, and also in many cases, appears to present the most difficulties. It is, of course, highly unlikely that graduates, before entering an organisation, will have had experience in this area and they are therefore dependent on either being able to cope with the management task, or on organisational training. It is interesting that a disparity of this nature should be thought to exist, for it could indicate that organisational personnel policies are based on an unrealistic assessment of the relative importance of factors making up organisational work roles,[32] and could also indicate a lack of congruence between organisational goals and values. In this context, graduates obviously regard the managing of subordinates as an essential and central part of their job, and would like to be regarded as such to a greater degree by those who review their performance and decide promotion; organisations are not seen to give sufficient attention to ability to manage, despite the fact that most young graduates are recruited for managerial functions.

Training in the graduates own field, is the second factor which was thought by the respondents to be not sufficiently recognised by organisations in assessing promotion, represents a slightly different problem from the one above. In this case, when examining the reasons why graduates should see such a disparity, it is important to understand the aims of organisations when recruiting graduates. It is probable that most graduates are recruited for managerial roles, and much of organisational training is essentially training for management, which means that an important part of assessment is in terms of potential for higher managerial positions. Whilst training in the graduate's own field, therefore, is most useful in assessing promotion potential in the early stages of a career where experience is limited and information on performance is similarly limited, when such information does become available, it is obviously important that such information is used to a considerable degree, with a consequent lessening of the importance given to training in the graduate's field. This explanation does provide a useful framework for examining the disparity; and it could be suggested that graduates who have invested a considerable amount of time in obtaining a specialist training will inevitably be reluctant to minimise the importance of the one thing that gives them a sense of security. The disparity, therefore, can be seen as arising out of the difference between the need felt for organisations to judge on ability and performance, and the desire of graduates to be judged on the very factor which has obtained them employment in the first place. Thus graduates are recruited on the basis of their qualifications and specialist training, but appear to be promoted on other factors, which is obviously something they find difficult to adjust to, although given the difference in the extent of the disparity between the different organisations it could be said that some organisations are more effective in helping graduates to adjust than are others.

The most significant feature of all lies in the disparity between the perceived importance of 'being in the right place at the right time' in an ideal system, and the perceived importance of the part this factor plays in the actual systems of promotion in existence. This can be seen as a measure of the inadequacies of organisational promotion policies, for it represents the role that the chance or luck element plays, or is seen to play, in promotion. Not surprisingly, graduates feel that this factor should play the least important role in promotion. One assumes that personnel policies of all kinds aim at eliminating, or at least greatly reducing the element of chance, in the sense that this will enable organisations to influence or control their organisational members more effectively, and so achieve a pattern of stability so necessary for the achievement of established goals. The expectations of individuals are all important in this context, and in relation to promotion it could be argued that the organisational system involves stable sets of expectations as to how a person must act in order to secure promotion, and how those responsible for promotion should bestow it. However, it might be useful to extend this to say that such expectations will come about not just as a result of an *awareness* of, or perception of, how a system actually works, but as a result also of how a system actually does work.

The chance element in promotion, be it perceived or actual, can have dysfunctional effects for the organisation, and certainly can be seen to represent an unjust or unfair element in organisational policy. In connection with this, the slight disparity as between an ideal and actual promotion system of the rating of the factor 'good relations with superiors' could be looked upon in similar terms. The connotation usually given to this factor is in terms of nepotism, or at least the over-importance of cultivated relationships at the expense of the fairer and juster features which have more to do with performance. This is not to say, of course, that good relations with one's superiors is not as much a question of ability as ability in managing subordinates, but the interviews did tend to indicate that such relationships could be, and often were, seen as being deliberately cultivated, often in terms of an attempt to obtain what was regarded as an unfair advantage.

ATTITUDES TOWARDS FEATURES OF GRADING SYSTEMS

It is not uncommon for many large organisations to have a system of grading similar to the traditional Civil Service model. In most cases, the grading system can be looked on as a manifestation of the formal hierarchical organisation, and can be looked on as a key element in organisation structure. Grading systems, too, provide an important base for other organisational personnel policies and procedures – for the delineation of status,[33] for the distribution of salaries,[34] and in relation to appraisal and promotion systems. A grading system, therefore, is a structural feature of an organisation, and can be looked at in terms of the way it affects the attitudes and behaviour of individuals, directly and indirectly, and the implications it has for other personnel policies and procedures.

In this context, the major interest was in the relative importance of factors seen by graduates to determine their position within the company, and also the reaction to grading systems as personnel institutions, in terms of the degree to which trading information was conveyed to, and between, individuals. The starting point, however, was to ascertain the proportions of respondents who were aware of the existence of a grading system in their organisations. Of the total of 186 respondents, 94% replied that there was a formal grading system in their particular organisation; there were variations according to organisational membership with positive replies from 88% of company A, 100% of company B, and 96% from company C. The results are, of course, extremely positive, but certainly one would expect this to be so, and perhaps the surprising and even disturbing feature is that anyone should not know of the existence of a grading system when one exists (as was the case in all these organisations).

The determination of ones organisational position or grade is likely to be based on a number of factors, the importance of which will differ from organisation to organisation. What was considered of particular interest here, was the degree of importance which the graduates thought was given to each of a number of such factors in determining their grade or position. Results (in rank order of importance) are shown in Table 4.8.

Table 4.8

THE PERCEIVED IMPORTANCE OF FACTORS DETERMINING
ORGANISATIONAL GRADE

Factors	*Order of Importance*			
	All	*A*	*B*	*C*
Job performance	1	1	1	1
Difficulty of job	3	3	3 =	2
Length of service	4	6	3 =	6
Age	6	5	2	5
General education	2	2	5	3
Specialist training	5	4	6	4

The stated importance of job performance as the major factor affecting grade, together with the similar importance of job difficulty, reflects the fact that grading is, in some ways, closely connected to the promotion system; and it will be remembered that job related factors were perceived as the most important factors affecting promotion. However, in this situation, grading is seen to be affected by general educational factors to a far greater extent than is promotion. The reason for this situation became apparent during the interview programme, for it transpired that though almost all the graduates were assigned a grade, they had not all had experience of promotion, mainly because of their short service. Educational factors were seen, therefore, as playing an important role in affecting grading, almost as an extension of the fact that educational qualifications were the most important criterion for initial recruitment. The fact that age was ranked overall as the least important fact, also tends to support this explanation.

There appeared to be a fairly positive correlation between the order of importance of factors in companies A and C ($r = 0.805$ and $r = 0.772$ respectively) and the overall ranking. Yet the correlation was small between company B ($r = 0.258$) and the overall situation. The major reason for this was the high ranking in company B of the age and length of service factors, which illustrates quite clearly the philosophy of this particular organisation (it is significant, too, that the correlation for company C as between ideal and actual promotion systems was the lowest of the three organisations, $r = 0.441$). Apparently non performance related factors are more significant for grade and advancement in company B than in the other two companies.

The other interesting feature about grading systems emerged in response to two questions relating to the secrecy surrounding the grades of respondents. The questions specifically asked how much secrecy was maintained firstly by the *company* about the grades of individuals, and secondly, how much secrecy was maintained by *individuals* about their own grades. Results are shown in Table 4.9.

Table 4.9

THE PERCEIVED EXTENT OF GRADE SECRECY

| *Degree of Secrecy* | *Extent of Company Secrecy* (%) | | | |
	All (186)	*A (70)*	*B (50)*	*C (30)*
Absolute secrecy	31	23	42	23
Some secrecy	39	35	42	33
Little secrecy	16	22	12	23
No secrecy	14	20	4	21
	Extent of Individual Secrecy (%)			
Absolute secrecy	6	5	0	0
Some secrecy	50	35	60	50
Little secrecy	32	38	36	30
No secrecy	12	22	4	20

Looking, firstly, at the secrecy thought by the respondents to be maintained by organisations over grading information, it is apparent that a good deal of information about grades is withheld by organisations. Thus, some 60% of all respondents thought that there was at least some secrecy maintained by their firm about their grade, with similar proportions for companies A and C, and a large proportion, 84% from company B. What such results essentially illustrate is a situation where although a grading system exists and is used for a number of personnel purposes, organisations practice, formally or informally, a policy of keeping such grade information from employees.

Significantly, too, a large proportion of respondents overall

(56%), thought that there was at least some secrecy maintained by individuals about their grades; although much of this response was confined to the category 'some secrecy' rather than 'absolute secrecy'. Thus, though there was thought to be less secrecy maintained about grades by individuals then by organisations, the general feeling was that individuals did tend to be secretive about their grades. Again, this was particularly so in company B which could be taken to indicate a tendency in this organisation towards the over-formalising of relationships, and a greater emphasis on structure than in the other organisations. It is certainly relevant at this stage to make the point that grades are representative of the status structure of organisations, and in this context, Caplow[35] has made the observation that the organisational status order is an array of positions, and differs from the systems of social ranking in being unequivocal, transitive and inclusive. The grades of individuals, therefore, have a distinct bearing on their status, and given the importance of status considerations for organisational members, it is interesting that organisations regard information on grades as being confidential, and accordingly withhold such information from employees. Grades can be looked at in career terms, and so regarded as elements of structure against which to judge progress, and in this respect the question of an individual's organisational identity, and his relative success or failure, becomes increasingly relevant.

THE IMPORTANCE OF SALARY

Grading systems often provide the basis for salary structures,[36] and the basis of such salary structures is often given much prominence in any discussion of behaviour in organisations. Salary can also be looked upon as an indicator of progress, and not solely progress within the organisation but with one's peers in other organisations. In addition, the motivational aspects of financial compensation cannot be ignored, although there is considerable controversy about the motivational significance of salary increases.[37] (It was interesting to find in the study of student career perceptions discussed in the previous chapter, that though salary prospects were thought by students to be of considerable importance to organisations, they themselves rated this factor as much less important.)

It is suggested here, that the major concern of employees with regard to salary are; firstly, the overall degree of satisfaction with the salary amount (in relation to their own organisation and also to their peers in other organisations); and secondly, the basis on which salary is determined, particularly in comparison with what is regarded as the basis on which salary should be determined – the difference, therefore, between the actual salary system and the ideal salary system. Regarding the satisfaction with salary, two sets of questions were asked; firstly the satisfaction of graduates with the salaries they received; and, secondly, the extent to which the salaries of respondents compared with those of other people in other companies doing similar jobs to them. Of the total respondents, 68% reported that they were at least fairly satisfied with their salaries, with results from the three major organisations varying from only 53% in company C, to 62% in company A, and 80% in company B feeling fairly satisfied or better with their salary situation. There is, therefore, a significant difference ($X^2 = 18.5$ $p = >0.001$) between degrees of satisfaction with salary in the three major organisations, which illustrates clearly the way in which organisations differ in terms of their personnel policy and practice – in this case salary policy; and further, the fact that if some organisations are more effective in this area than others that much of this is due to the satisfactory fulfilment of the needs and expectations of individuals.

With regard to the comparative element in salaries, 78% of the total respondents were of the opinion that their salaries compared at least reasonably well, or better, with the salaries of other people in other companies doing similar jobs. Again there was some disparity between the three major organisations, with 70% in company A, 94% in company B, and 83% in company C regarding their salaries as comparing reasonably well or very well with salaries paid to others in similar jobs elsewhere. This relatively large proportion expressing satisfaction, reflects the nature of the three main organisations in the study, all of whom can be looked upon as major employers, and it could be suggested that any comparison from within such organisations would tend to take this factor very much into account. However, there is a significant difference again ($X^2 = 18.9$, $p = >0.001$) between the proportions from each organisation thinking that their salaries compared favourably, which supports the earlier point about overall satisfaction with salary, namely that organisations through their salary policy do influence the attitudes of their members. It is similarly significant, that company B had the highest proportion of graduates thinking that their salaries compared favourably with those of other people doing similar jobs in other organisations, indicating that though some 20% were not satisfied with their salaries internally, the majority even of these recognised that they would be unlikely to do better elsewhere. The important thing about such results is that as well as highlighting the way in which organisations can control to differing extents the attitudes of members through specific personnel policies, they also indicate the importance for job and career attitudes of external or comparative factors.

The other important aspect of financial compensation and its distribution amongst organisational members, concerned the criteria used (or seen to be used) for salary determination, particularly in relation to the criteria which employees think should be used. A considerable disparity between the actual system and a perceived ideal system could be taken to indicate a source (or potential source) of dissatisfaction, which either by itself, or when combined with other such factors could lead to unfavourable organisational attitudes, and eventually to labour turnover. To examine the nature of this relationship between actual and ideal salary systems, and to ascertain the basis of salary determination, two separate questions were asked: the first relating to the importance of each of a number of listed factors in determining the salary of the graduate respondents in their organisation; and the second referring to the importance the graduate respondents thought should be given to each factor in determining their salary. As in the earlier and similar questions on the basis of promotion, scores were calculated for each factor, with four points for the most positive response, and one point for the least positive, and the factors then arranged in order of relative importance. Results are shown below in Table 4.10.

Table 4.10

THE PERCEIVED RELATIVE IMPORTANCE OF FACTORS
AFFECTING SALARY

Factor	Ideal System				Company System			
	All	A	B	C	All	A	B	C
Performance in the job	1	1	1	2	1	1	1	1
Number of subordinates	7	7	6	5	9	9	2	7
Difficulty of job	2	2	2	4	6	7	3	5
General education	6	6	7	6	2	2	8	6
Administrative ability	3	3	3	3	8	8	4	4
Specialist training	5	5	5	9	6	4	5	8
Length of service	9	9	9	8	4	5	2	9
Hard work	4	4	4	1	5	6	6	3
Relations with superiors	8	8	8	7	3	3	7	2

There appears to be no real correlation ($r = 0.06$) between the overall perceptions of the relative importance of factors in an ideal system and the actual importance of factors in the factual determination of salary. Yet, when a breakdown is attempted of the responses in each of the three major companies in the study, some interesting differences are revealed; the correlations for each of the companies being company A $r = 0.06$, company B $r = 0.39$, and company C $r = 0.69$. The fairly positive correlation obtained for company C particularly (and company B rather less so), indicates that here the expectations of graduates with regard to salary determination are to a reasonable extent being met. This compares most favourably with the situation in company A (and indeed with the other organisations included in the study) where there is little if any relationship between the importance graduates would like given to the listed factors, and the importance which they are actually given by the company in determining salary. One of the most interesting features about these particular results is the fact that in company C where there is the highest correlation between the company system and the graduate's ideal system, the satisfaction with the amount of salary received is the lowest of all the organisations in the study. One can, therefore, conclude that graduates in company C are less satisfied than most graduates in other companies with the amount of salary they receive, yet are more satisfied than graduates elsewhere with the way in which their salary is determined.

It is interesting to note that the factors rated most highly in the ideal system are all related to the job being performed. This would certainly tend to indicate the desire of graduates to be assessed and paid in relation to their job performance. The major discrepancies in the overall rankings for ideal and actual salary systems lay in the placing of the factors, job difficulty, general education, relations with superiors, and length of service, and it is proposed to discuss each of these factors in turn. The generally higher ranking of the job difficulty factor for an ideal system, appears to support the above point about the desire of graduates to be assessed and paid in relation to the actual job they are performing; it would seem that graduates feel that the actual salary systems in existence in their organisations are based more on factors not related to their actual job situation. It is important, here, to emphasise that the discrepancy was particularly large in company A (which contained the largest number of respondents) which obviously weighted the overall response, for though there was a disparity in the same direction in companies B and C, this was by no means as great. The above comments are, therefore, of particular relevance to company A.

The discrepancy existing over the rating of the general education factor – particularly in terms of the high rating this is given in company systems – is more difficult to understand. However, the points made in discussing the similar high rating given to this factor in relation to the determination of grades would appear to be relevant in this context. Thus, the company, in determining salary and grade in the absence of reliable and comprehensive information about job performance, is often forced into the position of basing both salary and grade on factors which are largely externally based; educational background is one of the most important factors affecting the hierarchical level an individual is recruited into, and for the early part of service this often continues. This is not to say, of course, that organisations do not carry this on for a considerable time, or even overemphasise this factor to the exclusion of others, but generally it could be suggested that this is a reasonable initial basis for salary determination (particularly given the difficulties in obtaining predictions of potential from existing selection techniques). Again, though it is necessary to point out that this discrepancy is very marked in the case of company A, much less so in company C, and in the case of company B there exists the interesting situation where the graduates thought that the company did not place enough emphasis on this factor. Thus, in an ideal system the ratings were very similar from graduates in all companies about the importance of the general education factor, yet in the company systems the rankings were both above and below those for the ideal system; indicating the perceived differences between the practice of different companies in this area.

The other two major discrepancies which existed, related to the rankings of the factors concerned with length of service and relations with superiors. Length of service was ranked lowest of all in an ideal system, whereas its overall ranking in the combined totals for the company systems was fourth out of nine. A similar disparity to the overall rankings existed in companies A and B (9:5 and 9:2 respectively), but significantly graduates in company C rated the length of service factor as being least important in their company system, and second lowest in their ideal system. Thus, in company C there is a close relationship between the perceived organisational view concerning length of servcie, and the graduate's own view, but this is in marked contrast to the situation in company A and particularly in company B where the importance given to length of service by the company is seen as being excessive and contrary to the views of graduate employees. An explanation for this situation might well take into account that all the graduates had less than five years service in their organisations, as well as the fact that an emphasis on length of service for advancement and compensation purposes is usually indicative of an organisational philosophy which underemphasises performance related factors.

The disparity between the ranking of the 'relations with superiors' factor in an ideal system, and in a company system, raises a number of interesting issues. This factor was ranked second lowest overall in an ideal system, and third overall in company systems, and similar results were revealed in companies A and C; in company B the disparity whilst existing was only slight. These particular results can be looked at from the standpoint of both the organisation and the individual, in order to provide some explanation of the differences. An organisation could legitimately argue that good relations with ones superiors was an important and essential part of work role performance, whilst individuals could point, also legitimately, to the fact that the cultivating of such relationships could result in this being the predominant factor when salary, promotion and other benefits are being considered. It is this latter viewpoint which is probably the more realistic, indicating that good relations with superiors was likely to lead to a better salary rise; certainly evidence exists to suggest tht informal factors such as this, play an important part in career achievement,[38] and Martin and Strauss,[39] and Sofer,[40] have discussed at length the role that sponsorship can play in career development. It is suggested here that a view of the organisation as a dynamic social system allows for a realistic assessment of the importance of such factors as social relations, power structures, and status, in any consideration of the determination of salary or promotion. In other words organisational policies should accept that this situation will occur, and if it is desired to minimise the unfair effects of such factors, then attention should be given to channelling such social relationships towards organisationally acceptable ends. Training programmes represent one way of attempting such a task, but it is suggested that what is really required is a comprehensive attempt to make clear the criteria which are used in assessment, and in salary and promotion determination. It is, in a sense, the task of ensuring the free flow of information regarding the careers of individuals wherever possible. The only qualification and it can be vital, is an economic one; organisations have an immense investment in human resources and if the withholding of career information at certain stages can lead to individuals staying or leaving, for example, and so increasing this investment, it could be argued on economic grounds, that such information should be withheld. Yet, equally, given the same situation, it could be argued that organisations do have social responsibilities, and that acceptance of such responsibilities, and the subsequent development of policies in line with this acceptance, will eventually give an economic return in creating improved employee relationships, and performance. Both arguments are meaningful, but the acceptance of one philosophy or the other by an organisation, which will depend on a variety of factors – some completely outside an organisation's control (such as historical factors) – can be justified on economic grounds; the difference arises out of the short- or long-term gain. Certainly, the philosophy to be chosen or to emerge will greatly influence the nature of organisational personnel policies, and subsequently the attitudes and behaviour of staff.

THE PROVISION OF SECURITY

Bass,[41] has pointed out that in our society job security has considerable sociopsychological meaning, and much of the discussion about the provision of this factor by organisations, and the design of individuals for job security, has centred on the concepts of motivation and job satisfaction. The work of such as Argyris,[42] McGregor[43] and Herzberg,[44] has implied that organisations ought to concentrate on the more intrinsic features of the job which are more likely to motivate individuals, and to provide job satisfaction, the implication being, therefore, as Parker[45] has suggested, that insecurity in a job adversely affects satisfaction. The provision of security by an organisation is often referred to as an 'extrinsic' job factor, relating to the conditions under which work is carried out. In the Shell study of graduates' job attitudes,[46] for example, the respondents appeared to be more concerned with 'intrinsic' features of jobs – features existing in the work itself – than with extrinsic features. Yet, there do exist, as Fox[47] has indicated, modern restatements of the doctrine that much work can be expected to yield only extrinsic satisfactions; the work of Dubin[48] and Goldthorpe[49] supports this argument, yet significantly, they are mainly concerned with the lower occupational levels. It is strongly argued here, though, that whatever the level being examined, the extrinsic factors in any work situation are of considerable importance, and further, that it could be suggested that without the provision of a minimum level of extrinsic rewards, then attempts to increase intrinsic satisfaction in a job are likely to fail. It is certainly possible to relate Mill's[50] emphasis on the significance of security to individuals in many situations, to the present position over executive and graduate employment in Britain. Given the increasing emphasis on more effective manpower utilisation, and reduction of manpower costs, there have been a large number of executive redundancies, and further indications that there has been a cut back in the numbers of graduates being recruited into industrial and commercial organisations; certainly relatively high graduate unemployment is a probability in the present situation. Given such a position there is strong justification for suggesting that security is an important, and sought after factor, particularly amongst those who do not have it.

The relative importance of job security as a feature of an individual's work situation will obviously depend on a variety of factors, but particularly his psychological characteristics and all aspects of the structure of the situation in which he finds himself. It would be realistic to suggest, that for most graduates, job security is not one of the more important features of their work goals – the evidence from the career perceptions of undergraduates reported in the previous chapter indicates this. Yet, organisations were perceived, in that same study, as placing a good deal of emphasis on security factors, and the evidence from this present study tends to indicate that security factors, such as length of service and good supervisor relations, play an important role in the determination of an individual's organisational position and progress. In this part of the study, which is concerned specifically with job security factors, questions were asked of the graduates about the extent of the emphasis placed by their organisations on the provision of job security, and on the importance of a number of listed factors in contributing to their feeling of security in a job.

The response to the first of these questions about the emphasis on job security provides considerable support for the foregoing argument that organisations do emphasise this factor. Of the total respondents, 57% indicated that their organisation placed considerable emphasis on job security and a further 35% thought that some emphasis was placed on its provision. Within the three major organisations there were some differences, with company A having 83% reporting a considerable emphasis compared with 62% in company B, and 60% in company C, but the great majority in all three organisations were obviously aware of the positive policy of their firm with regard to the provision of security.

Given this emphasis by the organisations in the study on job security, the methods by which they bring about this situation becomes of great significance, but it is necessary to make the point that this is closely related to the factors which individuals perceive as providing them with job security. In others words, the factors which individuals regard as important in providing job security, are the same factors which individuals perceive that the organisations emphasise in order to provide job security. The responses of graduates to this question are shown in Table 4.11.

Table 4.11

THE PERCEIVED RELATIVE IMPORTANCE OF FACTORS CONTRIBUTING TO FEELINGS OF JOB SECURITY BY RESPONDENTS

	Ranked Importance for Job Security			
Factors	*All*	*A*	*B*	*C*
Company's reputation	1	1	1	4
University degree	2	2	3	1
Experience with company	3	3	4	2
Specialised nature of work	4	4	2	3
Salary	5	5	5	5
Company pension scheme	6	7	6	6
Length of service	7	6	7	7

There is a very positive correlation between the rankings for all three companies (A, $r = 0.97$; B, $r = 0.89$; C, $r = 0.79$) illustrating the considerable agreement amongst graduates generally over the importance of factors contributing to job security. The implication is that graduates as a group are in accord over this, over and above anything the organisation might do to affect this situation, and this to a large extent is borne out of the results which show that the highest ranked factors are those related to the graduate's labour market security rather than with security within his organisation. The reputation of the company, which is ranked as the most important factor overall, and by graduates in the two largest organisations, reflects the existence of what might be termed a 'status hierarchy' of organisations. Certain organisations are regarded as prestige organisations by graduate applicants, and accordingly, have no shortage of good applicants – the same system operates with applications to universities, with some universities held in greater esteem than others. Given his perceived organisational hierarchy and the fact that employment in a high status organisation is perceived as increasing ones labour market value, it is readily understandable that graduates rate highly the reputation of the organisation as a factor contributing to their feelings of job security. The fact, also, that the three major organisations in the study could be realistically classified as prestige organisations – particularly so in the case of companies A and B – must be looked on as a further contributory factor.

The degree qualification, which is ranked as second in importance in contributing to the graduate's feeling of job security, can be looked upon as an objective measure of the investment made by both the graduate, and by society in his education. The acquisition of a university degree, whilst not an absolute guarantee of employment at a relatively high level, does open up a considerable number of opportunities, not readily available to a non-graduate, whilst at the same time it provides the strong likelihood not simply of employment, but employment at a salary, and at a level, significantly higher than that which could be expected by, say, a sixth form leaver, or an early university leaver. Of course, the degree qualification is often only a means of gaining entry at such a level, and advancement will generally depend on subsequent performance (although it would appear from the earlier results that qualifications and educational background continue to affect salary and promotion for at least the early years of service). It is significant, therefore, that the other two highly-rated factors in influencing feelings of security are both related to the work experience of graduates in their organisation – that is, general experience in the company, and the specialised nature of the work. Both these factors are related to the graduates' position in the labour market and like the two other important factors can be regarded as fairly objective criteria for external (or possibly internal) assessments of development. Formal organisations are major socialising agencies in society, and the job experiences of graduates in their companies can be regarded as elements in this socialisation process. The nature of this experience then becomes of significance for the graduate, in terms of his labour market position, and the perceived quality of this experience will to a large extent depend on the reputation of his organisation. The ranking of job specialisation as a feature of some importance for job security is understandable, in the sense that it can be seen as a further investment in particular skills, yet it is certainly the case that there are problems in over-specialisation which can greatly restrict subsequent job mobility. However, the dangers of over-specialisation would not necessarily be apparent to a graduate with a relatively limited work experience, and specialisation is obviously regarded more in the light of gaining what amounts to a higher qualification.

The attempts by organisations to promote a sense of job security usually centre on pension schemes, salary structures with regular increments, and rewards for length of service. It is, therefore, of some considerable interest to find that these standard organisational practices are rated as least important by graduates. This disparity reveals that though the aims of organisations might be clearcut, their attempts to achieve these aims are based on assumptions which are questionable. This misalignment between an organisational view of graduate's needs and attitudes, and the stated attitudes of graduates obviously leads to policies and procedures which bear little relation to the needs and realities of the situation. This misalignment is not confined to policies with regard to security, but is apparent in other areas, some of which have already been discussed. It does give further support though, to the basic argument that there is a need to clarify the relationship between organisational personnel policies and practices and the needs and expectations of staff. If, for example, the personnel policies of a particular company are based on a belief that employees were primarily concerned with security in the work situation, with the result that salary scales emphasised age and length of service, and that promotion was based on similar factors, and if this belief was misplaced and largely assumption, then it would not be difficult to predict a situation where the abler employees would leave the organisation altogether. The consequences of such unrealistic policies can be economically costly in the short term, and similarly detrimental, but also more far reaching in the long term.

ATTITUDES TO SUPERVISION AND SOME IMPLICATIONS

The importance of supervision as a determinant of attitudes and behaviour is a theme constantly stressed in behavioural science research and literature. Much of this work has been concerned to relate types, or styles, of supervision to the rather wide concept of employee satisfaction, but as Vroom[51] has pointed out, there is still some disagreement about the importance of immediate supervision for worker satisfaction. There is a good deal of evidence to suggest that a more democratic or participative leadership style is more conducive to a higher level of job satisfaction and lower levels of turnover and absenteeism, with much of this evidence stemming from the work of such as McGregor[52] and Likert.[53] However, the difficulty lies in attempting to generalise from such findings, which are often based on a psychologically orientated approach to leadership attitudes and behaviour, stressing the personal features and styles of leaders, the personal relations between supervisors and work groups, and assumptions about the attitudes and motivations of individuals - Fox,[54] particularly, has commented on the overemphasis given to such factors. Certainly, as Rhenman[55] has indicated, the hope that a democratic style of leadership would prove unquestionably best has not been fulfilled, and a major reason for this, it could be suggested, is the lack of attention given to structural features of the work situation, and the tendency to oversimplify, or attribute causality to, the relationship between job satisfaction as a concept and particular variables, such as leader attitudes and behaviour. Vroom,[56] in reviewing leadership research studies, has observed that there is some doubt as to the direction of causality in the case of supervisory style, and Child, in referring to the same problem has commented that 'supervision as a determinant of job satisfaction must be viewed in the context of the environing organisational structure'.[57] It is difficult to disagree with Roberts et al.'s findings,[58] which suggest a relationship between leadership attitudes, leadership behaviour, satisfaction, and performance, but it can be argued that any meaningful examination of the impact of various aspects of supervision on the attitudes and behaviour of employees should take place in a framework which accounts for employee attitudes towards other features of the work situation, as well as towards features of their work role and careers. The relevance of this argument can be supported by reference to the study by Miller,[59] of alienation among professional employees in a bureaucracy. The evidence from this study suggests that a participative style of leadership does not provide as much satisfaction or less alienation as a laissez-faire style, which is seen as allowing more autonomy in the work role. It could be suggested, therefore, that the attitudes of professional employees to types of supervision are very much affected by occupational values, and by attitudes towards other features of the job and work situation.

The above comments have highlighted some of the problems in defining the exact nature of the relationship between supervisory style and employee attitudes and behaviour, and have further suggested that supervisory style is just one of a number of organisational and job features which need to be considered when

attempting to understand such attitudes and behaviour. The signi-
cant point, however, in the present context, is the overall satisfaction felt by employees with their immediate supervision, for it
is the degree of satisfaction felt with immediate supervision which,
when examined in relation to attitudes towards other aspects of the
job and work situation – and also in relation to the needs and
expectations of employees – will provide an explanation of behaviour which might be manifested in the form of performance
change or mobility. In this sense, therefore, supervision can be
looked upon as a management or organisational policy, the
effectiveness of which will depend on the relationship between the
needs and expectations of employees, and the structural features
of the organisation.

The experience of graduates with the attitudes and behaviour of
their immediate supervisor, and the personal significance to them
of 'good' supervision, will obviously play an important part in the
formulation of their own attitudes and subsequent behaviour. It
was revealed in the study of the career perceptions of final year
students that two factors which related to supervision – freedom
from supervision, and the competence of management – were both
ranked a lot more highly in terms of their importance to the
students, than they were when applied to their perceived degree of
provision by industry. In others words, the graduates expectations
of supervision in industry did not match up to their aspirations with
regard to supervision. When considering the overall satisfaction
with supervision by graduates in the present study, this fact must
be borne in mind. Here, there were two questions asked of the
graduates in relation to supervision – the first concerned with
attitudes to immediate supervision, the second with attitudes
towards the competence of top management – and the results are
shown in Table 4.12.

Table 4.12

THE DEGREE OF SATISFACTION WITH ASPECTS OF
SUPERVISION

Degree of Satisfaction	Immediate Supervision (%)				Top Management Competence (%)			
	All (186)	A (70)	B (50)	C (30)	All	A	B	C
Highly satisfied	17	17	18	10	12	7	16	20
Fairly satisfied	50	40	62	43	56	50	64	50
Not very satisfied	26	33	16	35	26	36	12	20
Very dissatisfied	7	10	4	12	6	7	8	10

The results for the combined total of graduates who were generally satisfied, were remarkably similar with regard to both immediate supervision and top management competence, with 67 % of the respondents indicating that they were at least fairly satisfied with their immediate supervision, and 68 % that they were similarly satisfied with the competence of top management. However, it can be seen from the breakdown into the responses from graduates in the three major organisations, that there are grounds for considering these two aspects of organisational leadership as separate issues. This is particularly so in the case of company C, when there is a very significant difference between the degree of satisfaction felt with these two aspects of supervision ($X^2 = 12 \cdot 7$, $p = 0 \cdot 001$). The importance of immediate supervision as a factor influencing the attitudes and behaviour of graduates cannot be overestimated, and it was interesting to note that in the interviews held with the graduates, this factor was a major issue. The relationships of graduates with their immediate superiors is a significant part of their socialisation experience in the organisation, and satisfaction or dissatisfaction, as the case may be, with this relationship, can obviously have important consequences. The fact, therefore, that nearly one third of all respondents were not satisfied with their immediate supervision must be of some concern, with the situation in companies A and C even more disturbing, with 43 % and 47 % respectively not satisfied with their immediate supervision. It was stated earlier, that the exact role of supervisory factors influencing employee attitudes and behaviour is still the subject of considerable discussion, mainly concerned with the dichotomy between views suggesting that leadership factors are a major determinant of such behaviour, and views suggesting that such factors are merely contributory. The standpoint adopted here is that the relationship between a supervisor and a subordinate cannot be looked at in isolation – the wider context of such a relationship must be accounted for, and this would indicate characteristics of work roles, personnel policies and practices, and careers. In terms, therefore, of these distinct yet interrelated features, it is possible to examine the importance of immediate supervision for employee attitudes and behaviour. In the present context, it allows for the suggestion that if supervision is perceived as unsatisfactory then this will at least be a contributory factor, and could perhaps be a major factor, in such behavioural manifestations as labour turnover and performance.

A more detailed examination of the responses from the three major organisations reveals that there are important differences in

M

the degree of satisfaction with immediate supervision felt by graduates within these organisations. The difference is relatively slight between companies A and C, but there is a very signficant difference between Companies B and C ($X^2 = 15 \cdot 2$, $p = 0 \cdot 001$), and a similar difference between companies A and B ($X^2 = 14 \cdot 3$, $p = 0 \cdot 001$). The indication is, therefore, that there is far more satisfaction with supervision in company B than in the other organisations. This is unlikely to be coincidence, and must be attributed to the importance given in company B to supervision as an organisational policy. In this sense, the favourable response to immediate supervision by graduates in company B, could be said to reflect the company philosophy with regard to the importance of the managerial role, and also effectiveness of training in this field. It is certainly a fact that ability in managing subordinates is rated more highly in company B as a factor affecting salary, promotion and grade than in the other organisations, which would tend to give further support to the argument that competence in supervision is a major requirement in this company. It can perhaps, be argued, with reference to the above differences in graduates' satisfaction with their immediate supervision, that policies which stress the importance of supervision and leadership, and which are implemented through training programmes and subsequent practice, can lead to greater employee satisfaction and all that this might entail.

The above argument gains further support, when an analysis is made of the differences in responses from graduates in the three major organisations about their satisfaction with the competence of top management. There is a significant difference between the degree felt by graduates in companies A and B ($X^2 = 10 \cdot 2$, $p = 0 \cdot 01$), and also between companies A and C ($X^2 = 9 \cdot 1$, $p = 0 \cdot 01$), whilst the degree of satisfaction felt by graduates in companies B and C are very similar. Thus, whilst graduates in both companies B and C are generally satisfied with the competence of top management, the same cannot be said of the attitudes of graduates in company A. To some extent, a belief in the competence of top management must represent a belief in the effectiveness of the company as a whole, and also in its reputation. It could probably be said that the overall results regarding the competence of top management are relatively favourable, reflecting the generally high reputation of the companies in the study. In fact the three companies in the study represent an interesting contrast which might usefully be used to assist in explaining the results, for company A which is a major recruiter of graduates, had just prior to the study come in for some general criticism in relation to the performance of its top management – this was due to the influence of family connections and the increasing signs of labour problems. Company B, an extremely large graduate recruiter, was regarded, and still is, as being in the forefront in terms of personnel research and personnel policies, and its economic performance has for some time been extremely good, whereas company C, which again recruits a large number of graduates, although having the most impressive economic record of all three organisations is not generally thought highly of in relation to its personnel policies and practices. These suggested differences, which were crystallised in the interviewing programmes, shed some light on the two sets of results on attitudes to supervisory factors.

SOME FACTORS AFFECTING THE PERSONAL SATISFACTION OF GRADUATES IN THEIR WORK ROLES

The final section in this study of the attitudes of graduates towards various organisational personnel policies and practices, was concerned with two features of organisational life which have an important relationship with the nature of graduate's attitudes towards their jobs, work situation and career; the first is concerned with process of information flow, the second with the degree of autonomy in a work role. In addition, an attempt was made to assess, in relation to these two features, the attitudes of graduates towards their work role in terms of the demands the role makes upon them, the degree of achievement felt, and the level of job interest.

The amount of information available or made available to individuals about aspects of their work role, work situation and career, plays an important part in any individual choice decision or attitudes held as a result of obtained information. There is a considerable body of knowledge relevant to the significance of communications in industry, but this has largely concentrated on means of communication and communication structures: Leavitt,[60] for example, talks of communication networks; Friedlander[61] has summarised the available work on the appropriateness of communication patterns for different industrial environments and for the accomplishment of tasks within these environments; and Burns,[62] has described situations where communications patterns transcend departmental boundaries. The major concern here was not with how information is communicated but with the perceived adequacy of the information that was received. If inadequacies are perceived it can then be suggested that this could be either a result of positive company policy, or, alternatively, an indication of inadequacies in the system of information flow. Three 'information areas' were identified initially – overall company objectives, more specific company plans, and information on career prospects – and questions were asked in relation to the extent graduates thought information in each of these areas was adequate. The responses of graduates to the first two of these questions are shown in Table 4.13.

Table 4.13

THE PERCEIVED EXTENT OF THE ADEQUACY OF INFORMATION ON (*a*) COMPANY PLANS (*b*) COMPANY OBJECTIVES

Extent of Adequacy	*Company Objectives*				*Company Plans*			
	All	*A*	*B*	*C*	*All*	*A*	*B*	*C*
To a great extent	21	18	26	25	10	2	10	0
To some extent	43	32	50	50	42	66	48	8
To a small extent	26	30	16	15	30	12	32	53
Not at all	10	20	8	10	18	20	10	39

The objectives of the organisation refer to its overall goals or aims expressed in general rather than specific terms, whilst the organisation plans refer to the specific policies designed to achieve the organisational objectives. In the sense, therefore, that the two are separate entities even though they are interrelated, it is possible, theoretically and practically, to have a situation where employees are aware of organisational objectives yet relatively unaware of organisational plans, and vice versa – and this can be illustrated with reference to the results. In company A, for example, it appears that only 50% of the graduates think that the information on company objectives is adequate, compared with 68% who are relatively satisfied with information on company plans; the situation in company C on the other hand suggests that whilst 75% are satisfied with information given on company objectives, only 8% are satisfied with the information on company plans.

The general trend with the above results lies in the direction of a suggestion that, with the exception of company A, graduates are more satisfied with the adequacy of information they receive on company objectives than company plans (64% and 52% respectively). Yet it could be said, that a situation where over one third do not regard as adequate the information they receive on company objectives, and where nearly half are dissatisfied with information on company plans, is far from satisfactory and says little for the communication processes operative in organisations. The results do highlight specific problem areas for the three major organisations in the study, especially in the case of company C, and the highly significant difference shown between attitudes to this company's objectives and company plans wih regard to information flow ($X^2 = 98 \cdot 2$, $p = 0 \cdot 001$). The fact that 92 % of graduates in company C were dissatisfied with the information given on the company plans, certainly suggests that in this organisation, policies and plans are formulated and practised with little regard for employees; the interviews held with graduates in company C did highlight the relative ignorance of graduates about company policies, and the inadequacy of the knowledge of graduates in company C about the existing appraisal system which was discussed earlier, lends further support to this argument. The other major feature in these results, relates to the attitude of graduates in company A which is in contrast to the attitudes of graduates in the other organisations. Here there is a fairly significant difference ($X^2 = 5 \cdot 9$, $p = 0 \cdot 02$) between the adequacy of information on company objectives and company plans, but with information on company plans being perceived as more adequate.

The information which individuals receive or do not receive about their career prospects, plays a vital role in shaping their choice decisions. It is possible to discern two organisational approaches to the question of the nature and extent of the information which individuals should be given about their career prospects in the organisation; firstly, the view that organisations have a responsibility to their employees to provide them with all relevant information about their careers; and, secondly, the view that questions the wisdom of giving a lot of information on careers and suggests that it is in the organisation's interests to withhold some career information. The above approaches could be described as extreme, but nonetheless it is possible to suggest that organisational policies with regard to career information do tend towards one or other of the approaches, the first of which could be looked upon as motivated by social responsibility, the second by economic considerations. Interestingly enough, though, it could be argued that if a company adopted a policy based on the first approach the results might well be successful in economic terms, on the grounds that employees might well respond favourably to a company which placed such emphasis on its responsibilities to its employees. Similarly, if the second approach were adopted, on the grounds possibly, that if people were told that they had reached their career limit, or that there was a promotion blockage, they might then leave the organisation or perform sub-optimally, then the philosophy of the organisation with regard to the treatment of employees would quickly communicate itself, and the results could, in the long term, be economically unrewarding. The importance, therefore, of a balance between these two distinct approaches is obvious. Of course, the two approaches described above are representative of specific policy decisions, and it is important to point out that there is a further situation which can occur with regard to career information which could be described as a non-policy – the lack of an organisational policy in this area, probably due to a lack of awareness of the significance of career information for individuals; it could be suggested that either of the above approaches would be preferable to this *laissez-faire* situation.

In the final analysis, it is the attitudes of employees with regard to the information given that is of consequence, for it is on the basis of such attitudes that specific behaviour patterns will emerge. The graduates in this study were therefore asked a general question about career information which attempted to ascertain the extent they perceived the information they were given about their career prospects to be adequate. The responses to this question are shown in Table 4.14.

Table 4.14

THE PERCEIVED EXTENT OF THE ADEQUACY OF
INFORMATION ON CAREER PROSPECTS

Extent of Adequacy	All	A	B	C
To a great extent	4	3	2	0
To some extent	39	40	47	46
To a small extent	36	27	39	34
Not at all	21	30	12	20

The results are remarkably similar as between the three major organisations in the study, and they reflect the overall result which indicates that only 43% of the graduates were at least to some extent satisfied with the adequacy of information in career prospects. Given the importance of career considerations for graduates, these results represent a considerable indictment of the practice of organisations in this area. The significance of this can be appreciated by reference to the fact that, in the study of the career perceptions of final year students discussed in the previous chapter, career and promotion prospects was rated extremely highly in terms of importance to students, and was rated as the most important factor in terms of provision by industry and commerce. In other words, the expectations of graduates are that career and promotion factors are regarded by organisations as possibly the most important consideration in terms of personnel practice. The results of the present study suggests that these expectations are likely to suffer as a consequence of the inadequacy of information about career prospects. Whilst it would be wrong to suggest that organisations should acquiesce to all employee needs, aspirations, and expectations, it can be argued that organisations should be aware of such factors, and should at least attempt to move closer to a situation where there is a close relationship between such factors, and organisational policy and practice. It can certainly be suggested, that the disparity revealed above is far removed from such a situation. Without adequate career information an individual is unable to make effective career decisions, and in this sense, an individual in an organisation is in the same position as a school leaver faced with making a first career decision. For the individual in the organisation the situation could be regarded in terms of Blauner's concept of powerlessness, where such a person 'is an object controlled and manipulated by other persons, or an impersonal system';[63] given the nature of this concept, there would appear to be a good deal of evidence to suggest its existence in the present context.

One other aspect of powerlessness experienced by individuals in organisations, refers to their freedom to assert themselves, or to change or modify such domination,[64] and it is suggested here that this can be applied to the freedom, or control, individuals have over their own work role behaviour. The experiments with 'autonomous working groups',[65] in which groups of employees control the operations on the shop floor with only the broadest direction from management, represent an attempt to implement theoretical ideas about increasing the degree of control an employee has over his work role at shop floor level, and the desire for some degree of autonomy is no less important at managerial level. As Parker,[66] has pointed out in a review of job satisfaction studies, autonomy in the work situation – freedom to make decisions and take responsibilities – does appear to be positively related to job satisfaction. The argument that graduates generally desire what might be termed a reasonable degree of autonomy in the work situation, can be supported by reference to the study reported in the previous chapter, where final year students listed factors they thought important in a work situation. Out of nineteen factors listed in order of importance, three out of the first five listed – opportunity for initiative, authority for decision making, and the opportunity to plan ones own work – relate in some way to autonomy in the work situation, with a further rated factor – intellectual challenge – which could be regarded as contributory.

The present study was concerned with three particular aspects of the degree of autonomy perceived by graduates to exist in their work situation: the freedom to implement their own ideas, the freedom to plan their own work, and the freedom to consult outside sources of information. For each of these three areas, graduates were asked to specify the degree of perceived freedom, and the results are shown in Table 4.15.

Table 4.15

THE PERCEIVED DEGREE OF FREEDOM WITH ASPECTS OF
WORK AUTONOMY

| *Freedom to Implement Ideas* | *Degree of Freedom* | | | |
	A lot	*Some*	*Little*	*None*
All	30	47	17	6
A	25	50	19	6
B	37	51	9	3
C	16	51	25	8
Freedom to Plan Own Work				
All	39	43	11	7
A	30	45	20	5
B	47	43	5	5
C	40	40	15	5
Freedom to Consult Outside Sources of Information				
All	59	31	8	2
A	66	20	10	4
B	79	17	3	1
C	40	40	16	4

The overall results indicate that graduates perceive a relatively high degree of freedom in all three areas being given by organisations. There were, of course, overall differences within this generally high degree of freedom – for example, there is a significant difference between the degree of freedom to implement ideas and the freedom to consult outside sources of information ($X^2 = 5 \cdot 2$, $p = 0 \cdot 05$) – but the more important differences occurred between the three major organisations involved in the study. It is important however, to point out that all three organisations do conform to the overall pattern which shows that the least amount of freedom is found in the areas of implementation of ideas, and the greatest amount in the ability to consult outside sources of information.

There were significant differences between the reactions of graduates in all three major organisations with regard to freedom to implement their own ideas ($X^2 = 9.5$, $p = 0.05$), freedom to plan their own work ($X^2 = 6.63$, $p = 0.05$), and freedom to consult outside sources of information ($X^2 = 7.67$, $p = 0.05$). There were, in addition, even greater differences between the company perceived as giving the greatest amount of freedom and the company perceived as giving the least. Company B, in all three areas was perceived as giving the most freedom and it is interesting to note the degree of differences between company B and either company A or company C in relation to the three areas of work autonomy. With regard to freedom to implement ideas, the greatest degree of difference was between company B and company C ($X^2 = 9.0$, $p = 0.01$), for freedom to plan ones own work the greatest degree was between company B and company A ($X^2 = 4.7$, $p = 0.05$), and for freedom to consult outside sources of information the greatest difference was between company B and company C ($X^2 = 7.47$, $p = 0.01$). If, therefore, it is accepted that autonomy in the work situation is an important influence on the satisfaction graduates feel with their jobs, it could be suggested that company B was significantly better in the provision of such autonomy than company C and company A. There is some indication as to why this situation might arise, for company B had, for some time prior to the study been experimenting with the motivational aspects of work roles, and, in particular, had been concerned with developing the autonomy and achievement features of graduate jobs.

There has been considerable discussion in the behavioural science literature about the relationship between features of the job, or work situation, and job attitudes (usually discussed in terms of job satisfaction or dissatisfaction), and much of this discussion has centred on the distinction between factors which are either positively or negatively related to employee motivation. The two-factor theory of Herzberg[67] with reference to job attitudes and job motivation, has been particularly influential, with its distinction between 'motivating factors' (such as achievement, recognition and advancement) and 'hygiene factors' (such as work conditions, supervision and policy); the major hypothesis of this two-factor theory is that motivating factors are more important as determinants of job satisfaction, and less important as sources of dissatisfaction, and that hygiene factors demonstrate the reverse relationship. Basically, motivating factors refer to intrinsic aspects of the work itself, whereas hygiene factors are extrinsic. Such a distinction was used by the Shell organisation in their study of the job attitudes of their own graduates.[68] This concentration on the motivational bases of job satisfaction, can be said to have led to the development of ideas such as job enlargement and job enrichment; the latter concept which is more concerned with the quality of work experience has been referred to by Paul, Robertson and Herzberg, as involving 'building into people's jobs, quite specifically, greater scope for personal achievement and its recognition, more challenging and responsible work, and more opportunity for individual advancement and growth. It is concerned only incidentally with matters such as pay, working conditions, organisational structure, communication and training. . . .'[69]

The above outline, albeit brief, does highlight the major elements of what might be termed a motivational (or aspirational) approach to job attitudes and behaviour, and on the surface at least, the results of the previous study of the factors important to final year students in a job situation, would tend to give support to such an approach, since those factors relating to 'motivators' were generally rated highest. It is, however, suggested that the above motivational approach represents an extremely over-simplified view of the behavioural processes occurring as a result of job experience. One of the major weaknesses lies in the concentration on the performance of a work role, that is, on intrinsic job features, rather than on factors extrinsic to the work situation. What is lacking is any real attempt to examine the vital relationship between the work role, the work situation, and the careers of individuals; simply to examine the factors relevant to job performance in isolation, without reference to the way in which such factors are largely dependent on the other two dimensions, presents what could almost be called a false picture of the formation of job attitudes, and subsequent job behaviour. This is not to say that such intrinsic factors are not important, but that they must be seen in relation to factors which affect the overall work situation (personnel policies and programmes), and overall career considerations. It is perhaps, useful to look at some specific aspects of this relationship in order to illustrate the need for an integrated approach. Given, for example, that 'recognition' is important to individuals in a work situation, it is relevant to ask where this recognition is to come from; if, as seems likely it is organisational recognition, this would largely come through the medium of a supervisor – but, to follow the two-factor, or intrinsic/

extrinsic theories rigidly, it would appear that supervision is a hygiene, extrinsic, or non-motivating factor. In addition, it is relevant to point out that recognition of achievement might also be given in a more formalised way, than say the congratulatory behaviour of the supervisor; it could be, for example, that the recognition would be reflected in a salary increase, or in the form of a promotion, which would mean a commensurate rise in status. The forms, therefore, in which recognition might be crystallised have everything to do with the policies of the organisation, and have a good deal to do with the career of the individual, both inside and outside the organisation. It is the implication contained in the above motivational approaches that recognition, advancement or achievement are desired for their own sakes, that is seen in this context to be a major weakness, although such approaches have been criticised on other grounds, namely, methodological (Quinn and Kahn[70]), an emphasis on white collar employees (Centers and Bugental[71]), and the tendency for individuals to overemphasise motivating factors as a result of the social desirability of such responses (Wall and Stephenson).[72]

The approach adopted here, is that motivational considerations do play an important role in influencing job attitudes and behaviour, but that the nature and extent of this influence will be dependent on the structural features of organisational life (which would include the area of personnel policy and practice), the nature and extent of career considerations, the level of employee under consideration, and a variety of situational and environmental factors. It is useful at this point, to refer back to the framework of occupational choice outlined in Chapter 2, and to suggest that the arguments presented there as a basis for such a framework are equally applicable in the present context. A wide interpretation of occupational choice would allow for the inclusion of any decision to leave a work role, as well as any decision to take another, and would also allow for analysis of the decision-making process. Given this theoretical background to the work attitudes and behaviour of individuals, it is possible to examine within a comprehensive framework the wide-ranging influences on such behaviour, and to avoid oversimplification. Two examples, representing opposite approaches to the behaviour of individuals in work situations will serve to illustrate the dangers of oversimplification: firstly, Herzberg,[73] who implies that if intrinsic, or motivating, features of jobs are provided for, then satisfaction will occur (with the benefits that this might bring); and secondly, the approach of Goldthorpe et al.[74] who imply that the behaviour of an individual in a work situation is governed by his prior orientations to work. Thus, on the one hand the position is that organisations by providing for intrinsic job features can almost totally control the behaviour and attitudes of staff, and on the other, that no matter what organisations do in the way of providing opportunities, and improving the work situation, individuals will be generally unaffected since they see work in instrumental terms, as a means to the fulfilment of non-work ends. Both approaches oversimplify the real problems faced by organisations, in developing personnel policies which aim to influence the attitudes and behaviour of staff in accordance with both organisational and individual goals. Certainly, external environmental considerations are important, and would appear to be particularly so lower down the organisational hierarchy, but this does not negate the fact that experience within the organisation can influence and change attitudes in some way; and similarly, that the nature and extent of such influence and change will depend on a wide variety of motivational, environmental and career factors. The promotion of individuals to foremen, supervisors or any management role provides useful evidence that changing the work role often means changing attitudes and behaviour.

It is in the light of the above comments that the final part of this study will be discussed. This section refers to the attitudes of graduates towards their work role in terms of the demand the role makes upon them, the degree of achievement felt, and the level of job interest. Questions were asked about the demanding nature of the work in terms of making use of the abilities of the graduates, the extent to which the graduates obtained a feeling of achievement from their job, and the extent to which the graduates find their work interesting. The results are shown in Tables 4.16, 4.17 and 4.18.

Table 4.16

THE DEMANDING NATURE OF THE WORK IN TERMS OF
MAKING THE MAXIMUM USE OF GRADUATE'S ABILITIES

Degree	*Demanding Nature of Work* (%)			
	All	*A*	*B*	*C*
Very demanding	6	6	8	0
Quite demanding	52	22	68	45
Not very demanding	35	55	18	45
Undemanding	7	17	6	10
Total	100	100	100	100

Table 4.17

THE PERCEIVED EXTENT OF OBTAINING A FEELING OF
ACHIEVEMENT FROM THE JOB

Degree	Feeling of Achievement (%)			
	All	A	B	C
A great extent	24	15	28	20
Some extent	47	37	52	46
A small extent	23	40	16	19
Not at all	6	8	4	15
Total	100	100	100	100

Table 4.18

THE EXTENT TO WHICH THE WORK GRADUATES DO IS
PERCEIVED AS INTERESTING

Degree	Interesting Nature of Work (%)			
	All	A	B	C
Very interesting	37	19	42	33
Quite interesting	50	37	48	51
Not very interesting	10	40	8	12
Uninteresting	3	4	2	4
Total	100	100	100	100

In examining the overall results first of all it would appear that only 58% of the graduates thought their work reasonably demanding, whilst 71% thought they obtained a reasonable feeling of achievement from their jobs, and 87% thought their work at least reasonably interesting (the difference is significant, $X^2 = 21 \cdot 1$, $p = 0 \cdot 001$). The fact that only 58% of the graduates in the study thought their job demanding supports the findings of Pym,[75] who in a series of studies into the utilisation of professional manpower suggests that many professionals (who are often graduates) are employed on tasks not requiring them to make use of their abilities, and further, experience an absence of clearly defined work objectives, insufficient influence and control over work or resources, few prospects of promotion, and relatively poor pay. Whilst there would be variation in the degree of support for all Pym's findings by the present study, his major finding, as to the underutilisation of professional manpower would appear congruent with the above results. The implications of this, are, of course, far reaching, and would refer to the role and output of educational system in relation to the world of employment, the expectations and aspirations of graduates, and the personnel policies and practices of organisations.

The final point to be made about the above intrinsic features of jobs, and the attitudes of graduates to them, is that support is again available for the argument that organisations differ in respect of the way they influence and control graduate attitudes and behaviour by the manipulation of personnel policies. In each of the three areas of the demanding, achieving and interesting nature of jobs, there was a significant difference between the attitudes of graduates in the three major organisations, (demanding $X^2 = 46\cdot48$, $p = 0\cdot001$; achieving $X^2 = 18\cdot1$, $p = 0\cdot001$; interesting $X^2 = 33\cdot9$, $p = 0\cdot001$). The major differences occured in all three cases, between company B and company A, with company B consistently receiving highly favourable responses from their graduate employees, and company A receiving generally unfavourable responses in all three areas. Given that these three aspects of the jobs of graduates do have an important influence on their overall job, work situation and career attitudes, and also relate to the degree of utilisation of graduates, it is possible to at least be aware of some of the problems that company A is likely to have with its graduate staff.

A SUMMARY

The study of the job, work situation, and career attitudes of 186 recent graduates working in 8 industrial and commercial organisations, has been concerned to point out, that within a framework of motivational, environmental and career constraints, organisations do have the means at their disposal to influence the attitudes of graduate employees, and as a result, their behaviour. The means referred to are provided by personnel policies and practices, and to examine the nature of the relationship between such methods, and the attitudes of graduates, questions were asked of the graduates in order to ascertain their attitudes towards the use made of their skills, abilities and knowledge, appraisal systems, promotion determination and opportunities, grading systems, salary determination and satisfaction, job security, information flow, the degree of work autonomy, and the intrinsic features of jobs.

In all cases, the overall results were used as a basis for a consideration of the major trends to emerge, but a key part of the analysis was the comparison of the attitudes of graduates in the three major organisations in the study to the above factors. The overall results highlighted particularly the problem of recorrecting organisational policies and individual needs, whereas the analysis of the three major organisations provided strong evidence for the original hypothesis, that organisations can to varying degrees influence and control the attitudes, and subsequently the behaviour of their graduate employees.

It must be pointed out that this particular study has concentrated on the perceptions of various features of organisational control systems by a specific cohort group. The extent to which recent graduates are a distinct group with a distinct culture will obviously affect the degree to which it is possible to generalise from the specific result, here. We are, however, talking about individuals who have to varying degrees accommodated their graduate culture into a wider career and organisational culture and much of the above discussion, it is suggested, is relevant to the organisational experiences and career and work considerations of the wider managerial work force.

It is also important to stress that it has not been possible to attempt an intensive analysis of the major organisations in this study. The differences revealed in terms of employee reactions here point to important policy, practice, and culture differences in the organisations concerned. A further investigation would provide a useful and important analysis of the specific organisational reasons for differences in terms of the quality of organisational practice in the areas discussed.

CHAPTER 5

A Qualitative Approach to the Planning and Utilisation of Manpower – Some Theoretical and Practical Considerations

This book has been concerned with a number of distinct yet interrelated aspects of the process of personnel flow, and a major function of this final chapter is to integrate the ideas and research findings discussed in previous chapters. This would then allow for the analysis of the relationship between the control aspects of manpower planning (as manifested by personnel policies in their widest sense), and the choice behaviour of individuals.

As a prelude to the integration of the major issues raised, it is proposed to develop further some of the issues discussed in the previous chapter, where the attitudes of graduate staff were examined, in relation to certain features of their job, work situation and careers. This present discussion will outline some of the considerations for both individuals and organisations, arising from the attempts by organisations to influence and control human resources, and will be based on a pilot study of the job and career attitudes of middle and senior managers in two large organisations. It is necessary to point out that these studies are based on interviews with eighty managers (fifty in one organisation, thirty in another) selected to represent the various hierarchical levels in the organisations concerned. The same open ended interview schedule was used with all the managers, and interviews generally lasted about an hour. Detailed information was obtained on the personnel practice of the organisations concerned, and this, together with the information obtained in the depth interviews, does provide a useful insight into some of the factors affecting the attitudes of managerial staff, and further provides a useful base for further research into the relationship between employee attitudes and behaviour, and organisational attempts to influence such behaviour in line with organisationally acceptable goals.

PERSONNEL POLICIES AND MANAGERIAL REACTIONS – SOME ISSUES

The overall aim of the pilot investigation was to gain some insight into the effect on the individual manager of the structure and ideology of the organisations, current personnel practices, and relevant factors in the external social and economic environment. The aims reflect the distinction made in the previous chapter between the concepts of job, work situation, and career, and also the approach specified at the start of the book, that it is necessary to adopt, what might be termed an 'open systems' approach, in any study of the attitudes and behaviour of staff in organisations. It is possible to view personnel policies as optimal interventions in a dynamic system, and is suggested that this approach allows for a meaningful analysis of the process of mutual influence between policies and behaviour. The other important point to make at this stage refers to the fact that the management of human resources is, as Sofer[1] has pointed out, subject to conflicting pressures; on the one hand, there is pressure to obtain a maximim return on investment which results in systematic and objective policies and procedures for controlling and influencing human resources, and on the other hand, there is pressure from these very sources – organisational employees – arising out of needs, aspirations, personal relationships, and the importance of status, power and other social and psychological factors. The subsequent discussion, therefore, will reflect this essentially dynamic situation, and, though it will be necessary to examine each policy area individually in terms of the specific issues involved, the dominant theme will remain the interrelated nature of personnel policies. As Vetter has said, 'the planning approach brings about the interrelationship of the various activities of personnel management into clear focus, a result that constitutes one of the major benefits of manpower planning'.[2]

RECRUITMENT AND SELECTION – THE PROBLEM OF ORGANISATIONAL ENTRY

One major element of control which an organisation possesses is the ability to choose its employess. It could be said that to a large extent an organisation is only as good as its employees, and that in line with this, an efficient recruitment and selection policy is necessary to achieve an effective work force.[3] Certainly, decisions taken at this stage will influence the future manpower structure of the organisation for a considerable period of time (particularly so in organisations in the public sector where a policy of almost guaranteed job security is often practised). Both quantitative and qualitative considerations are relevant here, and it is important to point out that recruitment and selection does not take place in a vaccum, but in the context of both the external and internal labour market. It is, perhaps, useful to develop this latter point, and emphasise that much recruitment and selection is handled internally with decisions made to appoint from within; in fact, ability to promote from within could be said to indicate effective manpower and succession planning. However, it is equally important to point out that it is both necessary and possibly desirable to recruit in the outside labour market. The necessity for this refers to the impossibility of organisations filling all their vacant posts from within due to the operation of the personnel flow system, and also to the fact that there are certain categories of human resources over which organisations have no control, such as the output of the educational system. The desirability of recruiting in the outside labour market has particular relevance for the philosophy and nature of the organisation as based on the values, attitudes and expectations of the work force. If, for example, an organisation continually promoted from within this could have two effects: firstly, there would be no influx of new staff and hence no possibility of an influx of new ideas, and possible change in existing ideas and practices; and, secondly, it could lead to an acceptance amongst employees that promotion was inevitable if one stayed long enough in the organisation. There exist at present a number of organisations in traditional areas of industry and commerce with well established recruitment and promotion procedures which illustrate this particular problem. To take the example of a large insurance company (shipping companies, solicitors offices, and to some extent banks would have similar characteristics); this organisation has always recruited from the generally middle-class sixth form leavers in local schools, and the oldest outside recruit at present in their employment was aged thirty-one, at the time he was recruited, and this at a middle-management level and for a newly created specialist appointment. The nature of the policies of this company are, therefore, a reflection of the fact that long service is expected and rewarded, that all recruitment is from the traditional base, and that posts are always filled from within. It is, perhaps interesting to note that this particular organisation has recently introduced a graduate recruitment scheme and taken on thirty graduates for training without any research into the possible consequences of such an action; this action should provide some interesting consequences. Effectively they are imposing a totally different set of expectations on to a work force with well established expectation patterns.

Another interesting point of difference between the policies of organisations with regard to the recruitment of staff, is the way in which organisations tend either towards recruiting younger staff in numbers surplus to their requirements, or towards recruiting specifically for specific posts. Both situations, in their extreme form, could be said to be likely to lead to personnel problems. In the first situation where an organisation deliberately over-recruits on the ground that trained staff will always be available and that some of those who are dissatisfied as a result of this treatment will leave, which will ameliorate the situation for the organisation. This tends to happen particularly with graduates entering some large organisations, where they are not recruited for a specific job but for a general training, and then at some later stage the better graduates of the initially selected cohort are given specific, well-planned work roles leaving the remainder to either adapt to the fact that they are likely to be performing relatively less important work roles and having a relatively slower rate of promotion, or to reject the situation. The subsequent wastage rate is not, therefore, a major concern but is regarded as normal. The latter situation described above, where individuals are recruited for specific work roles or training programmes, is usually preceded by a very detailed and careful selection system. However, this could lead, as Sofer[4] has indicated to a situation where the initial investment is regarded as having been made in the formal selection procedure, with what happens subsequently being diminished by this fact. Both approaches outlined above can lead to problems for firms adopting the 'stockpiling' approach which could well find that they have difficulty in attracting good calibre staff due to their high wastage rates and reputation; and in the second instance, of firms adopting a highly specific approach to recruitment, staff might well find that this reflects a rigidity which might hinder considerably their future development.

The recruitment and selection process ostensibly exists to identify, attract and obtain individuals with the abilities and attributes desired by the organisation. However, there are a number of other aspects of recruitment and selection activities and policies which are important in this context. As was pointed out earlier, organisations do not recruit and select in a vacuum and the considerations of the labour market situation must be taken into account. In certain situations, therfore, it might be possible for organisations to dictate the proceedings, but where supply is scarce the opposite might be the case. In addition, the ability of organisations to attract staff will depend on a number of other factors, of which a key one would be the reputation of the organisation, for reputation will be strongly affected by policies and practices pursued by the organisation (which will obviously be compared with those of other recruiting organisations). The recruitment and selection procedures adopted by organisations also has far-reaching consequences, for it must be remembered that for many individuals, involvement with the recruitment and selection procedures of a firm will be their first real contact with the firm. Thus, the process takes on a significance for the applicant which is unfortunately, often not fully realised by organisations. This significance can be said to reflect the fact that the selection process is a two-way process often involving selection by both organisation and applicant, and, in addition to this, the experiences an individual undergoes during the whole recruitment and selection process will, together with his prior aspirations and attitudes, determine initially, his attitude to the organisation, and his expectations in relation to working within it. The information which an individual is given during the recruitment and selection process, the organisational representatives with whom he comes into contact, and the way he is treated will, therefore, have consequences far beyond the immediate situation.

Given the above implications of recruitment and selection for the nature, quality and attitudes of an organisation's work force, it could be strongly argued that policy with regard to recruitment and selection should be formalised. The establishment of a formalised policy in this area should, of course, be based on past experience, and an awareness of employment features (job, work situation and career) which are of importance to potential recruits. This inevitably means that policies developed to deal with organisational entry should be closely related to other features of organisational life which they reflect, and which they affect.

EDUCATION, TRAINING AND QUALIFICATIONS

The processes involved in developing individuals once they have joined an organisation play an important part in the creation of an effective work force, in promoting attitudes which rate highly personnel development, and in the fulfilment of the objectives of other personnel policies. The process of training can be looked on as a process of socialisation, defined in organisational terms by Caplow as 'the organisationally directed process that prepares and qualifies individuals to occupy organisational positions',[5] with a particular emphasis on the acquired nature of the behaviour as a positive aspect of the process. Much organisational training is supposedly designed to improve organisational effectiveness and individual performance in line with a relevant set of norms,[6] but there have been problems associated particularly with the value of formal training programmes in conveying appropriate skills and knowledge. However, it could be said that, though the manifest function of training activities might be educational in the sense that such formal skills and abilities are taught and learnt, there are a number of other functions of such programmes. Such latent functions might include the communication of organisational values and a variety of relevant career information which might include types of acceptable behaviour, sources of influence and the nature of power and status structures. In addition, formal training programmes, regardless of what is learnt or conveyed often serve functions similar to the acquisition of qualifications, which have a good deal to do with career progress and its acknowledgement.

The nature of training programmes varies considerably between organisations, but it is often strongly argued that if training is to be at all meaningful it should be firmly based on the requirements of the organisation. This argument is based on the fact that there is an important distinction between training and education primarily to the question of objectives. Thus, training could be said to refer to the provision of skills and abilities with respect to the performing of a specific job, whereas management education refers more to the development of the individual in terms of allowing him to widen his attitudes and knowledge (in a general sense) for possible promotion to a higher organisational role. Hunt,[7] in discussing the role of manpower as an asset in a growth economy expands on this distinction, and having done this presents a well-argued case for progression in both areas.

Both training and education programmes are generally formalised, whether they are conducted by the organisation or by some outside agency, and in this respect they serve important functions for the career of individuals in addition to the educational function mentioned above. Induction programmes represent the initial introduction into the organisation of the recruit, but often induction programmes are associated with organisational training programmes and can last for periods of up to one year, or even longer in extreme cases. However, given that there is a perceived and accepted hierarchy of organisations – in terms of their reputation for sound economic performance, and progressive personnel policies – then selection by one of these organisations, and the training that this means, acts in a similar way to attending a good university or taking a good degree, and becomes a current asset. Subsequent training and education programmes which are formalised also serve the same function; attendance at specific training programmes run by business schools, for example, represent assets in career terms.

The other interesting and relevant feature of education and training is the growth in the number of qualified staff in recent years. For example, in one of the organisations under discussion the increase in graduate staff was from 7% of the total staff in 1953 to 20% in 1966, and the decrease in the number of non-qualified staff was from 44% of the total staff in 1953 to 14% in 1966.

Several questions are raised as a result of this trend towards the increasing use of qualified personnel. The attitudes of non-qualified staff to qualified staff, and to their own position in the company and the labour market would seem in need of evaluation. It should also be possible to examine the attitudes of non-qualified staff to qualifications, qualified staff and their own lack of qualifications, and relate these attitudes to the importance placed on other job factors, for example, security or status. In the pilot interviews, the attitudes of non-qualified staff appeared fairly enlightened, but it was possible to detect in several cases some resentment, coloured perhaps by the rebuttal of 'experience' in the face of 'qualifications'. A further impression is that attitudes to different types of qualified staff are dissimilar, with graduates, for example, being seen in a much more unfavourable light than professionally qualified staff.

The great increase in the number of qualified people within these companies could possibly be seen in terms of creation of a 'qualifications barrier' to non-qualified people, with consequently a choice facing them of either attempting to obtain a qualification themselves, or else lowering their level of aspiration. There may well be difficulties in obtaining a qualification, not perhaps through lack of ability, but from adverse personal circumstances. The concept of the level of aspiration[8] might well be utilised in connection with non-qualified and poorly qualified staff, to examine, for example, the way in which the frustration tolerance, and the associated earlier frustration experiences of an individual, influence his setting of the level of aspiration.

In discussing qualifications in this context, one approach might be to examine exactly what is meant by the term. Without going into the rights and wrongs of the examination system, it might be usefully pointed out that the ability to pass examinations, and hence to obtain qualifications, might not indicate ability to do a particular job, though, of course, it does provide some objective measure. Similarly, an inability to pass examinations might mean only this, and in practice individuals falling into this category might perform excellently in a particular job, and also be of high potential. What would seem to be needed is some form of objective test(s), which could be utilised in appraisal systems, specifically for non-qualified staff. One further point is also relevant here; a professional course of study and subsequent examinations might well take a considerable amount of time (years), and techniques learned in such situations, and over such a period of time, might bear much less relevance than is generally thought in a situation where technical change is occurring.

In the light of what Crichton[9] has called the growth of professionalism within organisations, it is interesting to contemplate a possible dilemma facing the professional arising out of his membership of an industrial or commercial organisation. Of course, there are difficulties associated with defining exactly what constitutes a professional person, or a professional organisation, as Millerson[10] has indicated, but here the relevance is with what might be termed a responsibility to the profession or a professional ethic. Thus, the situation might arise, where there was a conflict between the responsibility of the professional to the firm or to the profession. As Blau and Scott have pointed out[11] the professional has internalised his own standards and has a reference point with his professional colleagues; this means that there is a dilemma faced by organisations in deciding how much professional freedom to allow and how much organisational influence to attempt.

The increase in qualified personnel and specialists appears to be creating a problem for individuals with regard to overspecialisation, and many of the managers interviewed were conscious of difficulties with regard to career development because of the narrowness of a particular specialism. If, for example, an individual is qualified in accountancy and all his experience has been in the finance function, the feeling exists that it is extremely difficult to move out of this function (and in this particular function the problem is exacerbated by the increasing role of the computer which is leading to feelings of insecurity). Certainly, most of the specialists interviewed were extremely aware of the dangers of becoming trapped in a particular function with only further specialist experience being gained. The barriers to cross-fertilisation between departments, functions, and divisions are a major cause of such apprehension, and it is important to point out that situations do develop where the placement policies of organisations, though based on the principles of job rotation and free internal personnel flow, are often found deficient in practice. allowing for the creation and maintenance of such internal barriers. It is, therefore, possible to highlight the existence of sub organisations, based on function and to identify rather narrow career paths.

Qualifications imply the acquisition of skills and the competence of an individual in a particular field. If individuals are not given the scope for applying such skills, as appeared to be happening in these cases, and in the case of many of the graduates in the previous study, the effect from an organisational standpoint could be inefficiency in the utilisation of manpower. However, the major effect could well be in terms of the reaction of the individual employee which could well be to leave the organisation entirely. The link between expectations and subsequent reality is particularly important here.

COMPENSATION POLICIES

The two aspects of financial compensation which are of relevance in this context are; firstly, the role of compensation in industrial motivation; and secondly, the behavioural consequences of salary structures. In a comprehensive review of the literature relating to the role of compensation in affecting the job behaviour of employees, Opsahl and Dunnette[12] have suggested that there are at least five theories or interpretations of this role, namely: money as a generalised conditioned reinforcer, money as a conditioned incentive, money as an anxiety reducer, money as a 'hygiene' factor, and money as an instrument for gaining desired outcomes – and they offer detailed criticisms of each of the five theories. Arising out of these general criticisms they make the important point that any interpretations attached to studies of the role of financial compensation must give careful attention to the interaction between job and personal variables.[13] Given the importance of this interaction – which has been continually stressed in this book – it is necessary to consider such factors as types of payment systems, the determination of salary level, the individual's salary progression, and the degree of secrecy surrounding salary policies, in relation to the perceived importance of financial compensation, the relationship between performance and payment, and the perceived importance of financial compensation in relation to the other job, work situation and career factors. Thus, on the one hand it is necessary to consider the objective features of payment systems, and on the other, the subjective reactions to such systems.

As an incentive, financial compensation tends to be associated with the assumptions underlying the 'economic man' principle, namely that man is rational and desires above all else to maximise his financial position. This conception is inadequate, in the sense that it fails to take account of individual differences, different situations, or theories of personality and motivation. However, despite the fact that the motivation effects of financial compensation will depend on the nature and importance of the factors, there can be little doubt as to the importance of such compensation for the overall job satisfaction of individuals.[14] Whether an increase in salary as a contribution to overall job satisfaction acts an incentive to better performance is another matter, and one which has caused much controversy in the literature.[15] Certainly, as Vetter[16] has pointed out, the motivational aspects of salaries and benefits require careful attention in any manpower planning exercise, together with the relationship of starting salaries to the existing salary structure, and a consideration of the replacement cost of experienced manpower.

The interviews with the managers in the two organisations, and the graduates in the previous study, revealed some interesting additional functions of financial compensation in that salary was regarded as an important indicator of progress (both within and outside the employing organisation), and that the nature of the salary structure revealed company ideology.

With the present hierarchical levels of qualifications and the great expansion of technical and higher education it is becoming increasingly easier for an individual to compare his progress with others on the basis of salary. Information is widely available about salaries paid to people at similar levels and ages in industry, and there is also the added dimension of increasing professionalisation enabling further comparisons to be made. That people make sure of comparative information can be illustrated by the fact that most of the managers and graduates interviewed regularly referred to the job advertisement sections of national newspapers and specialist journals. In addition, it could well be that the pressures on an individual to reach a certain salary 'barrier' by a certain age are considerable, and that an inability to reach this is intepreted as failure, having consequences for both the individual and the organisation. It would be relevant, for example, to ascertain the reactions of individuals to such failure.

The salary structure in both organisations was generally related to grade and age, from which it is possible to argue that if the grade level determined salary, then from the point of view of retaining or attracting staff it would be possible to look at different salary structures and their possible effects. For example, if the salary structure contained short scales with high increments (but possible delays in promotion), this might attract people with high potential (because they would be reasonably certain of promotion), but which for the majority, would mean probable frustration. Longer scales with increments relating to increases in the cost of living might encourage only the unambitious. Certainly it could be argued that age related salary scales will have important implications for the type of work force organisations attract and keep, and on a more general level, that any attempt to plan or manage manpower should be closely related to salary policy.

One of the intriguing points to emerge from the interviews, and from the graduate study in the previous chapter was the secrecy surrounding salaries and grades. Given that these factors are closely related it is relevant to comment on this situation and to highlight the frustration which developed as a consequence. There were a number of examples of individuals being unaware of their salary limits, many of those interviewed did not know what grade they were, and most of the others had found out by 'devious means'. There would seem to be an interesting split here between stated company policy and actual practice, for if the official view regarding knowledge of grade and salary limits is that if one asks, then one is told, and in practice, most people do not ask because the feeling is conveyed that it is 'not done' then there is a confusion which is highly likely to have dysfunctional consequences for the organisation. The significance of such secrecy lies in its effect on the individual who is interested in his career development, and hence, factors affecting his career situation, yet is unable to look ahead due to the lack of information.

Situations do occur where financial compensation is deliberately used to keep individuals within the organisation. Thus, where an artificially high salary is paid to an individual, his expectations will be based on this fact, which could create considerable mobility difficulties for him. There were a number of cases revealed in the interviews where this situation had arisen; the individuals concerned were very highly paid, lived up to their income, were dissatisfied with the jobs they were performing, and because of their financial situation were unable to leave. The other major feature of the financial compensation programme in the marketing organisation was the fact that there was little attempt to relate salary to performance and responsibility. Thus, a salary rise was expected every year, and though there were differences in the amounts given in the form of salary rises, the differences were marginal.

The need for effective salary administration cannot be overemphasised. Given both the intrinsic importance of financial compensation, and the process of comparison which takes place, it is, as Grant and Smith argue, 'essential that organisations . . . should provide an equitable system of grading and remuneration and should be willing to employ specialists to handle the problems involved'.[17]

GRADING SYSTEMS

The prevalence of systems for grading managerial staff, was revealed by a BIM study of staff grading schemes,[18] as was the fact that such systems were used in conjunction with other personnel policies, particularly those concerned with remuneration and appraisal. Grading systems, of course, relate closely to status systems, and in discussing status and status needs we are referring to the desire of employees for some form of organisational identity, which will reflect their role in the organisation. This identity might be provided through the department an individual is assigned to, his job title, job description, grade, and the set of privileges that are associated with the role. In this context, Caplow[19] has highlighted an important distinction between the status of an organisational position, which he defines as its place in the prescribed rank order of influence in the organisation, and 'status', which refers to the quantitative difference, however measured, between the ability of two individuals to modify each others behaviour, when they interact.

It could be said, that one of the important functions of a high status position or grade, is the control an individual has over his fate at work. This question of control is obviously important for any understanding of the relationship between status and job satisfaction, and one aspect of this, would be the way in which control over one's technical and social environment, and freedom from supervision, accompany higher status and contribute to job satisfaction.[20]

There are, of course, problems associated with organisational attempts to provide systems for grading managerial staffs. The question of secrecy, which was referred to earlier with regard to salary, is similarly relevant to grading systems. If it is accepted that insecurity amongst staff is often caused by a lack of information, and also by a feeling of powerlessness (of not being in control over ones future), then a policy (albeit unofficial), of secrecy over grades, would appear to satisfy both these criteria, and accordingly contribute to insecurity. Considerable secrecy was perceived by individuals in respect of grades in most of the organistions studied, and, as with salary secrecy, this was a source of frustration. The problem is often one of confusion, in terms of the amount and quality of information a manager feels he is able to disclose to his subordinates, and relates to the inadequacy of the communications system in many organisations. It is obviously important for employees to know their grade, and it is, perhaps, even more important that they know the limits of their grade in terms of salary, and further, that they know what other grade limits are, so as to be fully aware of what a move from one grade to another means. For executives to either be unaware of their grades, or else to have to resort to devious means to discover it, would seem to indicate a total lack of awareness on the part of the organisation, about the needs and expectations of managerial employees. An allied cause of frustration well highlighted by the interviews, was the situation where individuals were performing jobs which were at a higher grade than their actual grade. This 'temporary' situation (that apparently could go on for a long period of time) where official recognition is not given to level of responsibility could also be regarded as representative of unrealistic personnel policies.

The close association between grading systems and status systems, allows for mention of the fact that conflict aroused by status differences can be considerable, and that such status differences can have dysfunctional consequences for the organisation. Certainly, to judge from the interviews, status considerations play an important part in organisational life, and it would be useful in any future organisational analysis to ascertain the significance of the role of status in relation to effective organisational performance.

SYSTEMS OF APPRAISAL

Performance appraisal has been defined as 'a formal and systematic means of assessing the recent effectiveness of individual managers'.[21] It could, therefore, be seen as a means of identifying talent, given the situation where positions in organisations are continuously being vacated through the system of personnel flow.[22] If the overall purpose of appraisal schemes is to improve the efficiency of the organisation, by making the best possible use of human resources through the identification of ability, performance, and potential for advancement, there also exist a number of more specific uses of such schemes. These would include the contribution to salary reviews in terms of differential payments to be made, the identification of the development and training needs of the individual, assistance in planning job rotation, and assistance in making promotions.

Most appraisal systems are highly formalised and involve at least the completion of a regular written report on performance (usually annually) and often, in addition to this, an interview or, discussion between a superior and subordinate, which would involve discussion of the appraisal, and the general career considerations of the subordinate. Some schemes in existence also allow for another senior manager, who knows the individual being appraised, to be involved in the appraisal interview.

The appraisal interview often takes on considerable social and psychological significance for the individual being appraised. It is, perhaps, a sad comment on the quality of supervision in some of the organisations studied, that an appraisal was seen by many individuals as the only way in discussing their career aspirations and prospects in the organisation. Another point to emerge from the interviews in one of the organisations concerned, was an appraisal interview perceived as one of the few ways of obtaining a move out of the department. It might also be relevant to point out, that many of the interviewees commented that they *expected* to be appraised after joining the organisation; in other words, appraisals were regarded as standard and expected elements of organisational personnel policy, and it could be postulated that absence of such a system would be perceived as abnormal, and possibly, an indication of a poor, ineffective, or unfair organisation. Irrespective of the success or otherwise of an appraisal system it could be said to serve the function of demonstrating that an institutional mechanism for dealing with the fairness question exists.

There are a great many problems associated with appraisal systems, and it is pertinent to mention some of the major ones. The difficulties associated with the measurement of performance are severe, particularly at managerial levels where the element of subjectivity is high, and there are associated problems of perception differences. Certainly, if career development is to be meaningful, then much thought will have to be given to these differences, and to ways of overcoming them. The relationship of appraisals to the reinforcement of behaviour raises another set of questions, for example, if an appraisal is made once a year does the employee know what he is being reinforced for? or does the appraisal consider actual behaviour as opposed to personality traits? The question of personal relationships is also highly relevant, given the fact that the nature of superior-subordinate relationships might be affected by the appraisal interview.

The attitudes of the individuals to appraisal will be governed in the long run by the effectiveness of the system, and this means letting people see that appraisals are based on common standards, that they are closely related to performance, and that action is taken as a result of such appraisals. Most of the individuals interviewed all expected a salary rise at the end of every year, and most thought that the actual amount was probably related to performance, but nobody was *fully* aware of a link between appraisal and performance.

One final problem which could arise indirectly out of appraisal systems is worthy of mention, and relates to a situation where the probabilities for individual advancement are known. Assuming that individuals have different probabilities for advancement, there could be a problem for organisations when information became available about these probabilities, about whether or not to share with employees this information, which would mean making them aware of their career limits. The effects of this might be difficult to predict, but whether or not this information was shared, would reflect the personal philosophy of the organisation concerned.

PROMOTION AND PLACEMENT PROGRAMMES

One of the major concerns facing organisations is to develop programmes which are designed to provide a pattern to the mobility of managerial staff, and such programmes will be involved with promotion, lateral movement, demotion, and the management of wastage. The task for such programmes is to equate organisational goals (in manpower terms) with the career concerns and paths of individuals, and their success will be judged on the degree to which organisational roles are filled by competent individuals, and on the degree to which such individuals are satisfied with their career progress. Policies associated with the mobility of staff are subject to a number of considerations and constraints, and amongst the most important of these would be the bases on which individuals are selected for movement, the balance to be achieved between internal and external apointments, the difficulties of achieving equality in promotion opportunities, the formal and informal barriers to staff movement, and the question of employee expectations in respect of promotion opportunities.

The most immediate concern for organisations in formulating policies for staff movement is the balance to be achieved between promotion from within and recruitment from outside. The issues to be considered have been outlined in the earlier discussion of recruitment and selection policies, but it is useful to draw attention to the fact that the determination of mobility programmes will depend on a clarification of organisational policy on this particular question. This clarification will need to consider the fact that significant categories of employees expect and aspire to promotion, and a policy of internal promotions could be said to contribute considerably to motivation and satisfaction, as well as providing a process which might be termed selective socialisation. A policy of filling organisational positions from outside, on the other hand could obviously have deterimentral effect on the satisfaction and commitment of the existing staff, although this might be the only possible course of action open to an organisation if internal candidates are not suitable, and in addition, it might be thought important to have an infusion of new staff with new ideas to keep the system from becoming stagnant and conformist. The balance is obviously crucial here with the organisation, as Sofer[23] has pointed out, having to bear in mind the significance of the promotion system as an incentive system and as a sanctioning system.

Opportunities for promotion and movement in an organisation, are regarded as being of considerable importance, in job and career terms, by managerial staff. Certainly, the managers and graduates interviewed place much personal emphasis on such opportunities, and the final year students in the study discussed in Chapter 3, rated this as one of the most important factors in an industrial career. Given this situation, the criteria used to determine promotion, and other aspects of mobility, becomes a major issue for both organisations and individuals. For organisations, the choice usually revolves around evaluation of relative merit, ability, and length of service, and the weighing to be given to each of these factors in promotion decisions. This process, however, is not clear as it might appear, for though on the grounds of objectivity there might be pressure for ability factors to predominate, there are problems in identifying and measuring ability, particularly in terms of predicting potential performance. In addition, there is likely to be similar pressure for organisations to reward seniority emanating largely from the relationships that exist within the organisation and the responsibility felt by subordinates; there is too, the argument that seniority is a more objective criterion than the identification and measurement of ability.[24] From the standpoint of the individual the important feature is his perception of the factors actually determining promotion in his organisation, particularly in the light of his perception of what promotion should be based on. The results of the graduate study in the previous chapter, and the information obtained from the managerial interviews indicated some disparity between organisational promotion systems and what was regarded as an ideal system; it is generally true to say that most respondents desired a promotion system based more on ability factors than was the case in their present organisational system. Yet it would be equally true to say that since most of the respondents were relatively short-service employees their attitudes might well have been governed by this fact, and certainly the managerial interviews tended to suggest that seniority becomes more important in the thinking of employees about promotion the more senior the individual becomes in terms of age and length of service. The significant general point to emerge, though was the perceived prevalence of chance, luck and similar arbitrary factors in promotion decisions, which would seem to indicate rather ill-defined promotion policies. The reason for this situation, can it is suggested, be largely accounted for by the considerable influence of personal relationships in mobility patterns, and in this context, Dalton[25] has discussed at length the informal factors involved in career achievement, and Martin and Sims[26] have discussed the role that sponsorship and cultivated personal relationships can play.

It could be argued that the aim of promotion policies should be to substitute fairness for chance, but it is obviously necessary, if this is to come about, to define and communicate the criteria to be used in 'fair' systems. Individuals are usually aware of the criteria on which promotion is based, and a revealing picture of the way in which such promotional expectations can affect the manpower situation in organisations is provided by Young,[27] who describes what can happen when such expectations are not met due to an inability of organisations to maintain previous rates of promotion. Young suggests that a diminution of promotion opportunities leads to staff wastage, and certainly this is one way of an individual adapting to such a situation, though there may be others; as Argyris has pointed out 'individuals will adapt to frustration and conflict in formal organisations by creating any one of a combination of . . . informal activities'.[28] Similarly, Merton's[29] identification of modes of individual adaption, namely conformity, innovation, ritualism, retreatism and rebellion, could be useful in understanding employee reaction to mobility constraints.

There are, in addition to promotion as a form of planned mobility, other ways in which staff can be developed and moved in line with organisational goals. Promotion, for example, can be handled with a combination of lateral and vertical movement, and job rotation policies can be equally valuable in their own right. The concern here, as Vetter [30] has indicated is with designing cross training efforts at various levels in the light of future organisational needs and of the demands such needs will place on managers. In practice, there are often difficulties in fulfilling what would appear to be a sound policy, and such difficulties centre on the barrier to lateral movement which are created by sections, departments, functions and divisions, in the case of the marketing organisation a major cause of this situation was the power of selection vested in individual managers, and their insularity (in terms of their unit). The problem, therefore, for organisations lies in seeing that policies relating to internal mobility are carried through in practice, and ensuring that effective policies do exist to cater for even the most difficult manpower problems. A final example will serve to illustrate this point, and to illustrate the dilemma that organisations face in developing policies for the effective management of human resources which allow for the needs, feelings, aspirations and expectations of individuals. The problem of the relatively ineffective employee is one which most organisations face, and which often organisations fail to deal with, for it brings into conflict economic and social responsibilities; yet it could be suggested that organisations that are able to deal positively with this problem are those which have successfully reconciled their differing and often conflicting responsibilities. The ways in which demotion or career limitations are managed could include lateral movement, retraining, or the creation of a new appointment, but in a sense the methods are far less relevant than the determination

o

and ability of organisations to manage *all* aspects of personnel flow.

A SYNTHESIS

The above discussion of certain aspects of the relationship between organisational policies concerned with personnel flow, and the attitudes and behaviour of staff as highlighted by the research studies, reflects the major concern of this book. Wilson has argued that 'manpower planning, manpower research, manpower management and manpower policy are best regarded as interdependent aspects of the same process',[31] and the nature of the relationships suggested by this argument has been fully investigated in the preceding chapters. The purpose of this final section is to co-ordinate the theoretical ideas developed in Chapters 1 and 2, with the research findings and the related practical considerations.

Manpower planning has been shown to be concerned with two distinct yet interrelated activities, namely the prediction of manpower requirements and supply, and the control or influence of manpower flow. The process of personnel flow was shown to be operative at national (and international level), and at organisational level, and it was suggested that attempts to predict, influence and control this movement should be firmly located in behavioural science theory. An attempt was then made to construct a theory based on a consideration of the factors which affected the job choice decisions of individuals. Three major theoretical perspectives were identified and discussed with respect to occupational choice which reflected psychological, sociological and economic perspectives, and it was argued that for a meaningful interpretation of the occupational choice process an approach was required which allowed for an integration of such perspectives. Thus any choice decision would be seen in terms of the personal development and motivational characteristics of the individual, his perception of what constituted the total net advantage, and his contact with those aspects of the social structure which act as influences and constraints.

Most of the theory relating to choice decisions refers to movement from the education system into the employment system, that is, with first choice of occupation, but it has been suggested that an integrated theory should account for subsequent job mobility within the employment system. The research studies, therefore, have been concerned with factors affecting the career attitudes and choices of individuals faced with moving into the employment system (or higher education system) for the first time, and also with the job and career attitudes (seen in terms of their relationship to any choice decision) of graduates and managers working in industry and commerce. It is argued that the framework of occupational choice developed earlier does account for the results of the research in that psychological, economic and sociological factors operate in the processes of attitude formation and decision making at both the first choice, and subsequent choice levels. The description by Campbell *et al.* of job behaviour as 'a function of individual characteristics (abilities), volitions (motivation) and social and organisational characteristics (opportunity)',[32] would, therefore, be relevant to the behaviour of individuals faced with choosing a job for the first time.

The movement of individuals from the education system into the employment system can be seen on two levels, at a national level and at an organisational level. The problem for both sectors can be seen in terms of making more effective the flow of personnel from the education system into the employment system; from the standpoint of the individual the two corresponding problems, are; firstly, occupational choice; and secondly, organisational choice. The nature of the attempts of the nation on the one hand, and organisations on the other, to influence this movement, and to make it more effective, can be seen in the form of manpower (personnel) policies and programmes. It is important to point out, that such policies and programmes represent attempts to influence attitudes and behaviour by changing the structure of the situation in some way, and the extent of this influence will depend not only on how individuals react to and relate to such policies and programmes, but also on individual characteristics and volitions.

Given the importance of national manpower policies and programmes as influences on personnel flow, the major focus of attention here has been with organisational personnel policies and programmes, and their attitudinal and behavioural consequences. In this context, schools and universities could be regarded as organisations, and as the research results have shown, the various social and organisational characteristics of such organisations play an important role in the career choice process.

However, the approach adopted has been to look at manpower planning from the standpoint of employing organisations, and the suggestion made that such organisations do have the means to influence the attitudes and behaviour of staff. The process by which this takes place is highly complex, and involves the interaction of the various personnel policies and programmes, in accordance with the model developed in Chapter 1. Thus, the recruitment and selection of the right quantity and quality will depend on the effectiveness of other personnel policies, such as payment and promotion opportunities. Similarly, promotion will depend on the recruitment of staff, the identification of talent through appraisal, and the nature of the opportunities available. However, the other key element in the model is the reaction of individuals to the operation of such personnel policies and practices, and this will depend on a combination of factors including overall career considerations and aspirations, expectations (as a result of both external and internal events) and experience of their job and work situation. Thus the reaction of an individual to a decline in promotion prospects, or to a failure to obtain a salary rise, or to an ineffective appraisal system, will depend on the relative importance of these factors to him personally, in terms of the above considerations. The role, therefore, of organisational personnel policies in influencing staff attitudes and behaviour must be seen in the light not only of staff reaction to each policy, but also of staff reaction to the combined policies, and to both external structural features, and psychological characteristics. This is not to say that the role of such policies will be diminished rather that it must be seen in context. On the contrary, the results of the graduate research in Chapter 4 showed clearly that organisations do differ markedly in terms of the effectiveness or otherwise of their personnel policies; effectiveness in fact, can be judged by the closeness of the relationship between individual goals and expectations, and organisational goals and policies.

This latter point is the crux of the whole manpower planning problem. All too often policies are formulated without regard either for the realities of the situation or for the consequences of implementing such policies, with the result that reaction to events takes place at the expense of planning to avoid such situations. The recent decision of some universities in the light of the need for financial stringency to fill posts only at the lower end of each grade is a classic example of a reactive policy which will lead to manpower difficulties in the future. Perhaps the most depressing aspect of such decisions is the fact that often evidence is available to show the folly of such action (in the case of the university system, for example, Young[33] has painted a highly relevant picture of promotion blockages).

The nature of manpower planning processes has been described and examined. The relationship between manpower planning, manpower research, manpower management, and manpower policy has been highlighted, and the case for treating these as interrelated parts of the same process has been put. The major problem remains not only of obtaining widespread acceptance of such ideas, but of obtaining action. Given both motivation and action, the need is to ensure that the results of actions are fed back into the system and change introduced where it is thought desirable and necessary.

Of necessity, the studies in this book are limited in scope and are used specifically to highlight the role of expectations and aspirations on the part of employees and potential employees, the workings of systems for arranging personnel flow, and the different reactions that similar groups of employees will develop to various aspects of personnel policies in organisations. There is a need for wider research in this area to explore further some of the disparities and differences revealed, and to relate some of the issues highlighted here to different organisational levels. It would be useful to relate the notion of occupational choice to personnel policy considerations at all organisational levels and for different and probably conflicting organisational interest groups.

APPENDIX

TRENDS IN THE UK GRADUATE MARKET

(a)

Year	Men	Numbers Graduating Women	Total	Index
1964	18,396	7,022	25,418	100
1966	23,562	8,644	32,166	127
1968	30,151	12,464	42,615	168
1970	33,343	14,241	47,584	187

(b) Employment Obtained

Destination	1964 Men %	Women %	Total %	1966 Men %	Women %	Total %	1968 Men %	Women %	Total %	1970 Men %	Women %	Total %
UK Employment	40·3	30·9	38·0	42·9	31·9	40·0	44·9	31·9	41·0	40·6	28·3	37·0
Other training	5·9	10·4	7·0	5·6	10·6	7·0	5·1	10·5	6·0	5·9	10·8	7·0
Teacher training	12·2	32·7	18·0	9·9	28·7	15·0	9·3	27·7	15·0	9·0	28·0	15·0
Research/study	23·4	10·5	20·0	22·7	12·1	21·4	21·4	12·0	19·0	19·6	11·2	17·0
All others	18·2	15·5	17·0	18·9	16·7	18·0	19·3	17·9	19·0	24·9	21·7	24·0

(c) Graduates Entering Industry and Commerce

	1964	1966	1968	1970
Number	5,574	8,064	10,958	11,030
Index	100	144	197	198

Source: '*First Employment of University Graduates*' published by the University Grants Committee.

TREND IN THE GRADUATE REQUIREMENTS OF A SAMPLE OF
TWENTY-FIVE INDUSTRIAL ORGANISATIONS

Company	Industry	1964	1966	1968	1970	1972
The Bowater Org.	Publishing	15	NIL	35	40	25
British Aluminium	Engineering	20	30	40	40	40
GKN	Engineering	45	45	80	80	90
Babcock & Wilcox	Engineering	20	20	50	50	50
Dunlop	Engineering	45	45	90	100	100
Laing	Engineering	30	50	50	55	45
Hawker Siddley	Engineering	70	70	130	100	40
Westland Group	Engineering	20	20	20	40	30
Esso Petroleum	Oil	50	30	100	75	75
Shell-Mex & BP Ltd	Oil	30	50	50	50	50
Burroughs	Business machines	100	80	50	40	80
IBM	Computers	150	150	200	200	100
Ferranti	Electronics	40	40	50	40	50
EMI	Electronics	75	50	80	80	50
Beecham	Pharmacy	30	25	70	100	70
Fisons	Pharmacy	30	40	50	30	20
The Rank Org.	Films	20	40	70	110	100
British Oxygen	Industrial gases	60	60	55	75	50
Cadbury's	Confectionery	15	20	30	30	30
Lewis's	Retailing	30	30	60	40	25
Kodak	Photography	10	30	80	70	70
Courtaulds	Textiles	60	60	60	200	12
Legal & General	Insurance	30	45	30	35	700
BMC	Cars	50	50	70	200	175
Ford	Cars	70	75	125	125	NIL
Total graduate requirement		1,115	1,155	1,725	2,005	1,555
Index		100	104	155	179	139
Civil service requirement		800	1,100	2,000	2,000	2,000
Index		100	138	250	250	260

Source: The Directory of Opportunities for Graduates (Cornmarket Press).

REFERENCE NOTES

CHAPTER 1
1 Eli Ginzberg, *The Development of Human Resources* (McGraw-Hill Inc., 1966), p. 1.
2 Eric W. Vetter, *Manpower Planning for High Talent Personnel* (Univ. of Michigan, 1967), p. 12.
3 A. R. Smith, 'An Introduction', *Manpower Research*, N. A. B. Wilson (ed.), English Univ. Press, 1970, pp. 3–5.
4 J. K. Galbraith, 'The Principle of Consistency', *Personnel Administration* (Jan./Feb. 1970).
5 D. Newton, 'What Manpower Planning Means', *Management Today* (July 1970), p. 8.
6 D. Newton, 'Controlling and Evaluating Personnel Strategy', *Long-Range Planning*, vol. 4, no. 1 (June 1969), pp. 24–35.
7 See for a useful discussion of this Garth L. Mangum, *The Goals of Manpower Policy* (Prentice-Hall Inc., 1969)
8 R. L. Ackoff, *A Concept of Corporate Planning* (John Wiley, 1970).
9 H. Igor Ansoff, 'A Quasi-Analytic Method for Long-Range Planning' *Modern Financial Management*, B. V. Carsberg and H. C. Eden (eds), (Penguin, 1969), p. 304.
10 A. Chambers, 'Planning and Achieving Profitable Growth' *Aspects of Corporate Planning* (ICWA 1970), p. 36.
11 See for example, T. Lupton, *Industrial Behaviour and Personnel Management* (IPM London, 1964).
12 Described in J. Kelly, *Organisational Behaviour* (Irwin, 1970).
13 P. M. Blau, *The Dynamics of Bureaucracy: A Study of Interpersonal Relationships in Two Government Agencies* (Univ. of Chicago Press, 1955).
14 A. W. Gouldner, *Patterns of Industrial Bureaucracy* (Routledge & Kegan Paul, 1955).
15 See, for example, W. Kochler *The Place of Values in the World of Fact* (Liveright, 1938), Ch. 8, pp. 314–28; and L. Von Bertanlanffy, 'The Theory of Open Systems in Physics and Biology', *Science* vol. 3 (1950), pp. 23–9.
16 F. E. Emery and E. L. Trist, 'Socio-Technical Systems' *Management Science, Models and Techniques*, C. W. Churchman and M. Verhulst (eds), vol. 2 (Pergamon, 1960), pp. 83–97.
17 D. Katz and R. L. Kahn, *The Social Psychology of Organisations* (Wiley, 1966), Ch. 2, pp. 14–29.
18 See, for example, A. K. Rice, *Productivity and Social Organisation: The Ahmedabad Experiment* (Tavistock, 1958); and E. L. Trist and K. W. Bamforth, 'Some Social and Psychological Consequences of the Longwall Method of Coal Mining', *Human Relations*, vol. 4 (1955).
19 Katz and Kahn, op. cit., p. 29.
20 J. Fieblemann and J. W. Friend, 'The Structure and Function of Organisation', *Philosophical Review*, vol. 54 (1945), pp. 19–44.

21 Department of Employment and Productivity, *Company Manpower Planning*, Manpower Papers, no. 1 (HMSO, 1968).
22 James W. Walker, 'Forecasting Manpower Needs', *Harvard Business Review* (March/April 1969), pp. 152–64.
23 E. Geisler, *Manpower Planning: An Emerging Staff Function* (New York, AMA, 1967), p. 8.
24 D. Barber, *The Practice of Personnel Management* (IPM, 1970).
25 D. Hood, 'Practical Manpower Planning', *Personnel and Training Management* (June 1968), pp. 12–15.
26 I. Gascoigne, 'Manpower Forecasting at the Enterprise Level: A Case Study', *British Journal of Industrial Relations*, vol. 6., part 1 (1968), pp. 94–106.
27 K. F. Lane and J. E. Andrew, 'A Method of Labour Turnover Analysis' *Royal Statistical Society, Journal Series A*, 118 (1955), pp. 296–323.
28 Vetter, op. cit., p. 15.
29 D. Pym, 'Technical Change and the Misuse of Professional Manpower: Some Observations', *Occupational Psychology*, vol. 41, no. 1 (Jan. 1967), pp. 1–16.
30 D. J. Bell, W. R. Hawes, C. G. Lewis and C. J. Purkiss, 'Manpower Planning at the level of the firm' *Manpower Planning: A Bibliography*, C. G. Lewis (ed.) (English Univ. Press, 1969).
31 G. McBeath, *Organisation and Manpower Planning* (Business Publications, 1966).
32 R. A. Denerley and R. P. Plumbley, *Recruitment and Selection in a Full Employment Economy* (IPM, 1967).
33 Walker, op. cit.
34 Frank H. Cassell, 'Government and Managerial Manpower Planning' *Managerial Manpower Planning* (Educational Testing Service, Princeton, 1967), pp. 57–72.
35 This in turn has interesting consequences for sectional behaviour within and between universities.
36 E. Ginzberg, 'A Manpower Policy for Canada', lecture to Canadian Imperial Bank of Commerce, 1969.
37 J. R. Miller, 'Computer Simulation of Human Behaviour in Organisations', *Industrial Management Review*, (Winter 1970), p. 25.
38 Vetter, op. cit.
39 M. Haire, 'A New Look at Human Resources' *Industrial Managerial Review* (Winter 1970), pp. 17–23.
40 G. L. Buckingham and D. T. B. North, *Productivity Agreements and Wage Systems* (Gower Press, 1969).
41 C. Sofer, *Men in Mid Career* (Cambridge Univ. Press, 1970), p. 15.
42 Shell Refining Company, *Statement of Objectives and Philosophy*, Internal document.
43 W. A. Faunce, *Problems of an Industrial Society* (McGraw-Hill, 1968).
44 R. A. Lester, *Manpower Planning in a Free Society* (Princeton Univ. Press, 1966).
45 Edinburgh Group, *Perspectives in Manpower Planning* (Institute of Personnel Management, 1968).
46 DEP op. cit.
47 For a full discussion of the problems facing trade unions, see A. J. M.

Sykes, *The Problems facing British Trade Unions*, Univ. of Strathclyde working paper 1965.
48 Walker, op. cit.
49 D. H. Gray, *Manpower Planning* (IPM London, 1966), p. 9.
50 M. Stycos, 'Problems of Fertility Control in Underdeveloped countries' *Town Planning Review* (1966).
51 Gray, op. cit., p. 16.
52 Walker, op. cit.
53 A. Moss, 'An Approach to Manpower Forecasting' *The Business Economist*, vol. 2, no. 2 (1970).
54 Moss, ibid.
55 Alan Fox, *Industrial Sociology and Industrial Relations*, Royal Commission on Trade Unions and Employers Associations, Research Paper no. 3 (HMSO, 1965).
56 Eric Rhenman, *Industrial Democracy and Industrial Management* (Tavistock, 1967).
57 Michael Hall, 'Towards a Manpower Grid', *Personnel Management* (June, 1965), pp. 72–8.
58 J. R. Crossley, 'Essential Statistics for Manpower Forecasting', *Manpower Policy and Employment Trends* B. C. Roberts and J. H. Smith (eds) (Bell Pub. Co. for LSE, 1966).
59 Ministry of Labour Manpower Research Unit, *The Pattern of the Future*, Manpower Studies no. 1 (HMSO, 1964).
60 See, e.g. UK Committee in Manpower Resources for Science and Technology *Report of the 1965 Triennial Manpower Survey of Engineers, Technologists, Scientists and Supporting Staff*, Cmnd 3103 (HMSO, 1966).
61 The Department of Economic Affairs, *The National Plan* (HMSO, 1965).
62 Ministry of Labour Manpower Research Unit, op. cit.
63 E. Evans, 'Budgeting for Manpower' *Planning Industrial Training* (NIAE, 1968).
64 C. Leicester, 'Manpower Planning at the National Level', *Manpower Planning – A Bibliography*, C. G. Lewis (ed.), (English Univ. Press, 1969).
65 Hall, op. cit.
66 Edinburgh Group, op. cit.
67 T. L. Johnston, 'State Policy Company Practice', *Personnel Management* (1968), pp. 28–31.
68 L. C. Hunter and G. L. Reid, *Urban Worker Mobility* (OECD, Paris, 1968).
69 Hunter and Reid, ibid.
70 Cassell, op. cit.
71 Johnston, op. cit., p. 28.
72 See, e.g. *The Intermediate Areas*, Report of a Committee under the Chairmanship of Sir Joseph Hunt, Cmnd 3998 (HMSO, 1969).
73 For example, the Royal Mint in Wales, the Giro in Bootle, the Post Office in Scotland.
74 Johnston, op. cit.
75 See, e.g. UK Estimates Committee of House of Commons, 9th Report, *Manpower Training for Industry* (HMSO, 1967).
76 See, e.g. G. Hansen, 'Now we are Six', *Personnel Management*

(August 1970), pp. 12–17 and W. J. Giles, 'Training after the Act' *Personnel Management* (June 1969), pp. 20–7.

77 G. A. Yewdall, 'Manpower Planning at Industry Level', *Manpower Planning: A Bibliography* C. G. Lewis (ed.) (English Univ. Press, 1969).

78 Amalgamated Engineering Union, *Evidence to Royal Commission on Trade Unions and Employers' Association* (HMSO, 1965).

79 J. Jones, 'A Trade Union Attitude to the More Efficient Use of Manpower', *Management and Manpower Utilisation* (DEP/IPM/BIM, Harrogate, 1968), pp. 11–15.

80 Edinburgh Group, op. cit., p. 28.

81 Newton, op. cit. (1970), p. 8.

82 Hall, op. cit., p. 74.

83 Newton, op. cit. (1970), p. 8.

84 Jean Cox, 'Manpower Planning at National and Company Level', unpublished paper (1970).

85 Hall, op. cit., p. 74.

86 Vetter, op. cit., p. 84.

87 PIB, *Report* No. 8, Cmnd 2873 (Jan. 1966).

88 PIB, *Report on Overtime Working in Britain,* no. 161, Cmnd 4554 (Dec. 1970).

89 Pym, op. cit.

90 Edinburgh Group, op. cit., p. 44.

91 See, e.g. V. H. Vroom, *Work and Motivation* (Wiley, 1967).

92 See, e.g. J. H. Goldthorpe, 'Attitudes and Behaviour of Car Assembly Workers', *British Journal Sociology* (Sept. 1966), pp. 227–44.

93 See, e.g. A. Fox, *Industrial Sociology and Industrial Relations*, Royal Commission on Trade Unions and Employers' Association, Research Paper no. 3 (1965).

94 Newton, op. cit. (1969).

95 Edinburgh Group, op. cit., p. 45.

96 Walker, op. cit., p. 160.

97 Vetter, op. cit., p. 181.

98 H. G. Heneman Jnr and G. Seltzer, *Manpower Planning and Forecasting in the Firm: An Exploratory Probe* (Univ. of Minnesota, 1968).

99 E. S. M. Chadwick, 'Manpower Planning in the BP Company', *Manpower Research*, N. A. B. Wilson (ed.) (English Univ. Press, 1970).

100 Newton, op. cit. (1969).

101 P. R. Hodgson, 'Manpower Planning at the Level of the Firm', *BACIE Journal* (1967).

102 D. Wedderburn, *Co-ordinated and Technical Manpower Planning for Change* (OECD, Paris, 1967).

103 J. W. Kuhn, *Scientific and Managerial Manpower in the Nuclear Industry* (Columbia Univ. Press, New York, 1966).

104 D. T. Bryant, 'A Survey of the Development of Manpower Planning Policies', *British Journal of Industrial Relations,* vol. 3 (1965), pp. 279–90.

105 A. K. Rice, J. M. M. Hill and E. L. Trist, 'The Representation of Labour Turnover as a Social Process', *Human Relations* 3 (1950), pp. 349–72.

106 H. Silcock, 'The Phenomenon of Labour Turnover', *Royal Statistical Society*, Journal Series, A, 117 (1954).

107 F. J. Gaudet, 'The Literature on Labour Turnover', *Industrial Relations Newsletter Inc.* (New York 1960).

108 M. Hedberg, 'The Turnover of Labour in Industry: An Actuarial Study', *Acta Sociologica*, vol. 5 (1961), pp. 129–43.

109 Silcock, op. cit.

110 Chadwick, op. cit., p. 54.

111 D. J. Bartholomew, *Stochastic Models of Social Processes* (Wiley, New York, 1969).

112 Bartholomew, 'Note on the Measurement and Production of Labour Turnover', *Royal Statistical Society*, Journal Series A, 122 (1959), pp. 232–9.

113 D. J. Bartholomew, 'A Multi-Stage Renewal Process', *Royal Statistical Society*, Journal Series B, 25 (1963), pp. 150–68.

114 D. J. Bartholomew, 'Renewal Theory Models for Manpower Systems' *Manpower Research*, N. A. B. Wilson (ed.) (English Univ. Press, 1970), pp. 120–8.

115 A. Young, 'Demographic and Ecological Models for Manpower Planning', *Manpower Planning*, D. J. Bartholomew (ed.) (1972).

116 M. G. Kendall, 'Mathematical Models for Manpower Planning', *Manpower Research*, N. A. B. Wilson (ed.), pp. 114–19.

117 W. R. Dill, D. P. Gaver and W. L. Weber, 'Models and Modelling for Manpower Planning', *Management Science* 13 (1966), pp. 13–142.

118 S. Eilon, 'OR – An Approach to Problem Solving', *Personnel Management* (July 1970), pp. 30–4.

119 A. Young, 'Models for Planning Recruitment and Promotion of Staff', *British Journal of Industrial Relations*, vol 3, part 3 (1965), pp. 301–10.

120 M. Haire, 'A New Look at Human Resources', *Industrial Management Review* (Winter 1970), pp. 17–23.

121 Edinburgh Group, op. cit., p. 55.

122 J. R. Miller, op. cit. p. 25.

123 M. L. Lavin, 'Strategy in Modelling Manpower Problems', *Industrial Management Review* (Winter 1970), p. 50.

124 Miller, op. cit., p. 29.

125 W. G. McCelland, 'Career Patterns and Organisational Needs', *A.T.M. Occasional Papers* (September 1968), pp. 19–33.

126 A. Cox, 'Personnel Planning, Objectives, and Methods', *Management International Review*, vol. 4/5 (1968), pp. 104–14.

127 M. Hedberg, 'The Turnover of Labour in Industry: An Actuarial Study', *Acta Sociologica*, vol. 5, pp. 129–43.

128 Young, op. cit. (1972).

129 J. Woodward (ed.), *Industrial Organisation: Behaviour and Control* (Oxford Univ. Press, 1970).

130 C. Perrow, *Organisational Analysis: A Sociological View* (Tavistock, 1970).

131 G. K. Ingham, *Size of Industrial Organisation and Worker Behaviour* (Cambridge Univ. Press, 1970).

132 J. H. Goldthorpe, D. Lockwood, F. Bechhofer and J. Platt, *The Affluent Worker: Industrial Attitudes and Behaviour* (Cambridge Univ. Press., 1968.

133 Vroom, op. cit.

134 C. Argyris, *Personality and Organisation* (Harper and Row, 1957).

135 D. McGregor, *The Human Side of the Enterprise* (McGraw-Hill, 1960).
136 Fox, op. cit.

CHAPTER 2

1 F. G. Harbison and C. A. Myers, *Education Manpower and Economic Growth* (McGraw-Hill, 1964).
2 Harbison and Myers, op. cit., p. 2.
3 A. Crichton, *Personnel Management in Context* (Batsford, 1968), p. 170.
4 R. King, *Education* (Longmans, 1969), p. 1.
5 C. Leicester, *Manpower Planning: A Bibliography* (English Univ. Press, 1969), p. 3.
6 N. Sanford (ed.), *The American College* (Wiley, 1962).
7 The Edinburgh Group, *Manpower Planning in Perspective* (Institute of Personnel Management, 1969).
8 D. McDowell, Review of J. S. Coleman, 'Education and Political Development' *Higher Education Review* (Autumn 1969), p. 79.
9 J. K. Galbraith, *The Affluent Society* (Penguin, 1962).
10 M. Carter, *Into Work* (Penguin, 1969), p. 28.
11 Carter, op. cit., p. 29.
12 Schools Council Working Party, *Curriculum Reform in Sixth Form Education* (HMSO, 1970).
13 T. Gretton, 'The Job Market for Graduates', *New Society* (June 1969).
14 R. S. Adams, 'Analysing the Teacher Role', *Educational Research* (Feb. 1970).
15 F. Eggan, *in* McDowell op. cit., p. 79.
16 M. Shanks, *The Innovators: The Economics of Technology* (Penguin, 1967), p. 107.
17 King, op. cit.
18 Carter, op. cit., p. 32.
19 Adams, op. cit.
20 'The Employment Frontier' (Editorial), *Trends in Education* (Jan. 1967), p. 3.
21 E. Ginzberg and associates, *Manpower Strategy for the Metropolis* (Columbia Univ. Press, New York, 1968).
22 M. Blaug, J. E. Peston and D. Eiderman, *The Utilisation of Educated Manpower in Industry* (Oliver and Boyd, 1969).
23 Carter, op. cit., p. 29.
24 Report of the Committee on Higher Education under the Chairmanship of Lord Robbins, *Higher Education*, Cmnd 2154 (HMSO, 1963).
25 W. P. Kuvlesky and R. C. Bealer, 'A Clarification of the Concept of Occupational Choice', *Rural Sociology*, vol. 31, no. 3 (1966), p. 265.
26 A. Roe, *The Psychology of Occupations* (Wiley, 1956), p. 251.
27 V. H. Vroom, *Work and Motivation* (Wiley, 1964).
28 L. T. Keil, D. S. Riddell and B. S. R. Green, 'Youth and Work – Problems and Perspectives', *Sociological Review*, vol. 14 (1966), pp. 117–37.
29 J. Ford and S. Box, 'Sociological Theory and Occupational Choice', *Sociological Review*, vol. 15, no. 3 (1967), p. 287.

30   F. Katz and H. W. Martin, 'Career Choice Processes', *Social Forces*, vol. 41 (1962), pp. 149–54.
31   T. H. Caplow, *The Sociology of Work* (McGraw-Hill, 1963).
32   Ford and Box, op. cit.
33   R. S. Sherlock and D. A. Cohen, 'Recruitment into Dentistry', *Social Forces*, vol. 41 (1962).
34   G. Psathas, 'Towards a Theory of Occupational Choice for Women', *Sociology and Social Research*, vol. 52, no. 2 (1962).
35   L. G. Reynolds, *The Structure of Labour Markets* (Greenwood, Connecticut, 1951).
36   P. M. Blau, J. W. Gustad, R. Jesser, H. S. P. Ames, and R. C. Wilcock, 'Occupational Choice: A Conceptual Framework', *Industrial and Labour Relations Review*, vol. 9, no. 4 (1956).
37   Ford and Box, op. cit.
38   Vroom, op. cit.
39   R. K. Merton, *The Student-Physician* (Free Press, New York, 1957), p. 68.
40   S. Rottenberg, 'On choice in Labour Markets', *Industrial and Labour Relations Review*, vol. 9 (1965), pp. 183–99.
41   A. Smith, *An Inquiry into the Nature and Causes of the Wealth of Nations* (Modern Library Edition, 1937).
42   Vroom, op. cit.
43   Blau *et al.*, op. cit., p. 537.
44   Kalder and D. G. Zytowski, 'Occupational Decision Making', unpublished working paper (Iowa State Univ.).
45   Kuvlesky and Bealer, op. cit.
46   S. White, 'The Process of Occupational Choice', *British Journal of Industrial Relations*, vol. 6, no. 2 (1968), pp. 166–84.
47   Vroom, op. cit.
48   White, op. cit.
49   White, ibid., p. 166.
50   E. Ginzberg *et al.*, *Occupational Choice: An Approach to a General Theory* (Columbia Univ. Press, New York, 1951).
51   D. E. Super, *The Psychology of Careers* (Harper & Row, 1957).
52   Ginzberg, *et al.*, op. cit.
53   Ginzberg, *et al.*, ibid., p. 49.
54   White, op. cit., p. 170.
55   Ginzberg, *et al.*, op. cit., p. 57.
56   K. Roberts, 'The Entry into Employment', *Sociological Review*, vol. 2 (1968), pp. 165–84.
57   L. G. Burchinal, 'Career Choices of Rural Youth in a Changing Society' Minnesota Agr. Exp. Station, NCRP 142 (1962).
58   Kuvlesky and Bealer, op. cit.
59   White, op. cit., p. 168.
60   Super, op. cit.; and also 'A Theory of Vocational Development', *American Psychologist*, vol. 6 (1953), pp. 185–90.
61   Super, ibid., p. 190.
62   Vroom, op. cit., p. 74.
63   R. L. Morrison, 'Self Concept Implementation in Occupation Choice', *Journal of Counselling Psychology,* vol. 9 (1962).
64   J. Holland, 'A Theory of Vocational Choice', *Journal of Counselling Psychology*, vol. 6 (1954), pp. 35–45.

65 Roe, op. cit.
66 E. H. Erikson, 'The Problem of Ego Identity and Growth and Crisis of the Health Personality', *Psychology Issues*, vol. 1, no. 1 (1959), p. 45.
67 White, op. cit.
68 V. S. Sommers, 'Vocational Choice as an Expression of Conflict in Identification', *American Journal of Psychotherapy*, vol. 10 (1956), pp. 520–35.
69 M. D. Galinsky and I. Fast, 'Vocational Choice as a Form of Identity Search' *Journal of Counselling Psychology*, vol. 13, no. 1 (1969), pp. 89–92.
70 F. E. Katz and J. W. Martin, 'Career Choice Processes', *Social Forces*, vol. 41 (1962), pp. 149–54.
71 Katz and Martin, ibid., p. 149.
72 Blau *et al.*, op. cit., p. 536.
73 Ford and Box, op. cit.
74 Roberts, op. cit.
75 R. M. Stephenson, 'Realism of Vocational Choice: a Critique and an Example', *Personnel and Guidance Journal*, vol. 35 (1957), pp. 482–8.
76 Kuvlesky and Bealer, op. cit.
77 Kuvlesky and Bealer, ibid., p. 267.
78 A. O. Haller and I. W. Miller, 'The Occupational Aspiration Scale: Theory, Structure and Correlates', Michigan Agr. Exp. Station, no. 288 (1963).
79 Kuvlesky and Bealer, op. cit., p. 274.
80 F. G. Caro and C. T. Philblad, 'Aspirations and Expectations', *Sociology and Social Research*, vol. 49 (1964–5), pp. 465–74.
81 F. Heider, *The Psychology of Interpersonal Relations* (Wiley, 1958).
82 Caro and Philblad, op. cit., p. 469.
83 W. B. Cannon, *The Wisdom of the Body* (Norton, New York, 1932).
84 L. Festinger, *A Theory of Cognitive Dissonance* (Stanford Univ. Press, California, 1957).
85 K. Davis and N. F. Moore, 'Some Principles of Stratification', *American Sociological Review*, vol. 10 (1954), pp. 245–9.
86 R. Stagner and N. Rosen, *The Psychology of Union-Management Relations* (Tavistock, 1966), p. 21.
87 Roe, op. cit.
88 D. G. Zytowski, *The Concept of Work Values*, unpublished paper (Iowa State Univ.).
89 See, for example, C. H. Miller, 'Occupational Choice and Values', *Personnel and Guidance Journal*, vol 35 (1956), pp. 244–6. J. L. Schwarzweller, 'Values and Occupational Choice', *Social Forces*, vol. 30 (1960), pp. 126–35. R. C. Simpson and I. H. Simpson, 'Values, Personal Influence and Occupational Choice', *Social Forces*, vol. 39 (1960), pp. 116–25. J. A. Davis, *Undergraduates Career Decisions* (Aldine, 1965).
90 Vroom, op. cit.
91 D. C. McLelland, 'Some Social Consequences of Achievement Motivation' *Symposium on Motivation*, M. R. Jones (ed. (Nebraska Univ. Press, 1955).
92 J. W. Atkinson, 'Motivational Determinants of Risk Taking Behaviour', *Psychological Review*, vol. 64. (1957), pp. 359–72.

93 E. Burnstein, 'Fear of Failure, Achievement Motivation, and Aspiring to Prestigeful Occupations', *Journal of Abnormal Social Psychology*, vol. 67 (1963), pp. 189–93.

94 J. G. Seashore, 'Validation of the Study of Values for Two Vocational Groups at the College Level', *Educational and Psychological Measurement*, vol. 7 (1947), pp. 757–63.

95 M. Rosenberg, *Occupations and Values* (Free Press, New York, 1957).

96 Vroom, op. cit., p. 62.

97 Vroom, ibid, p. 64.

98 B. R. Forer, 'Personality Factors in Occupational Choice', *Educational Psychological Measurement*, vol 13 (1953), p. 361.

99 J. Veroff *et al.*, 'The Use of Thematic Apperception to Assess Motivation in a Nationwide Interview Study', *Psychological Monographs* vol. 74, no. 12 (1960).

100 H. H. Meyer, W. B. Waler and G. H. Litwin, 'Motive Patterns and Risk Preferences Associated with Entrepreneurship', *Journal of Abnormal Social Psychology*, vol. 63 (1961), pp. 570–4.

101 D. C. McLelland, *The Achieving Society* (Van Nostrand, 1961).

102 Roe, op. cit.

103 Holland, op. cit., p. 35.

104 Vroom, op. cit., p. 82.

105 Zytowski, op. cit., p. 4.

106 Blau *et al.*, op. cit., p. 533.

107 Vroom, op. cit., p. 88.

108 Atkinson, op. cit.

109 D. R. Kaldor and D. G. Zytowski, *An Economic Model of Occupational Decision Making*, unpublished paper (Iowa State Univ.).

110 Rottenberg, op. cit., p. 56.

111 C. Kerr, 'Labour Markets: Their Character and Consequences', *American Economic Review* (May 1950), p. 278.

112 Rottenberg, op. cit., p. 87.

113 L. G. Reynolds and J. Shister, *Job Horizons* (Wiley, 1949).

114 C. Sofer, *Men in Mid Career* (Cambridge Univ. Press, 1970), p. 47.

115 Roe, op. cit.

116 Vroom, op. cit., p. 6.

117 Festinger, op. cit.

118 Sofer, op. cit., p. 45.

119 Keil, Riddell and Green, op. cit., p. 123.

120 P. Kelvin, *The Bases of Social Behaviour* (Holt, Reinhart & Winston, 1970).

121 D. C. Miller and W. H. Form, *Industrial Sociology* (Harper and Row, 1951).

122 Keil, Riddell and Green, op. cit., p. 123.

123 P. Musgrave, 'Towards a Sociological Theory of Occupational Choice', *Sociological Review*, vol. 15, no. 1 (1967).

124 Musgrave, ibid.

125 N. A. Coulson, E. T. Keil, D. S. Riddell and J. S. Struthers, 'Towards a Sociological Theory of Occupational Choice: A Critique', *Sociological Review*, vol. 15, no. 3 (1967), p. 301.

126 Keil, Riddell and Green, op. cit., p. 123.

127 Ford and Box, op. cit., p. 293.

128 Kaldor and Zatowski, op. cit.

129 Rottenberg, op. cit.
130 Psathas, op. cit.
131 Reynolds, op. cit.; Keil, Riddell and Green, op. cit.
132 B. Ashley, H. Cohen, D. McIntyre and R. Slatter, 'A Sociological Analysis of Students' Reasons for Becoming Teachers', *Sociological Review*, vol. 18, no. 1 (1970), pp. 53–69.
133 T. Parsons and E. A. Shills, *Towards a General Theory of Action* (Harper & Row, 1951), p. 190.
134 Psathas, op. cit., p. 253.
135 Roberts, op. cit.
136 Roberts, ibid., p. 172.
137 T. Veness, *School leavers* (Methuen, 1962).
138 Rosenberg, op. cit.
139 R. K. Kelsall, 'Self Recruitment in Four Professions', *Social Mobility in Britain* V. D. Glass (ed.) (Routledge & Kegan Paul, 1954).
140 R. Bendix, S. M. Lipset and F. T. Malm, 'Social Origins and Occupational Career Patterns', *Industrial and Labour Relations Review*, vol. 7 (1954).
141 W. Sewell, A. D. Haller and M. Strauss, 'Social Status and Educational and Occupational Aspirations', *American Sociological Review*, vol. 22 (1957), pp. 67–73.
142 W. Liversedge, 'Life Chances', *Sociological Review*, vol. 10 (1962), pp. 17–34.
143 White, op. cit., p. 182.
144 See, for example S. M. Chown, 'The Formation of Occupational Choice Among Grammar School Pupils', *Occupational Psychology*, vol. 32 (1958), pp. 171–82; and G. Jahoda, 'Job Attitudes and Job Choice Among Secondary Modern School Leavers', *Occupational Psychology*, vol. 26 (1952), pp. 125–40.
145 Report of the Central Advisory Council for Education, *15 to 18*, The Crowther Report (HMSO, 1959).
146 J. W. Carper and H. S. Becker, 'Adjustment to Conflicting Expectations in the Development of Identification with an Occupation', *Social Forces*, vol 36 (1957–8), pp. 51–6.
147 King, op. cit., p. 10.
148 The Robbins Report, op. cit., p. 45.
149 J. E. Floud, A. M. Halsey and F. M. Martin, *Social Class and Educational Opportunity* (Heinemann, 1956).
150 Kelsall, op. cit.
151 B. Bernstein, 'Some Sociological Determinants of Perception', *British Journal of Sociology*, vol. 9 (1958).
152 J. W. B. Douglas, *The Home and the School* (McGibbon and Kee, 1964).
153 Keil, Riddell and Green, op. cit., p. 129.
154 O. Banks, *Parity and Prestige in English Secondary Education* (Routledge & Kegan Paul, 1955).
155 A. Crichton, *Personnel Management in Context* (Batsford, 1968), p. 172.
156 M. P. Carter, *Home, School and Work* (Pergamon, 1962).
157 Liversedge, op. cit., p. 33.
158 King, op. cit., p. 8.

159 E. Durkheim, *The Division of Labour in Society* (Free Press, New York 1933).

160 T. Blackstone, 'The Plowden Report', *British Journal of Sociology*, vol. 18 (1967), pp. 291–302.

161 Veness, op. cit.

162 A. Rodger, *The Recruitment and Training of Youth Employment Officers* (Youth Employment, 1954).

163 J. Maizels, 'The Entry of School Leavers into Employment' *British Journal of Industrial Relations*, vol. 3, no. 1 (1965).

164 T. G. P. Rodgers and P. Williams, *The Recruitment and Training of Graduates* (IPM, 1970).

165 L. Taylor, *Occupational Sociology* (Oxford Univ. Press, 1968), p. 216.

166 Vroom, op. cit.

CHAPTER 3

1 The Edinburgh Group, *Perspective in Manpower Planning* (IPM, 1967), p. 85.

2 S. R. Parker, R. K. Brown J. Child and M. A. Smith, *The Sociology of Industry* (George Allen & Unwin, 1967), p. 31.

3 P. E. Drucker, 'The Educational Revolution', *Education, Economy and Society*, A. H. Halsey, J. E. Floud and C. A. Anderson (eds), (Glencoe Press, New York, 1962), p. 15.

4 A. H. Halsey, 'The Changing Functions of Universities', *Education, Economy and Society*, A. H. Halsey *et al.* (eds), op. cit., p. 463.

5 Drucker, op. cit. p. 4.

6 R. K. Merton, *Social Theory and Social Structure* (Free Press, New York, 1957), presents this useful distinction between 'manifest' and 'latent' functions.

7 F. E. Harbison and C. A. Myers, *Education, Manpower and Economic Growth* (McGraw-Hill, 1964).

8 S. R. Timperley and A. M. Gregory, 'Some Factors Affecting the Career Choices and Career Perceptions of Sixth Form School Leavers' *Sociological Review*, vol. 19, no. 1 (1971), pp. 95–114.

9 L. Taylor, *Occupational Sociology* (Oxford Univ. Press, 1968), p. 216.

10 Careers Research and Advisory Centre, *Beyond a Degree* (Whitefriars Press, 1970), pp. 42–64.

11 This figure includes CNAA graduates.

12 T. G. P. Rogers and P. Williams, *The Recruitment and Training of Graduates* (IPM, 1970).

13 CRAC, op. cit., p. 44.

14 P. R. Plumbley, 'Graduate Recruitment in the Seventies', *Management Decisions* (Spring, 1970), pp. 11–15.

15 Taylor, op. cit., p. 215.

16 P. Daws, 'What are you looking for?' CRAC, op. cit., pp. 6–11.

17 D. M. Monk, 'The Social Survey in Manpower Research', *Manpower Research*, N. A. B. Wilson (ed.) (English Univ. Press, 1969).

18 The Annual Report of the University of Liverpool Appointments Board for the year 1 October 1969–30 September 1970 shows that out of 1,723 students completing first and higher degree courses in 1970, 1,134 registered with the Board.

19 Timperley and Gregory, op. cit.
20 See, for example, W. H. Liversedge, 'Life Chances', *Sociological Review*, vol. 1 (1962), pp. 17–34.
21 F. Musgrave, 'Social Class and Levels of Aspiration in a Technological University', *Sociological Review*, vol. 15, no. 3 (1967), p. 311.
22 See, for example, K. Roberts, 'The Entry into Employment', *Sociological Review*, vol. 2 (1968), pp. 165–84; and P. W. Musgrave, 'Towards a Theory of Occupational Choice', *Sociological Review*, vol. 15, no. 1 (1967).
23 Committee of Manpower Resources for Science and Technology, Report of the Working Group on Manpower for Scientific Growth, *The Flow into Employment of Scientists, Engineers and Technologists*, Cmnd 3760 (HMSO, 1968). (Cited as the Swann Report.)
24 Council for Scientific Policy, *Enquiry into the Flow of Candidates in Science and Technology into Higher Education*, Cmnd 3541 (HMSO, 1968). (Cited as the Dainton Report.)
25 Committee on Manpower Resources for Science and Technology, Report of the Working Group on Migration, *The Brain Drain*, Cmnd 3417. (Cited as the Jones Report.)
26 K. G. Gannicott and M. Blaug, 'Manpower Forecasting since Robbins: A Science lobby in Action', *Higher Education Review* (Autumn, 1969), pp. 56–74.
27 Musgrave, op. cit., for example, talks in terms of 'prior role rehearsal'.
28 It is perhaps necessary to distinguish between types of work experience. Formal work experience is provided by sandwich courses for example, informal by vacation work for monetary purposes only, and there is a type of experience which comes midway between the formal and informal, namely vacation employment which is planned and which fulfils the criteria used for both formal and informal experiences.
29 Musgrave, op. cit.
30 K. Roberts, 'The Entry into Employment', *Sociological Review*, vol. 2 (1968), p. 165–84.
31 P. M. Blau, J. W. Gustad R. Jesser, J. S. P. Ames, and R. C. Wilcock, 'Occupational Choice: A Conceptual Framework', *Industrial and Labour Relations Review*, vol. 9, no. 4 (July 1956).
32 V. Vroom, *Work and Motivation* (Wiley, 1966).
33 Cambridge University Management Group, *Attitudes to Industry* (BIM, 1969).
34 University Grants Committee, A Report by the Rt. Hon. Lord Heyworth, University Appointments Boards, 50 Code No. 63–176 (HMSO, 1964).
35 Confederation of British Industry, A Report by a CBI Working Party, *Careers Guidance* (August 1969), p. 6.
36 See, for example, Blau *et al.*, op. cit.
37 Plumbley, op. cit.
38 Heyworth Report, op. cit.
39 P. Daws, 'What are you looking for?' *Beyond a Degree*, Careers Research and Advisory Centre (1970), pp. 6–11.
40 R. H. Turner, 'Modes of Social Ascent through Education: Sponsored and Contest Mobility' *American Sociological Review*, vol. 25 (1960).
41 See, for example, A. Young and G. Almond, 'Predicting Distribution of Staff', *The Computer Journal*, vol. 3, no. 4; and A. Young, 'Models

for Planning Recruitment and Promotion of Staff', *British Journal of Industrial Relations,* vol. 3, no. 3 (1965).

42   See, for example, F. Herzberg, *Work and the Nature of Man* (World Publishing Co., 1966).

43   W. Liversedge, 'Life Chances', *Sociological Review,* vol. 10 (1962).

44   Cambridge University Management Group, op. cit.

45   S. R. Timperley, 'The Recruitment and Training of Graduates: Some Issues', *Industrial Training International,* (November 1970), pp. 498–9.

46   Rogers and Williams, op. cit., p. 57.

47   Monk, op. cit.

CHAPTER 4

1   L. Taylor, *Occupational Sociology* (Oxford Univ. Press, 1968), p. 267.

2   H. L. Wilensky, 'Work, Careers and Social Integration', *International Social Science Journal,* vol. 12 (1960), pp. 543–60.

3   R. Dubin, *The World of Work* (Prentice-Hall Inc., 1958).

4   See, for example, D. Silverman and J. H. Goldthorpe, 'Formal Organisations or Industrial Sociology: Towards a Social Action Analysis of Organisations', *Sociology,* 2.2 (1968), pp. 221–38. 'Attitudes and Behaviour of Car Assembly Workers: A Deviant Case and a Theoretical Critique', *British Journal of Sociology,* XVII, 3 (1966), pp. 227–44.

5   J. H. Goldthorpe, D. Lockwood, F. Bechhoffer, and J. Platt, *The Affluent Worker: Industrial Attitudes and Behaviour* (Cambridge Univ. Press, 1968).

6   J. Child, *The Business Enterprise in Modern Industrial Society* (Collier-McMillan, 1969), p. 63.

7   S. R. Parker, 'The Subjective Experience of Work', *The Sociology of Industry,* S. R. Parker, R. K. Brown, J. Child and M. A. Smith (George Allen & Unwin, 1967), pp. 156–7.

8   R. H. Hall, *Occupations and the Social Structure* (Prentice-Hall Inc., 1969), p. 314.

9   Child, op. cit., p. 82.

10   C. Sofer, *Men in Mid Career* (Cambridge Univ. Press, 1970), p. 14.

11   J. D. Thompson, R. W. Avery and R. Carlson, *Occupations, Personnel and Careers* (Univ. of Pittsburgh, 1962).

12   J. P. Campbell, M. D. Dunnette, E. E. Lawler and K. E. Weick, *Managerial Behaviour, Performance and Effectiveness* (McGraw-Hill, 1970).

13   J. Woodward, 'Resistance to Change', *Management International Review,* 4/5 (1968).

14   T. Kynaston Reeves, 'A Model for Organisational Behaviour', *British Journal of Industrial Relations* (1968).

15   For a good discussion of the relationship between attitudes and behaviour see P. Kelvin, *The Bases of Social Behaviour* (Holt, Rinehart & Winston, 1969).

16   T. G. P. Rogers and P. Williams, *The Recruitment and Training of Graduates* (IPM, 1969), p. 55.

17   D. Pym, 'The Misuse of Professional Manpower' *Industrial Society,* D. Pym (ed.) (Penguin, 1968), p. 106.

18 Sofer, op. cit., p. 25.
19 E. Kay, H. H. Meyer, and J. R. P. French, 'Effects of Threat in a Performance Appraisal Interview', *Journal of Applied Psychology*, vol. 49, no. 5 (1965).
20 P. H. Thompson and G. W. Dalton, 'Performance Appraisal: Managers Beware', *Harvard Business Review* (Jan./Feb. 1970), pp. 149–57.
21 Thompson and Dalton, ibid., p. 149.
22 E. W. Vetter, *Manpower Planning for High Talent Personnel* (Univ. of Michigan, 1967), p. 77.
23 P. Pigors and C. A. Myers, *Personnel Administration*, 5th edn. (McGraw-Hill, 1965), p. 401.
24 Hall, op. cit., p. 307.
25 Vetter, op. cit., p. 63.
26 W. G. McLelland, 'Organisational Necessities and Individual Needs', *A.T.M. Journal* (1968).
27 Sofer, op. cit., p. 17.
28 T. Caplow, *Principles of Organisation* (Harcourt, Brace and World Inc., 1964), pp. 116–18.
29 F. Herzberg, *Work and the Nature of Man* (Staples Press, 1968).
30 W. R. Dill, T. L. Hilton, and W. R. Reitman, *The New Managers: Patterns of Behaviour and Development* (Prentice-Hall, 1962).
31 P. R. Hill, 'What Graduates Want from Shell', *The Financial Times* (Wednesday 28 May 1969), p. 15.
32 See for example, A. Pettigrew, 'Inter Group Conflict and Role Strain', *Journal of Management Studies*, vol. 5, no. 2 (1969); and R. L. Kahn *et al., Organisational Stress* (Wiley, 1964).
33 Young, e.g. uses grading systems as a basis for his technique of status profile analysis, see A. Young, 'Models for Planning Recruitment and Promotion of Staff', *British Journal of Industrial Relations*, vol. 3 (1965), pp. 301–10.
34 BIM, *Staff Grading Schemes* (1959).
35 Caplow, op. cit., p. 68.
36 BIM, op. cit.
37 See, for example, R. L. Opsahl and M. D. Dunnette, 'The Role of Financial Compensation in Industrial Motivation', *Psychological Bulletin*, vol. 66 (1966), pp. 94–118; M. Haire, 'The Incentive Character of Pay', *Managerial Compensation*, R. Andrews (ed.) (Ann Arbot, Michigan, 1965), pp. 13–17.
38 M. Dalton, 'Informal Factors in Career Achievement', *American Journal of Sociology*, vol. 56 (March 1961).
39 N. H. Martin and A. L. Strauss, 'Patterns of Mobility within Industrial Organisations', *Journal of Business*, vol. 29 (April 1956).
40 Sofer, op. cit., p. 25.
41 B. Bass, *Organisational Psychology* (Allyn & Bacon Inc., New Jersey, 1965), p. 99.
42 C. Argyris, *Personality and Organisation* (Harper & Row, 1957).
43 D. McGregor, 'The Human Side of Enterprise' (McGraw-Hill, 1960).
44 Herzberg, op. cit.
45 Parker, op. cit., p. 157.
46 Hill, op. cit.

47   A. Fox, *A Sociology of Work in Industry* (Collier-Macmillan, 1961), p. 7.

48   R. Dubin, 'Industrial Worker's Worlds: A Study of the Central Life Interests of Industrial Workers', *Social Problems*, vol. 3, no. 1 (1956), pp. 131–42.

49   J. H. Goldthorpe, D. Lockwood, F. Bechhofer and J. Platt, *The Affluent Worker: Industrial Attitudes and Behaviour* (Cambridge Univ. Press, 1968).

50   C. W. Mills, *White Collar* (Oxford Univ. Press, 1956).

51   V. H. Vroom, *Work and Motivation* (Wiley, 1964), p. 105.

52   McGregor, op. cit.

53   R. Likert, *The Human Organisation: Its Management and Value* (McGraw-Hill, 1967).

54   A. Fox, *Industrial Sociology and Industrial Relations*, Research Paper No. 3, Royal Commission on Trade Unions and Employers Associations (HMSO, 1966).

55   E. Rhenman, *Industrial Democracy and Industrial Management* (Tavistock, 1968), p. 91.

56   Vroom, op. cit.

57   Child, op. cit., p. 69.

58   K. Roberts, R. E. Miles, and L. Blankenship, *Organisational Leadership, Satisfaction and Productivity: A Comparative Analysis* (Univ. of California, 1969), Reprint No. 337.

59   G. A. Miller, 'Professionals in Bureaucracy: Alienation amongst Industrial Scientists and Engineers', *American Sociological Review*, vol. 32, no. 5 (1967), pp. 755–68.

60   H. H. Leavitt, 'Some Effects of Certain Communication Patterns on Group Performance', *Journal of Abnormal and Social Psychology*, vol. 46, no. 1 (1951).

61   F. Friedlander, 'The Relationship of Task and Human Conditions to Effective Organisational Structure', *Managing for Accomplishment*, B. M. Bass, R. Cooper, J. A. Haas (eds). (Heath and Lexington Books, 1970), pp. 111–38.

62   T. Burns, 'What Managers Do', *New Society* (17 Dec. 1954), pp. 8–9.

63   R. Blauner, *Alienation and Freedom* (Univ. of Chicago Press, 1964), p. 32.

64   Blauner, ibid., p. 32.

65   E. L. Trist, G. W. Higgin, H. Murray and A. B. Pollock, *Organisational Choice* (Tavistock, 1963).

66   Parker, op. cit., p. 157.

67   Herzberg, op. cit.

68   Hill, op. cit.

69   W. J. Paul, K. B. Robertson, F. Herzberg, 'Job Enrichment Pays Off', *Harvard Business Review* (March/April 1969), p. 61–79.

70   R. P. Quinn and R. L. Kahn, 'Organisational Psychology' *Annual Review of Psychology*, 18 (Annual Reviews Inc., 1967), pp. 437–66.

71   R. Centers and D. E. Bugental, 'Intrinsic and Extrinsic Job Motivations among Different Segments of the Working Population', *Journal Applied Psychology*, 50 (1966), pp. 193–7.

72   T. D. Wall and G. M. Stephenson, 'Herzberg's Two Factor Theory of Job Attitudes: A Critical Evaluation and Some Fresh Evidence', *Industrial Relations Journal* (Dec. 1970), pp. 41–65.

73 Herzberg, op. cit.
74 Goldthorpe *et al.*, op. cit.
75 Pym, op. cit.

CHAPTER 5

1   C. Sofer, *Men in Mid Career* (Cambridge Univ. Press, 1970), p. 14.
2   E. W. Vetter, *Manpower Planning for High Talent Personnel* (Univ. of Michigan, 1967), p. 53.
3   J. V. Grant and G. Smith, *Personnel Administration and Industrial Relations* (Longman, 1969), p. 62.
4   Sofer, op. cit., p. 17.
5   T. Caplow, *Principles of Organisation* (Harcourt, Brace and World Inc., 1964), p. 169.
6   A. Zaleznik, 'Managerial Behaviour and Interpersonal Competence', *Behavioural Science*, vol. 9, no. 2 (1964).
7   Sir Joseph Hunt, *Manpower as an Asset in a Growth Economy*, Willis Jackson Memorial Lecture (BACIE, 1970).
8   K. Lewin, T. Dembo, L. Festinger and P. S. Sears, 'Level of Aspiration', *Personality and the Behaviour Disorders*, J. Mev. Hunt (ed.), vol. 1 'Ronald, 1944).
9   A. Crichton, *Personnel Management in Context* (Batsford, 1958), p. 259.
10 G. Millerson, *The Qualifying Associations* (Routledge & Kegan Paul, 1964).
11 P. M. Blau and R. W. Scott, *Formal Organisations* (Routledge & Kegan Paul, 1963).
12 R. L. Opsahl and M. D. Dunnette, 'The Role of Financial Compensation in Industrial Motivation', *Psychological Bulletin*, vol. 66 (1966), pp. 94–118.
13 Opsahl and Dunnette, ibid., p. 100.
14 G. Strauss and L. R. Sayles, *Personnel: The Human Problems of Management* (Prentice-Hall, 1960), p. 631.
15 See for example, M. Haire, E. E. Ghiselli, L. W. Porter, (Psychological Research on Pay: An Overview', *Industrial Relations*, vol. 3, no. 1 (1963), pp. 3–8; and V. H. Vroom, *Work and Motivation* (Wiley, 1964).
16 Vetter, op. cit., p. 67.
17 Grant and Smith, op. cit., p. 250.
18 BIM, *Staff Grading Schemes* (1959).
19 Caplow, op. cit., p. 102.
20 R. Blauner, 'Work Satisfaction and Industrial Trends in Modern Society', *Labour and Trade Unionism*, W. Galenson and S. M. Lipset (eds), (Wiley, 1960).
21 T. M. Husband, 'Spotlight on Managers', *Personnel Management* (May, 1970), p. 18.
22 Sofer, op. cit., p. 25.
23 Sofer, op. cit., p. 18.
24 Strauss and Sayles, op. cit., p. 492.
25 M. Dalton, 'Informal Factors in Career Achievement', *American Journal of Sociology*, vol. 56 (March, 1951).
26 N. H. Martin and J. H. Sims, 'Thinking Ahead: Power Tactics', *Harvard Business Review*, vol. 34, no. 6 (1956).

27 A. Young, *Models for Planning Recruitment and Promotion of Staff*, unpublished paper (Univ. of Liverpool, 1968).

28 C. Argyris, 'The Individual and the Organisation: An Empirical Test', *Administrative Science Quarterly*, vol. 4 (Sept., 1959), p. 149.

29 R. K. Merton, *Social Theory and Social Structure* (Free Press, 1957).

30 Vetter, op. cit.

31 N. A. B. Wilson, 'Manpower Planning: An Overview', *Manpower Planning*, A. R. Smith (ed.) (English Univ. Press, 1970).

32 J. P. Campbell, M. D. Dunnette, E. E. Lawler, and K. E. Weick, *Managerial Behaviour Performance and Effectiveness* (McGraw-Hill, 1970).

33 A. Young, Report on University Staffing A.U.T. (Autumn 1967).

INDEX